and the flowers **showered...**

OSHO

Extemporaneous talks given by Osho at
the OSHO International Meditation Resort, Pune, India

and the flowers **showered...**

The Freudian Couch and Zen

ZEN STORIES, ZEN MASTERS AND LOVING LIFE

OSHO

This book is a transcript of a series of original talks by Osho, given to a live audience. All of
Osho's talks have been published in full as books, and are also available as original audio
recordings. Audio recordings and the complete text archive can be found via the online OSHO
Library at www.osho.com/library

Osho comments in this work are based on excerpts from:
Zen Buddhism, first published in 1959 by Peter Pauper Press, Inc., White Plains, New York, U.S.A.
Used by permission. www.peterpauper.com.
Zen Flesh, Zen Bones, by Paul Reps. © Tuttle Publishing. Reprinted by permission of Tuttle
Publishing.
Zen: Poems, Prayers, Sermons, Anecdotes, Interviews, 2nd Edition. Selected and translated
by Lucien Stryk and Takashi Ikemoto. Reprinted with the permission of Swallow Press/Ohio
University Press, Athens, Ohio (www.ohioswallow.com)
Suzuki, Daisetz.; Zen and Japanese Culture. © 1959 by Bollingen Foundation, Inc. New York,
1987 renewed Princeton University Press. Reprinted by permission of Princeton University Press.

OSHO MEDIA INTERNATIONAL
New York • Zurich • Mumbai
an imprint of
OSHO INTERNATIONAL
www.osho.com/oshointernational

Distributed by Publishers Group Worldwide
www.pgw.com

Library of Congress Catalog-In-Publication Data is available

Printed in India by Manipal Technologies Limited, Karnataka

ISBN 978-0-9844444-9-6
Also available as eBook ISBN 0-88050-257-6

contents

		preface	the potency of emptiness	vii
Chapter	1	the potency of emptiness	1
Chapter	2	all knowledge is borrowed	19
Chapter	3	that which doesn't change	37
Chapter	4	the path is just in front of you	57
Chapter	5	death is no ordinary phenomenon	77
Chapter	6	the perfect man is centered	97
Chapter	7	let the moment decide	115
Chapter	8	philosophy solves nothing	135
Chapter	9	a different way of being	151
Chapter	10	it is right before your eyes	175
Chapter	11	not mind, not buddha, not things	193

about Osho — 210

OSHO international meditation resort — 212

more OSHO books — 214

for more information — 216

preface

Zen insists on emptiness, that's why in Buddhism there is no concept of God, it is not needed. People in the West cannot understand how a religion exists without the concept of a God. Buddhism has no concept of any God – there is no need, because Buddhism insists on simply being empty, then everything follows. But who bothers? Once you are empty, things will take their own course. A religion exists without God. This is simply a miracle. In the West, people who write about religion and the philosophy of religion are always in trouble about how to define religion. They can define Hinduism, Mohammedanism, Christianity, easily, but Buddhism creates trouble. They can define God as being the center of all religion, but then Buddhism becomes a problem. They can define prayer as the essence of religion, but again Buddhism creates trouble, because there is no God and no prayer, no mantra, nothing. You have only to be empty. The concept of God will not allow you to be empty; prayer will be a disturbance; chanting will not allow you to be empty. Simply being empty, everything happens. Emptiness is the secret key of Buddhism. Be in such a way that you are not.

Osho
And the Grass Grows by Itself...

the potency of emptiness

Subhuti was one of Buddha's disciples. He was able to understand the potency of emptiness – the viewpoint that nothing exists except in its relationship of subjectivity and objectivity.
One day, when Subhuti was sitting under a tree in a mood of sublime emptiness, flowers began to fall around him. "We are praising you for your discourse on emptiness" the gods whispered to him. "But I have not spoken of emptiness" said Subhuti. "You have not spoken of emptiness, we have not heard emptiness" responded the gods. "This is true emptiness."
And blossoms showered upon Subhuti like rain.

Yes, it happens. It is not a metaphor, it is a fact – so don't take this story metaphorically. It is literally true...because the whole existence feels happy, blissful, ecstatic when even one individual soul achieves the ultimate.

We are part of the whole. And the whole is not indifferent to you, cannot be. How can a mother be indifferent to a child – her own child? It is impossible. When the child grows, the mother also grows with him. When the child is happy, the mother is also happy with him. When the child dances, something in the mother also dances. When the child is ill, the mother is ill. When the child is miserable, the mother is miserable...because they are not two, they are one. Their hearts beat in a rhythm.

The whole is your mother. The whole is not indifferent to you. Let this truth penetrate as deeply as possible in your heart, because even this awareness, that the whole feels happy with you, will change you. Then you are not alienated, then you are not a foreigner here. Then you are not a homeless wanderer, then this is a home. And the whole mothers you, cares about you, loves you. So it is natural that when somebody becomes a buddha, when somebody reaches the ultimate peak, the whole existence dances, the whole existence sings, the whole existence celebrates. It is literally true. It is not a metaphor; otherwise you will miss the whole point.

Blossoms shower, and then they go on showering – they never stop. The blossoms that showered for Buddha are still showering. The blossoms that showered for Subhuti are still showering. You cannot see them, not because they are not showering but because you are not capable of seeing them. Existence goes on celebrating infinitely for all the buddhas that have happened, for all the buddhas that are happening, and for all the buddhas that will happen – because for existence, past, future and present don't exist. It is a continuity, it is eternity. Only the now exists, infinite now.

They are still showering, but you cannot see them. Unless they shower for you, you cannot see them; and once you see them showering for you, you will see then that they have been showering for every buddha, for every enlightened soul.

The first thing: existence cares what happens to you. Existence is continuously praying that the ultimate should happen to you. In fact, you are nothing but a hand extended by the whole to reach the ultimate. You are nothing but a wave coming from the whole to touch the moon. You are nothing but a flower opening, so that the whole is filled with fragrance through you.

If you can drop yourself, those flowers can shower this very morning, this very moment. Gods are always ready, their hands are always full with flowers. They simply watch and wait. Whenever somebody becomes a Subhuti, empty, whenever somebody is absent, suddenly the flowers start showering.

This is one of the basic facts. Without it there is no possibility of trust; without it there is no possibility of your ever reaching the truth. Unless the whole helps, there is no possibility for you to reach – how can you reach? And ordinarily, our minds think just the opposite. We think of the whole as the enemy, not as the friend, never as the mother. We think about the whole as if the whole is trying to destroy us. We look at the whole through the door of death, not through the door of birth. It looks as if the whole is against you, fighting you, not allowing you to reach your goals and aims, not allowing you to be fulfilled. Hence you go on constantly warring with it. And the more you fight, the more your misconception proves to be true – because if you fight, your own fight is reflected through the whole.

The whole supports you, remember. Even when you fight, the whole supports you; even when you fight and you are wrong, the whole supports you. This is a second truth to be understood well. If you don't understand, it will be difficult for you to proceed further. Even if you fight with the whole, the whole supports you – because the whole cannot do anything else than support. If you go wrong, still the whole cares about you. Even if you go wrong, the whole moves with you. If a child goes wrong, the mother still cares. If a child becomes a thief and is ill, the mother will still care. She cannot give poison to the child. If the child goes completely wrong, astray, the mother will still pray for him. That is the meaning of Jesus' story of the two brothers.

One brother went away – not only away but astray from the father, and wasted his part of the heritage and became a beggar, a gambler, a drunkard. The other remained with the father, helped the business, worked on the farm and the gardens, increased the heritage, helped in every way, served in a surrendering spirit to the father. And then suddenly the news came that the other brother had become a beggar, that he was begging on the streets, and the father's whole heart started aching for him, and all his prayers were for him. He completely forgot the one who was near; he remembered only the one who had gone distant. In his dreams at night the other was present, but not the one who was close and working for him, who was good in every way.

And then one day the beggar son came back and the father arranged a big feast. The good son was coming home from the farm and somebody told him, "Look at the injustice of your father! You love him, you care for him and serve him and you have remained with him, been absolutely good, moral, never done anything against his wish, but never was a feast arranged for you. The fattest lamb has been murdered for your brother who has gone astray. He is coming like a beggar, and the whole house is celebrating!"

The son, the good son, felt very much hurt: this was absurd! He went back home angry. He talked to his father: "What are you doing? Never has a feast been given for me – and I have been serving you! What has this other son done for you? Just wasted the heritage, gambled everything, and now he has come home a beggar."

The father said, "Yes, because you are so close and you are so good and you are so happy, I need not worry about you. But the one who has gone astray – my prayers follow him and my love follows him."

Jesus used to tell this story again and again to his disciples because, as he said, God can forget the saints, there is no need to remember them, but God cannot forget the sinners. If he is a father...and I tell you he is not a father, he is a mother; a father is not such a deep phenomenon as a mother. That's why Hindus call him the mother – God is mother, a mothering. Jesus said whenever it happens that a shepherd is coming back home and a sheep is lost, he leaves all the other sheep in the forest, in the dark night, and goes to search and seek for the lost one. And when the lost sheep is found, he carries the lost sheep on his shoulders and he rejoices and he comes back home feeling very happy, because one who was lost has been found.

Whenever it happens – we are all lost sheep – whenever a sheep is found again, the shepherd rejoices. Flowers start showering.

Deities, gods, are not persons in the East, they are natural forces. Everything has been personified just to give a heart to it, a heartbeat – just to make it more caring. So Hindus, Buddhists, they have converted all the natural forces into gods, and they are right! When Subhuti attained to emptiness, gods started showering. And the meaning is very beautiful: the sun is a god for Hindus and Buddhists, the sky is a god; every tree has its own god, deity. The air is god, the earth is god. Everything has a heart – that is the meaning. Everything feels – that is the meaning. Nothing is indifferent to you – that is the meaning. When you attain, everything celebrates. Then the sun shines in a different way; the quality has changed.

To those who are ignorant, everything remains the same. The sun shines in the old way because the change of quality is very subtle, and only one who is empty can feel it. It is not gross, the ego cannot feel it; the gross is the field of the ego. The subtle can be felt only when there is no ego, because it is so subtle that if you are there you will miss it. Even your presence will be enough disturbance.

When one is totally empty, the quality of the sun immediately changes. It has a welcoming poetry about it. Its warmth is not only warmth, it has become a love – a loving warmth. The air is different, it lingers a little more around you, it touches you with more feeling, as if it has hands. The touch is totally different; now the touch has a sensitivity around it. The tree will flower, but not in the same way. Now the flowers are coming out of the tree as if they are jumping.

It is said that whenever Buddha passed through a forest, trees would start blossoming even when it was not the season for them. It has to be so! Man can err in recognizing Buddha but how can trees err? Man has a mind and the mind may miss, but how can the trees miss? – they don't have any minds, and when a buddha walks in a forest they start blossoming. It is natural, it has to be so! It is not a miracle. But you may not be able to see those flowers, because those flowers are not really physical. Those flowers are the feelings of the trees. When Buddha passes, the tree trembles in a different way, throbs in a different way, is no longer the same. This is the meaning. The whole cares for you, the whole is your mother.

Now try to understand this parable – one of the best.

Subhuti was one of Buddha's disciples.

Buddha had thousands of disciples. Subhuti was just one of them, nothing special about him. Really nobody knows much about Subhuti, this is the only story about him. There were great disciples, well known, famous – great scholars, princes. They had big kingdoms, and when they left them and renounced and became disciples of Buddha, they had a name around them. But flowers didn't shower on them. Flowers chose this Subhuti who was just one of the disciples, nothing special about him.

Only then do flowers shower; otherwise you also can become special around a buddha – and you can miss! You can feel egoistic about being near a buddha also, you can create a hierarchy; you can say, "I am not an ordinary disciple, I am something special. I am just next to Buddha. Others are just ordinary, a crowd, but I am not a crowd; I have a name, an identity of my own. Even before I came to Buddha I was somebody" – and you remain somebody.

Sariputta came to Buddha. When he came it was with five hundred disciples of his own. He was a master – of course an unenlightened master, knowing nothing, and still feeling that he knew because he was a great scholar. He knew all the scriptures. He was born a brahmin and a very talented one, a genius. From his very childhood he was known for his great memory – he could memorize anything. Only once he had to read a scripture, and it was already memorized. He was known all over the country; when he came to Buddha he was somebody. That somebodyness became the barrier.

These gods seem to be very irrational – they have chosen a disciple, Subhuti, who was just one in the crowd, nothing special about him. These gods seem to be crazy! They should have chosen Sariputta, he was the man to be chosen. But they have not chosen him. They have not chosen Ananda, Buddha's cousin-brother, Buddha's shadow continuously for forty years – for forty years, not for a single moment was he away from Buddha. He slept in the same room; he moved with Buddha, continuously by his side. He was the most well-known person. All the stories that Buddha told he starts by telling them to Ananda. He says, "Ananda, it happened this way…Ananda, once it happened." Ananda and Ananda and Ananda – he goes on repeating his name. But these gods are crazy, they have chosen Subhuti – a nobody!

Remember, only nobodies are chosen – because if you are somebody in this world you are nobody in the other world. If here you are a nobody, you become somebody in the other world. Values differ. Here, gross things are valued; there, subtle things are valued. And the most subtle, the subtlest, is *not to be*. Subhuti lived in the crowd – nobody even knew his name – and when this news reached that flowers were showering on Subhuti everybody wondered,

"Who is this Subhuti? We have never heard about him. Has it happened by some accident? Have the gods chosen him wrongly?" – because there were many who were higher in the hierarchy. Subhuti must have been the last. This is the only story about Subhuti.

Try to understand it well. When you are near a great master be a nobody. Gods are crazy, they will chose you only when you are not. And if you try to be, the more you succeed in being somebody, the more you will miss. This is what we are doing in the world and this we start doing around a buddha also. You crave riches. Why? – because with riches you become someone. You crave prestige and power. Why? – because with power and prestige you are not ordinary. You crave learning, scholarship, knowledge. Why? – because with knowledge you have something to be proud of.

But gods will not choose you that way. They have their own way of choosing. If you are beating your own drum too much, there is no need for gods to shower flowers on you – you are throwing flowers upon yourself! There is no need. When you stop being proud about anything, suddenly the whole existence starts being proud of you. Jesus says, "Those who are first in this world will be the last in the kingdom of my God, and those who are last will be the first."

It happened that a very rich man died and on the same day a beggar in the town also died. The name of the beggar was Lazarus. The rich man went directly to hell and Lazarus directly to heaven. The rich man looked up and saw Lazarus sitting near God, and he cried to heaven, "It seems that something has gone wrong. I should be there and this beggar Lazarus should be here!"

God laughed and he said, "Those who are last shall become the first, and those who are first shall become the last. You have enjoyed being first enough, now let Lazarus enjoy it a little."

And the rich man was feeling very hot – of course in hell you don't have any air-conditioning yet – burning hot. He was feeling very thirsty and there was no water. So he again cried and said, "God, please at least send Lazarus with a little water, I am feeling very thirsty."

And God said, "Lazarus was thirsty many times, just dying at your door, and you never gave him anything. He was dying, hungry at your door and there was a feast every day, and many were invited, but he was always chased away from the door by your servants because guests were coming, powerful guests, politicians, diplomats, rich men, and a beggar standing there would look awkward. Your servants chased him away and he was hungry, and the people who were invited were not hungry. You never looked at Lazarus. Now it is impossible."

And it is said Lazarus laughed.

This became a deep story for many many Christian mystics to ponder over. It became just like a Zen koan, and in monasteries Christian mystics have been asking again and again why Lazarus laughed.

He laughed at the absurdity of things. He never knew that a nobody like Lazarus, a leper, a beggar, could ever enter heaven. He could never have believed that this would happen. And he could not believe the other thing also – that a rich man, the richest in the town, should go to hell. He laughed.

And Lazarus still laughs. He will laugh when you die also: if you are a somebody he will laugh, because you will be thrown out. If you are nobody, just ordinary, he will laugh because you will be received.

In this world, because egos exist, all valuations belong to the ego. In the other world, the other dimension, valuation belongs to egolessness. Hence Buddha's emphasis on no-selfness, *anatta*. He said, "Don't believe even that 'I am a soul,' because that too can become a subtle ego. Don't say '*aham brahmasmi* – I am brahman, I am the ultimate self.' Don't say even that, because the 'I' is very tricky. It can deceive you. It has deceived you for many many lives. It can go on deceiving you. Simply say 'I am not' and remain in that not-ness, remain in that nothingness – become empty of the self."

One has to get rid of the self. Once the self is thrown away, nothing is lacking. You start overflowing and blossoms start falling on you.

Subhuti was one of Buddha's disciples.

Remember...*one of.*

He was able to understand the potency of emptiness.

He was just one of many, that's why he was able to understand the potency of emptiness. Nobody talked about him, nobody knew about him. He walked with, he followed Buddha on many many paths in his travels. Nobody even knew that he was there; if he had died nobody would have become aware. If he had escaped nobody would have known, because nobody ever knew that Subhuti was there. He knew – by and by, being nobody, he knew the potency of emptiness.

What is the meaning of it? ...Because the more he became a nonentity, the more he felt that Buddha was coming closer to him. Nobody else was aware, but Buddha was aware. Everybody wondered when these flowers showered on him, but it was not a surprise to Buddha. When it was reported to him that something had happened to Subhuti, Buddha said, "I was waiting. Any moment it was going to happen, because he has erased himself so much; any day it was going to happen. There is no surprise in it for me."

He was able to understand the potency of emptiness.

– by being empty! You don't know the power of emptiness. You don't know the power of being totally absent within. You know only the poverty of the ego.

But try to understand. With ego have you ever felt really powerful? With ego you always feel impotent. That's why the ego says, "Make your empire a little bigger so that you can feel you are powerful. No, this house won't do, a bigger house is needed; no, this much bank balance won't do, a bigger bank balance is needed; no, this much fame won't do, a little more."

The ego always asks for more. Why? If it is powerful, why go on asking for more? The very craving for more says, shows, that the ego feels impotent. You have a million rupees and you are impotent. The ego says, "No, one million won't do, have ten million rupees." And I tell you – with ten million rupees you will be tenfold more impotent, that's all. And then the ego will say, "No, this won't do…"

Nothing will do with ego. Everything proves only that you are impotent, powerless. The more power you gain the more powerless you feel in contrast. The richer you become the poorer you feel. The more healthy you are, the more afraid of death; the younger, the more you feel old age is coming nearer. The opposite is just around the corner, and if you have a little understanding, the opposite is just reaching you – around your neck. The more beautiful you are, the more you feel the inner ugliness.

Ego has never felt powerful. It only dreams of power, it thinks of power, it contemplates power – but those are simply dreams and nothing else. And dreams are there just to hide the impotence that is within you. But dreams cannot hide the reality. Whatsoever you do, from here or from there, through a loophole, again the reality comes in and shatters all dreams.

Ego is the most impotent thing in the world. But nobody realizes it, because it goes on asking for more, it never gives you a space to look at the situation. Before you become aware, it pushes you further and further somewhere. Always the goal is somewhere near the horizon. And it is so near, you think, "By the evening I will reach."

The evening never comes; the horizon remains always at the same distance. The horizon is an illusion; all the goals of ego are just illusions. But they give hope, and you go on feeling, "Some day or other I will become powerful." Right now you remain powerless, impotent, inferior, but in the future, in the hope, in the dream, you become powerful. You must be aware that many times, just sitting on your chair, you start daydreaming: you have become the emperor of the whole world or the president of the United States, and immediately you start enjoying it. Everybody looks at you, you have become the focal point of everyone's attention. Even that dream gives you exhilaration, intoxication. If you dream that way, you will walk in a different way.

This is how it is happening to everybody: your potency remains in the dreams, you remain impotent. The truth is just the opposite: when you don't seek, it comes; when you don't ask it is given; when you don't hanker it is there; when you don't go to the horizon, suddenly you realize that it has been always yours – only you never lived it. It is there inside, and you seek it outside. It is there within you and you go without. You are carrying it: the supreme-most power, the divine itself, is in you. And you are looking here and there like a beggar.

He was able to understand the potency of emptiness.

Just being empty, you will understand – there is no other way of understanding. Whatsoever you want to understand, be that, because that is the only way. Try being an ordinary man, nobody, with no name, no identity, with nothing to claim, with no power to enforce on others, with no effort to dominate, with no desire to possess, just being a nonentity. Try it – and see how powerful you become, how filled with energy and overflowing, so powerful that you can share your power, so blissful that you can give it to many, to millions. And the more you give, the more you are enriched. The more you share, the more it grows. You become a flood.

He was able to understand the potency of emptiness –

just by being nobody –

– the viewpoint that nothing exists except in its relationship of subjectivity and objectivity.

This is one of the deepest meditations Buddha discovered. He says everything exists in relation, it is a relativity; it is not an absolute, substantial thing.

For example: you are poor, I am rich. Is it a substantial thing or only a relative thing? I may be poor in relation to somebody else, and you may be rich in relation to somebody else. Even a beggar can be rich in relation to another beggar; there are rich beggars and poor beggars. A rich man in comparison to an even richer man is a poor man. You are poor – is your poverty existential or just a relationship? It is a relative phenomenon. If there is nobody to be related to, who will you be, a poor man or a rich man?

Think…suddenly the whole of humanity disappears and you are left alone on the earth: which will you be, poor or rich? You will be simply you – not rich, not poor – because how to compare? There is no Rockefeller to compare with, there is no beggar to compare with. Will you be beautiful or ugly when you are alone? You will be neither, you will be simply you. With nothing to compare with, how can you be ugly or beautiful? So it is with beauty and ugliness, richness and poverty and with all things. Will you be wise or a fool? Foolish or wise? Neither!

So Buddha says all these things exist in relationship. They are not existential, they are just concepts. And we are so much bothered about these things which are *not*. You are too much bothered if you are ugly. You are too much bothered if you are beautiful. The worry is created by something which is not.

A relative thing is not. It is just a relationship, as if you have drawn a design in the sky, a flower of air. Even a bubble in water is more substantial than relativities. Who are you if you are alone? Nobody. Somebodyness comes in relationship with somebody.

That means, just to be nobody is to be in nature; just to be nobody is to be in existence.

And you are alone, remember. The society exists only outside you. Deep within you are alone. Close your eyes and see whether you are beautiful or ugly; both the concepts disappear, inside there is no beauty, no ugliness. Close your eyes and contemplate who you are. Respected, not respected? Moral, immoral? Young, old? Black, white? A master or a slave? Who are you? Close your eyes and in your aloneness every concept drops. You cannot be anything. Then emptiness arises. All concepts nullified, only your existence remains.

This is one of the deepest meditations Buddha discovered: To be nobody. And this has not to be forced. You are not to think that you are nobody, you have to realize it; otherwise your nobodyness will be too heavy. You are not to think that you are nobody, you have to simply realize that all things that you think you are, are relative.

And truth is absolute, it is not relative. Truth is not relative: it does not depend on anything, it is simply there. So find out the truth within you and don't bother about relationships. They differ, interpretations differ. And if interpretations change, you change. Something is in fashion – if you use it you are modern, appreciated. Something has gone out of fashion – if you use it you are out of date, you are not respected. Fifty years before, that was in fashion and you would have been modern. Fifty years later on, it may come again in fashion and then again you will be modern. Right now you are out of date. But who are you – changing fashions, changing concepts, relativities?

One of my friends was a communist, but a very rich man – and he never felt the contradiction. He was a bourgeois, well fed, never worked with his hands. He had many servants; he belonged to an old royal family. And then he went to Russia in 1940. When he came back he told me, "Wherever I went, I started feeling guilty – because whenever I shook hands with anybody, I could feel immediately that the other felt that my hands didn't carry any marks of a laborer. They are not proletarian, they are bourgeois: soft, feminine. And immediately the other person's face would change, and he would let go of my hand as if I was untouchable." He told me, "In India, whenever I shake hands with anybody my hands are appreciated. They are beautiful, feminine, artistic. In Russia, I felt so guilty about my hands that I even started to think how to destroy their softness, so that nobody would look at me as an exploiter – a bourgeois, a rich man."...Because there, labor had become a value. If you were proletarian in Soviet Russia you were somebody; if you were a rich man you were a sinner. Anything is just a relative concept.

In India, we have respected *bhikkhus*, swamis, sannyasins. And that has been so in China also – before Mao. A man who renounced the world was the most respected man and the society cared about him. He was the highest peak of humanity. And then communism came to China and thousands of monasteries have been destroyed completely, and all the monks, respected men of the past, have become sinners. They have to work. You can eat only if you work, and begging is exploitation. It has been prohibited by the law; now nobody can beg.

If Buddha is born in China, it will be very difficult for him now. He will not be allowed to beg, he will be thought of as an exploiter. Even if Marx is born in China or Russia he will be in difficulty because his whole life he never did anything other than reading in the British Museum Library. He was not a proletarian, he was not a laborer – and his friend and collaborator, Friedrich Engels, was a very rich man. They are worshipped like gods there. But if Friedrich Engels went to visit Soviet Russia, he would be in difficulty. He never worked, he lived on others' labor, and he helped Marx; without his help Marx could not have written *Das Kapital* or the *Communist Manifesto*. But in Soviet Russia, he will be in difficulty, the fashion has changed. Concepts change. Remember this: that which changes is relative, and that which remains unchanging is absolute – and your being is absolute; it is not part of relativity.

...the viewpoint that nothing exists except in its relationship of subjectivity and objectivity.

If you understand this standpoint well, contemplate it, meditate on it, suddenly you are illuminated within and you see that everything is empty.

One day, when Subhuti was sitting under a tree in a mood of sublime emptiness...

Remember the words *sublime emptiness*, because sometimes you also feel empty – but that is not sublime. Sometimes you also feel empty, but not ecstatic emptiness – a depression, a negative emptiness, not a positive emptiness. This distinction has to be remembered.

A negative emptiness means you are feeling a failure, not understanding. You have tried to achieve something in the world and you have not achieved it. You feel empty because the thing you desired you couldn't get; the woman you wanted you couldn't get – you feel empty. The man you were after escaped; you feel empty. The success that was in your dreams could not happen; you feel empty. This emptiness is negative. This is a sadness, a depression, a frustrated state of mind. If you are feeling empty that way, remember, flowers will not shower on you. Your emptiness is not real, not positive. You are still after things, that's why you are feeling empty. You are still after the ego; you wanted to be somebody and could not. It is a failure, not an understanding.

So remember, if you renounce the world through a failure it is not renunciation, it is not sannyas, it is not true. If you renounce the world through understanding, that is totally different. You don't renounce it as a sad effort, with frustration within, failure all around. You don't do it like a suicide, remember. If your sannyas is a suicide, then flowers will not shower on you. Then you are leaving because...

You must have heard Aesop's fable. A fox was passing, and there were grapes, but the vine was high on a tree. She tried and tried and jumped but they were beyond her reach. So she went away saying, "They are not worth anything, they are not yet sweet and ripe. They are sour." She couldn't reach.

But it is difficult for the ego to realize that, "I am a failure." Rather than recognizing that, "I have failed, they were beyond my reach," the ego will say, "They were not worth..."

Your many sannyasins, so-called saints, are just like that Aesop's fox. They have renounced the world not because they understood the futility of it but because they were failures and it was beyond their reach – and they are still filled with grudge and complaint. You go to them and they will still be against it, saying, "Wealth is dirt; and what is a beautiful woman? – nothing but bones and blood!" Who are they trying to convince? They are trying to convince themselves that the grapes are sour and bitter.

Why talk about women when you have left the world? Why talk about wealth when you have no concern about it? A deep concern still exists. You cannot accept the failure yet and understanding has not arisen.

Whenever you are against something, remember, understanding has not arisen – because in understanding, for and against both disappear. In understanding you are not inimical to the world. In understanding you are not condemning the world and the people there. If you go on condemning, your condemnation shows that somewhere there is a wound, and you are feeling jealous – because without jealousy there can be no condemnation. You condemn people because somehow, somewhere, unconsciously you feel they are enjoying themselves and you have missed.

You go on saying this world is just a dream, but if it is really a dream then why insist that it is a dream? Nobody insists about dreams. In the morning you wake up and you know it was a dream – finished. You don't go telling people that whatsoever they are is a dream.

Remember one trick of the mind: you try to convince people about something just to convince yourself, because when the other feels convinced you feel okay. If you go and tell people that sex is sin and they are convinced, or they cannot refute you, you become happy. You have convinced yourself. Looking into others' eyes, you are trying to cover your own failure.

Negative emptiness is useless. It is simply the absence of something. Positive emptiness is presence of something, not absence; that's why positive emptiness becomes a power. Negative emptiness becomes a sad, depressed state of mind – you simply cave in, that's all. Feeling a failure, feeling dejected, feeling everywhere the wall that you cannot cross, feeling impotent, you denounce, you condemn.

But this is not a growth, this is a regression. And deep inside you cannot flower, because only understanding flowers, never depression. And if you cannot flower, existence is not going to shower flowers on you. Existence simply responds to you: whatsoever you are, existence gives you more of that. If you have many flowers within your being flowering, a million times more flowers will shower on you. If you have a deep depression, the existence helps that too – a million times more depression will come to you. Whatsoever you are will knock at your door. Whatsoever you are will be given to you more and more.

So be careful and be alert. And remember, a sublime emptiness is a positive phenomenon. One is not a failure, one simply looks at the thing and understands that dreams cannot be fulfilled. Then one never feels sad, one feels happy that, "I have come to this understanding that dreams cannot be fulfilled." One never feels depressed, hopeless, one feels simply happy and blissful because, "I have come to an understanding. Now I will not try the impossible, now I will not try the futile." And one never says that the object of desire is wrong; when you are in positive, sublime emptiness, you say desire is wrong, not the object of desire – this is the difference. In negative emptiness you say the object of desire is wrong, so change the object. If it is wealth, money, power – drop it. Make the object God, liberation, heaven instead – change the object.

If emptiness is perfect and sublime and positive, you don't see the object as wrong. You simply see that desire is futile; objects are okay, but desire is futile. Then you don't change your desire from one object to another object, you simply drop the desire itself.

Non-desiring, you flower. Desiring, you become more and more paralyzed and dead.

> *One day, when Subhuti was sitting under a tree in a mood of sublime emptiness...*

...Empty but happy, empty but filled; empty but not lacking, empty but overflowing; empty but at ease, at home.

> *...flowers began to fall around him.*

He was surprised, because he was nobody. He never expected it. If you expect, the flowers never shower; if you don't expect, they shower – but then you are surprised. Why? Subhuti must have thought something had gone wrong. Showering on Subhuti, a nobody, no one, and that too when he was empty? Not even thinking of God, not even thinking of liberation, not even meditating – because when you are meditating you are not empty, you are doing something and filled with your effort. Not doing anything? Subhuti must have become alert that something had gone wrong: The gods have gone crazy! Why these flowers? And it is not the season – he must have looked at the tree and he must have looked at himself again: "On *me*, flowers are showering?" He could not believe it.

Remember, whenever the ultimate happens to you, you will be surprised because you never expected it. You were not waiting for it even, you were not hoping. And those who are expecting and waiting and hoping and praying and desiring – it never happens to them because they are so tense. They are never empty, never relaxed.

The universe comes to you when you are relaxed, because then you are vulnerable, open – all doors open. From anywhere, God is welcome. But you are not praying, and you are not asking for God to come; you are not doing

anything. When you are not doing anything, just in a mood of sublime emptiness, you become the temple and he comes.

In a mood of sublime emptiness, flowers began to fall around him...

He looked all around – what is happening?

"We are praising you for your discourse on emptiness," the gods
whispered to him.

He couldn't believe it. He was never expecting it. He couldn't believe that
he was worthy, or he was capable, or he had grown.

"We are praising you for your discourse on emptiness," the gods
whispered to him.

They have to whisper. They must have looked at the amazed eyes of this
Subhuti, so surprised. They said, "We are praising you. Don't be so surprised
and don't be so amazed. Be at ease! We are just praising you for your discourse
on emptiness."

"But I have not spoken of emptiness," said Subhuti –

"I have not spoken anything!"

"You have not spoken of emptiness, we have not heard emptiness,"
responded the gods. "This is true emptiness."
And blossoms showered upon Subhuti like rain.

Try to understand. They said, *"We are praising you for your discourse on
emptiness,"* and he was not talking to anybody, there was nobody. He was not
talking to himself, because he was empty, not divided. He was not talking at all,
he was simply there. Nothing was being done on his part – no clouds of thought
were passing in his mind, no feelings arising in his heart: he was simply as if
not. He was simply empty.
   And the gods said: *"We are praising you for your discourse on emptiness."*
   So he was more surprised and he said, "What? *I have not spoken of emptiness,* I have not said anything!"
   They said, "You have not spoken and we have not heard. *This is true emptiness."* You cannot discourse on emptiness, you can only be empty – that is

the only discourse. Everything else can be talked about, everything else can become a sermon, the object of a sermon, everything else can be discussed, argued – but not emptiness, because the very effort to say anything about it destroys it. The moment you say it, it is not there. Even a single word is enough and the emptiness is lost. Even a single word can fill you and the emptiness disappears.

No, nothing can be said about it. Nobody has ever said anything about it. You can just be empty and that is the discourse. *Being* is the discourse.

Emptiness can never become an object of thought, thoughtlessness is its nature. So the gods said, "You have not said anything and we have not heard. That is the beauty of it! That's why we are praising you. Rarely does it happen that somebody is simply empty. *This is true emptiness.*" And Subhuti was not even aware that it was emptiness, because if you are aware, something foreign has entered into it: you are divided, you are split. When one is really empty, there is nothing else than emptiness, not even the awareness of emptiness. Not even the witness is there. One is perfectly alert, one is not asleep – but the witness is not there. It goes beyond witnessing, because whenever you witness something there is a slight tension inside, a subtle effort, and then emptiness is one thing and you are something else. You witness it, you are not empty; then emptiness is again just a thought in the mind.

People come to me and say, "I have experienced one moment of emptiness." And I tell them, "If you have experienced it then forget about it, because who will experience it? The experiencer is enough, enough of a barrier. Who will experience it?" Emptiness cannot be experienced. It is not an experience, because the experiencer is not there: the experiencer and the experience have become one. It is an experiencing.

Allow me to coin this word: it is an *experiencing*, it is a process, undivided. Both the poles have disappeared, both the banks have disappeared, and only the river exists. You cannot say, "I experienced," because you were not there – how can you experience it? And once you enter it, you cannot make it a past experience; you cannot say, "I experienced." Then it becomes a past memory.

No, emptiness can never become a memory, because emptiness can never leave a trace. It cannot leave any footprints. How can emptiness become a past memory? How can you say "I experienced"? It is always in the now, it is experienc*ing*. It is neither past nor future, it is always an ongoing process. Once you enter you have entered. You cannot even say "I experienced" – that's why Subhuti was not even aware of what was happening. He was not there. Any distinction between him and the universe was not there. No distinction, all boundaries dissolved. The universe started melting in him, he melted into the universe, merging, melting, oneness. And the gods said, "This is true emptiness."

And blossoms showered upon Subhuti like rain.

This last line has to be understood very, very carefully, because when some-body says that you are empty, immediately the ego can come back – because you will become aware, and you will feel something has been achieved. Suddenly the gods will make you aware that you are empty.

But Subhuti is rare, extraordinarily rare. Even though the gods shouted around him, whispered in his ears, and the flowers were showering on him like rain, he didn't bother. He simply kept silent. They said, "You have spoken, you have given a discourse!" He listened without coming back. They said, "You have not spoken, we have not heard. *This is true emptiness!"* There was no ego saying, "The true happiness happened to me. Now I have become enlightened" – otherwise he would have missed at the last point. Immediately, flowers would have stopped showering, if he had come back. No, he must have closed his eyes and he must have thought, "These gods are mad and these flowers are dreams – don't bother."

The emptiness was so beautiful that now nothing could be more beautiful than that. He simply remained in his sublime emptiness – that's why blossoms showered upon Subhuti like rain. Now they were not falling a few here and a few there, now they were showering like rain.

This is the only story about Subhuti, nothing is said about him anymore. Nowhere is he mentioned again. But I tell you the flowers are still showering. Subhuti is no longer under any tree – because when one becomes really, totally empty, one dissolves into the universe. But the universe still celebrates it. The flowers go on showering.

But you will be able to know them only when they shower for you. When God knocks at your door only then do you know that God is, never before. All arguments are futile, all discourses not to the point, unless God knocks at your door. Unless it happens to you, nothing can become a conviction.

I talk about Subhuti because this happened to me, and this is not a meta-phor; it is literal. I had read about Subhuti before, but I thought that it was a metaphor – beautiful, poetic. I never had even a slight notion that this actually happens. I never thought that this was a realistic phenomenon, a real thing that happens. But now I tell you it happens. It happened to me, it can happen to you...but a sublime emptiness is needed.

And never be confused. Don't ever think that your negative emptiness can ever become sublime. Your negative emptiness is like darkness; sublime emptiness is like light, it is like a rising sun. Negative emptiness is like death. Sublime emptiness is like life, eternal life. It is blissful.

Allow that mood to penetrate you deeper and deeper. Go and sit under trees. Just sit, not doing anything. Everything stops – when you stop, every-thing stops. Time will not be moving, as if suddenly the world has come to a peak and there is no movement. But don't bring in the idea, "Now I am empty," otherwise you will miss. And even if gods start showering flowers on you, don't pay much attention.

And now you know the story, don't even ask why. Subhuti had to ask, you need not. Even if they whisper by themselves, "We have heard true emptiness and the discourse on it," don't bother, and the flowers will shower like rain on you, too.

Enough for today.

all knowledge is borrowed

*When Yamaoka was a brash student he visited the master Dokuon.
Wanting to impress the master he said: "There is no mind, there is no
body, there is no buddha. There is no better, there is no worse. There is
no master, there is no student. There is no giving, there is no receiving.
What we think we see and feel is not real. None of these seeming things
really exists."
Dokuon had been sitting quietly smoking his pipe, and saying nothing.
Suddenly he picked up his staff and gave Yamaoka a terrible whack.
Yamaoka jumped up in anger.
Dokuon said: "Since none of these things really exists, and all is
emptiness, where does your anger come from? Think about it."*

Knowledge is not of much help. Only being can become the vehicle for
the other shore. You can go on thinking, accumulating information –
but those are paper boats, they won't help in an ocean voyage. If you
remain on the shore and go on talking about them, it is okay – paper boats
are as good as real boats if you never go for the voyage. But if you go for the
voyage with paper boats then you will be drowned. And words are nothing but
paper boats – not even that substantial.

When we accumulate knowledge, what do we do? Nothing changes inside;
the being remains absolutely unaffected. Just like dust, information gathers
around you – just like dust gathering around a mirror. The mirror remains the

same, only it loses its mirroring quality. Your consciousness remains the same; what you know through the mind makes no difference, in fact it becomes worse. Accumulated knowledge is just like dust around your mirroring consciousness; the consciousness reflects less and less and less.

The more you know, the less aware you become. When you are completely filled with scholarship, borrowed knowledge, you are already dead. Then nothing comes to you as your own. Everything is borrowed and parrotlike.

Mind is a parrot. I have heard – it happened in the days of Joseph Stalin – a man, a very prominent communist, came to the Moscow police station and reported that his parrot was missing. Because this man was a very prominent communist, the chief at the police station inquired about the parrot, for it was significant and had to be searched for. In his inquiries he asked, "Does the parrot talk?"

The communist, the comrade, felt a slight fear, and then he said, "Yes, he talks. But note it down: whatever political opinions he has, they are completely his own."

But how can a parrot have opinions of its own? A parrot cannot have opinions of its own – and neither can the mind, because the mind is a mechanism. A parrot is more alive than a mind. Even a parrot may have some opinions of its own, but the mind cannot. Mind is a computer, a biocomputer. It accumulates. It is never original, it cannot be. Whatsoever it has is borrowed, taken from others.

You become original only when you transcend mind. When the mind is dropped, and the consciousness faces existence directly, immediately, moment to moment in contact with existence, you become original. Then for the first time you are authentically your own. Otherwise all ideas are borrowed. You may quote scriptures, you may know by heart all the Vedas, the Koran, the Gita, the Bible, but that makes no difference – they are not your own. And knowledge that is not your own is dangerous, more dangerous than ignorance, because it is a hidden ignorance and you will not be able to see that you are deceiving yourself. You are carrying false coins and thinking you are a rich man, carrying false stones and thinking they are Kohinoors. Sooner or later your poverty will be revealed. Then you will be shocked.

This happens whenever you die, whenever death comes near. In the shock that death gives to you, suddenly you become aware that you have not gained anything – because only that is gained which is gained in being.

You have accumulated fragments of knowledge from here and there, you may have become a great encyclopedia, but that is not the point. And particularly for those who are in search of truth, it is a barrier, not a help. Knowledge has to be transcended.

When there is no knowledge, knowing happens, because knowing is your quality – the quality of consciousness. It is just like a mirror: the mirror reflects whatsoever is there; consciousness reflects the truth that is always in front of you, just at the tip of your nose.

But the mind is in between – and the mind goes on chattering, and the truth remains just in front of you and the mind goes on chattering. And you go with the mind. You miss. Mind is a great missing.

Before we enter this beautiful anecdote, a few more things. First: knowledge is borrowed, realize this. The very realization becomes a dropping of it. You don't have to do anything. Simply realize that whatsoever you know you have heard, you have not known it. You have read it, you have not realized it; it is not a revelation to you, it is a conditioning of the mind. It has been taught to you – you have not learned it. Truth can be learned, cannot be taught.

Learning means being responsive to whatsoever is around you – that which is, to be responsive to it. This is a great learning, but not knowledge.

There is no way to find truth – except through finding it. There is no short cut to it. You cannot borrow, you cannot steal, you cannot deceive, to get to it. There is simply no way unless you are without any mind within you – because mind is a wavering, mind is a continuous trembling; mind is never unmoving, it is a movement. Mind is just like a breeze, continuously flowing, and the flame goes on wavering. When mind is not there the breeze stops, and the flame becomes unmoving. When your consciousness is an unmoving flame, you know the truth. You have to learn how not to follow the mind.

Nobody can give you the truth, nobody, not even a Buddha, a Jesus, a Krishna – nobody can give it to you. And it is beautiful that nobody can give it to you, otherwise it would become a commodity in the market. If it can be given, then it can also be sold. If it can be given, then it can also be stolen. If it can be given then you can take it from your friend, borrow it. It is beautiful that truth is not transferable in any way. Unless you reach it, you cannot reach. Unless you become it, you never have it. In fact, it is not something you can have. It is not a commodity, a thing, a thought. You can be it, but you cannot have it.

In the world, in *this* world, we can have everything – everything can become part of our possessions. Truth can never be possessed, because there are two things which can be possessed: thoughts and things. Things can be possessed, thoughts can be possessed – truth is neither. Truth is being. You can become it, but you cannot possess it. You cannot have it in your safe, you cannot have it in your book, you cannot have it in your hand. When you have it, you are it. You become truth. It is not a concept, it is a being itself.

The second thing to remember: this is a human tendency, to try to show you have that which you don't have. If you have it, you don't try to show it, there is no point. If you don't have it you try to show it, as if you have it. So remember, whatsoever you want to show to people, that is the thing you don't have.

If you go to a rich man's house and become his guest – nothing changes; if he is really rich nothing changes, he simply accepts you. Go to a poor man's house – he changes everything. He may borrow furniture from his neighbor, a carpet from somebody else, curtains from somebody else. He would like to impress you that he is rich. If you are not rich you would like to impress people that you are rich. And if you don't know, you would like people to think that you know. Whenever you want to impress somebody, remember this: it is a human tendency to impress, because nobody wants to look poor – and more so where things of the other world are concerned.

You can be a poor man as far as things of this world are concerned, that is not much of a poverty; but as far as God, the soul, liberation, truth are concerned – it is too much to bear, to be poor is too much to bear. You would like to impress people that you have something, and it is difficult to impress them as far as things of this world are concerned, because those things are visible. It is easy to impress people about things of the other world because they are not visible. You can impress people that you know, without knowing.

The problem arises because when you impress others, there is a possibility that you may be impressed yourself by their eyes and their convictions that you have something. By and by, if many people are convinced that you know, you will be convinced that you know – there is the problem, because deceiving others is not much of a problem. But if you are deceived by your own effort, then it will be almost impossible to bring you out of your sleep, because you think it is not a sleep at all! You think you are fully awake. It will be difficult to bring you out of your ignorance because you think you are enlightened already. It will be difficult to bring you out of your disease because you believe that you are healthy and whole already!

The greatest barrier that stands between you and the truth is that you have convinced yourself via others that you already have it. So it is a vicious circle. First: you try to convince others – and you can convince others because the thing is invisible. Second: others don't have it either, so they don't know. If you go and start talking about God, and go on talking, sooner or later people will start thinking that you know about God – because they don't know either. Except for the word *god* they don't know anything about it, and you can be very clever and cunning, cunning about theories and philosophies, argumentative. And if you go on and on, just out of sheer boredom they will say, "Yes, we believe that you know, but be finished."

I have heard, once it happened:

There was one great mystic, Baal Shem, a Jew, a Hassid. A scholar came to see him, a pretender – and all scholars are pretenders, because by "scholar" I mean someone who knows something through the scriptures, words, language, who has not encountered the reality himself – and he started talking about old prophets, and the Old Testament, and commenting about them… everything borrowed of course, unoriginal; foolish on his part because he was talking to a man who knows.

Baal Shem listened out of compassion, and then in the end he said, "Too bad, too bad; had the great Maimonides known you…"

Maimonides is a Jewish philosopher, a very great philosopher, so the pretender was very happy, overjoyed with this compliment, that had great Maimonides known him… So he asked, "I am so happy that you recognize me and you have given me recognition. Just one thing more: why do you say, 'Too bad, too bad; had the great Maimonides known you…?' What do you mean? Please tell me this, what do you mean?"

Baal Shem said, "Then you would have bored him, not me."

Just out of sheer boredom people start believing, "Yes, you know – but keep quiet." And then moreover, they don't know, they are as ignorant as you. There is only one difference: you are more articulate, you have read more, you have accumulated a little more dust, and they cannot argue, and you can put them in their place and make them silent. They have to believe that you know, and it doesn't make any difference to them whether you know it or not.

Be happy if you think you know, but you are creating such a stone wall it will be difficult for you to break it – because if you convince others, you become convinced that, "Yes, I know". That's how there are so many so-called masters. They don't know anything, but they have followers, and because of the followers they are convinced that they know. Take away their followers and you will see their confidence is gone.

Deep down, depth psychologists say that people accumulate followers just to convince themselves that they know. Without followers, how will you convince yourself? There is no way – you are alone! And it is difficult to deceive oneself directly, it is easy to deceive oneself via others. When you talk to someone and you see the light in his eyes, you are convinced that you must have something, otherwise, "Why did this light come to his eyes, his face? He was impressed." That's why we hanker so much to impress people. The mind wants to impress people so that it can be impressed via them, and can then believe in its borrowed knowledge as if it is a revelation. Beware of this. This is one of the trickiest traps. Once you fall into it, it will be difficult for you to come out.

A sinner can reach more easily to the truth than a scholar, because a sinner feels deep down that he is guilty, he can repent, and he feels he has done something wrong. You cannot find a sinner who is basically happy. He feels the guilt; he has done something wrong and he repents in the unconscious; he wants to undo whatsoever he has done to bring about the balance in his life, and some day or other he will bring the balance. But if you are a scholar, a man of words, theories and philosophies, a great pundit, then it is difficult, because you never feel guilt about your scholarship, you feel happy and egoistic about it.

Remember one thing: whatsoever gives you a feeling of ego is a barrier; whatsoever gives you a feeling of egolessness is the way.

If you are a sinner and you feel guilty, that means your ego is shaken. Through sin you cannot accumulate ego. It has happened many times that a sinner has taken the jump in a moment and has become a saint. It happened to Valmiki, an Indian saint, the first to tell the story of Rama. He was a robber and a murderer, and in a single moment the transformation happened. It has never happened like that to any pundit ever – and India is a great country of pundits: the brahmins, the scholars. You cannot compete with Indian scholars – they have a long heritage of thousands of years, and they have lived on words and words and words. But it has never happened that a scholar in a single moment took a jump, exploded, was broken from the past and became totally new. It has never happened that way. But it has happened many times with sinners, in a single moment, because deep down they were never able to make arrangements for their ego with whatsoever they were doing. Whatsoever they were doing was ego-shattering and ego is the wall, the stone wall.

If you feel you are a moralist, a puritan, you will create a subtle ego. If you think you are a knower, you will create a subtle ego. Remember, there is no sin except the ego, so don't accumulate it; and it is always accumulated through false things, because real things always shatter it. If you really know, the ego disappears; if you don't know, it accumulates and becomes bigger and bigger and stronger. If you are really a pure man, a religious man, ego disappears; but if you are a puritan, a moralist, then ego is strengthened. This should always be the criterion to judge whether whatsoever you are doing is good or wrong: judge it by the ego. If ego is strengthened, then it is wrong: drop it as soon as you can, drop it immediately! If ego is not strengthened, it is good.

If you go to the temple every day, or to church every Sunday, and you feel ego is strengthened, don't go to church – stop; don't go to the temple, it is not helping you, it is a poison. If you feel by going to church that you are religious, you are something extraordinary, greater, purer than others, holier-than-thou, if this attitude comes to you, holier-than-thou, then drop it, because this attitude is the only sin in the world that exists. All else is child's play. This is the only sin – this attitude of holier-than-thou.

Do only that which doesn't strengthen your ego, and sooner or later you will become enlightened, because when the ego is not, if even for a single moment it leaves you – suddenly the eyes open and you have seen it. Once seen, it is never forgotten. Once glimpsed, it becomes such a powerful magnet in your life that it goes on drawing you nearer and nearer to the center of the world. Sooner or later you will be merged into it.

But the ego resists, the ego resists surrender. It resists love, it resists prayerfulness, it resists meditation, it resists the divine. Ego is a resistance, a fight against the whole; that's why it is a sin. And ego is always interested in impressing people. The more you can impress people, the more ego gets food. It is a fact. If you cannot impress anybody, the supports are withdrawn and the ego starts trembling. It has no base in reality, it depends on others' opinions.

Now try to enter this anecdote:

"The brash student" – it is a contradiction, because a student cannot be brash, and if he is, he cannot be a student. A student cannot be impudent, he cannot be rude, he cannot be an egoist. If he is, he cannot be a student, because to be a student means to be receptive, to be ready to learn. And what is readiness to learn? Readiness to learn means: I know that I am ignorant. If I already know that I know, how can I learn? The doors are closed, I am not ready to learn; really, I am ready to teach.

It happened once in a Zen monastery: a man came and he wanted to be initiated. The master said, "We have two categories of initiates here. I have five hundred inmates in the ashram, in the monastery, and we have two categories: one is that of disciple, and one that of master. So which category would you like to join?"

The man was absolutely new, and even he felt a little hesitation. He said, "If it is possible then I would like to be initiated as a master."

The master was just joking. He was just joking – and wanted to look into the deeper unconscious of this man.

Everybody would like to be a master, and even if you become a disciple you become one only as a means, just as a means to become a master: you have to pass through it, it is compulsory; otherwise how can you become a master? So you have to be a disciple, but the search of the ego is to be the master. The ego would like to teach, not to learn, and even if you learn it is learning with the idea of how to get ready to teach.

You listen to me. With listening I have two categories also: you can listen like a disciple or you can listen like a would-be master. If you listen like a would-be master you will miss, because you cannot listen with that attitude. If you are just waiting to get ready to jump into being a master and teach others, you cannot be receptive. You can learn only if you are a disciple with no thought of becoming a master. This was one of the oldest traditions in the East – that a person would not start teaching unless his master told him to.

There was one disciple of Buddha who remained for many years with him; his name was Purna. He became enlightened, and he still remained with Buddha. After his enlightenment he would also come every day in the morning to listen to Buddha. He himself was now a buddha; nothing was lacking, he stood now in his own right, but he continued to come.

One day Buddha asked Purna, "Why do you go on coming? Now you can stop."

Purna said, "Unless you say so, how can I stop? If you say so, it is okay." Then he stopped coming to Buddha's lectures, but he remained just like a shadow moving with the *sangha*, with the order. Then after a few years, again Buddha said, "Purna, why do you go on following me? You go and teach people! You need not be here with me."

And Purna said, "I was waiting. When you say so, I will go. I am a disciple, so whatsoever you say I will do. If you say so, it's okay. So where should I go? Which direction should I go? Whom should I teach? You simply direct me and I will follow! I am a follower."

This man must have listened to Buddha totally, because even when he becomes enlightened he remains a disciple. And there are people who are absolutely ignorant and they are already "masters." Even if they are listening, they are listening with an attitude that sooner or later they have to teach. You listen just to tell others what you have learned! Drop that idea completely from the mind, because if that idea is there, if the would-be master is there, the disciple cannot exist with that idea; they never coexist.

A disciple is simply a disciple. One day it happens that he becomes a master – but that is not the end, that is just a consequence. Just by being a learner one becomes wise. That is a consequence, not the goal. If you learn simply to become wise you will never learn, because to be wise is an ego-goal, an ego-trip. And if you are just waiting to ripen, mature, and become a master, and this disciplehood is just a passage to be passed through – the sooner the better, it has to be finished, you are not happy in it, you would like to end it – then you are not a disciple, and you will never be a master. ...Because when a disciple ripens, he becomes a master spontaneously. That is not a goal to be followed, it happens as a byproduct.

The brash student – impudent, rude, thinking that he already knows… and that is the only impudence that can happen to a mind, to think that you already know.

> *When Yamaoka was a brash student he visited the master Dokuon.*
> *Wanting to impress the master he said…*

These Yamaokas come to me almost every day. I have met many, this Yamaoka is a type. People come to me and sometimes I enjoy it very much.

Once it happened: a man came; he talked for one hour – talked the whole Vedanta, and he had been asking for an interview for many days, writing letters to me, and he had traveled far, and he had been saying that he would like to ask a few questions. When he came he forgot about the questions, he started giving me answers – and I had not asked anything! For one hour he talked and talked and talked, there was not even a gap so I could interrupt him. No, he wouldn't listen even, so I had to say yes, yes, yes. And I listened to him and enjoyed it, and after one hour he said, "Now I will have to go, my time is finished but I learned so many things from you. And I will remember this meeting for ever and ever. I will cherish this memory – and you have solved all my problems."

Really, this was his problem: that he wanted to talk and say things and give some knowledge to me. And he was very happy because I listened. He remained the same, but he went away happy.

People come to me and they say that of course they know that "All is brahman." India is burdened too much with knowledge, and fools have become greater fools because of that burden because they all know, and they talk as knowers. They say that all is brahman, that reality is non-dual, and then in the end they ask, "My mind is very tense. Can you suggest something?"

If you know that existence is non-dual, if you know that the two does not exist, how can you be troubled and tense? If you know this, all trouble has gone, all worry dissolved, anguish disappears! But if you say to them, "You don't know," they won't listen. And if you just go on listening to them, in the end the real will come out automatically.

In a court, it happened: a man was charged with stealing a pocket watch. The man whose watch was stolen was a little shortsighted, his eyes were weak and he could see only with specs. He had forgotten his specs somewhere, and then on the street this man cut his pocket and took the watch. When the judge inquired, "Can you recognize that this is the man who has taken your watch?" the robbed man said, "It is difficult, because my eyes are weak, and without specs I cannot see rightly, everything is a little blurred. So I cannot say exactly whether it is this man or not, but my watch is stolen and I feel it is this man."

But because there was no other eyewitness or anything, and it could not be proved, the magistrate had to free the man. He said, "Now you can go, now you are free."

But the man looked a little puzzled. The judge said, "Now you can go, you are free!" The man still looked puzzled, and the judge asked, "Do you want to ask anything?"

He said, "Yes, can I have the watch? Can I keep it?"

This is what is happening...people go on talking, and if you go on listening to them, in the end you will find all their Vedanta is useless. In the end they ask something that shows their reality. The other was just language, verbalization.

This Yamaoka visited the master Dokuon – Dokuon was an enlightened man, one of the most loved in Japan, one of the most respected.

Wanting to impress the master he said...

When you want to impress a master you are a fool, you are a perfectly stupid man. You may want to impress the whole world, but don't try to impress a master; at least there, open your heart. Don't talk nonsense; at least there, be true.

If you go to a doctor you expose all your diseases to him, you allow him to diagnose, to examine, you tell everything, whatsoever is there, you don't hide anything. If you hide from a doctor, then why go to him in the first place? Go on hiding! But how do you expect him to help you if you hide?

To a doctor you tell everything about the body, to a master you have to tell everything about the soul; otherwise no help is possible. When you go to a master, go completely! Don't create a barrier of words between you and him. Say only whatsoever you know. If you don't know anything, say, "I don't know."

When P. D. Ouspensky came to Gurdjieff he was a great scholar, already world famous – more known in the world than Gurdjieff himself. Gurdjieff was an unknown *fakir* in those days; he became known through Ouspensky. Ouspensky had written a great book before he met Gurdjieff. The book is really rare because he talks as if he knows, and he is such an articulate man that he can deceive. The book is *Tertium Organum,* third canon of thought, and really one of the rarest books in the world. Even ignorance can sometimes do things; if you are skillful you can do things even in your ignorance.

Ouspensky claims in that book – and his claim is right – that there exist only three real books in the world: one is Aristotle's *Organum*, the first canon of thought; second is Bacon's *Novum Organum*, new canon of thought, the second canon of thought; and the third is his own *Tertium Organum*, third canon of thought. And really these three books are rare. All the three authors are ignorant, none of them knows anything about truth, but they are very articulate men. They really have done miracles: without knowing about truth they have written beautiful books. They have almost come around, approximately they have reached.

Ouspensky was a name; when he came to Gurdjieff, Gurdjieff was nobody. Of course he came with the knowledge that Gurdjieff was a man of being – really a man of no knowledge, but of very substantial being. What did Gurdjieff do? He did something beautiful: he remained silent. Ouspensky waited and waited and waited, became fidgety, started perspiring before this man because he simply remained silent, looking at him, and it was so awkward, and his eyes were very, very penetrating. If he wanted to he could burn you with his eyes. His face was such that, if he wanted to, he could simply shake you out of your being with his face. If he looked into you, you would feel very uneasy. He remained like a statue, and Ouspensky started trembling, a fever came over him. Then he asked, "But why are you silent? Why don't you say something?"

Gurdjieff said, "First one thing has to be decided, absolutely decided; only then will I say even a single word. Go into the other room, you will find a piece of paper there; write on it whatsoever you know, and also that which you don't know. Make two columns: one of your knowledge, one of your ignorance, because whatsoever you know I need not talk about. We are finished with it; you know it, there's no need to talk about it. Whatsoever you don't know, I will talk about."

Ouspensky has reported that he went into that room, sat on a chair, took the paper and the pencil – and for the first time in his life realized that he didn't know anything. This man Gurdjieff destroyed his whole knowledge because, for the first time with awareness, he was going to write: "I know God." How to write that? – because he didn't know. How to write: "I know truth?" Ouspensky was authentic; he came back after half an hour, gave the blank sheet of paper to Gurdjieff and said, "Now you start work. I don't know anything."

Gurdjieff said, "How could you write *Tertium Organum*? You don't know anything, and you have written the third canon of thought!"

It's as if people go on writing in their sleep, go on writing in their dreams. As if they don't know what they are doing, they don't know what is happening through them.

> *Wanting to impress the master, Yamaoka said, "There is no mind, there is no body, there is no buddha. There is no better, there is no worse. There is no master, there is no student. There is no giving, there is no receiving. What we think we see and feel is not real. None of these seeming things really exists."*

This is the highest teaching, the ultimate truth. This is the essence of the whole tradition of Buddha, that Buddha says everything is empty. That's what we were talking about when I discussed Sosan with you: everything is empty, everything is just relative, nothing exists absolutely. This is the highest realization. But you can read it in a book, and if you read it in a book and say it, it is simply stupid.

"There is no mind, there is no body, there is no Buddha."

Buddha has said, "I am not." But when Buddha says it, it means something. When Yamaoka says it, it means nothing. When Buddha says it, it is very significant: "I am not." He says, "Even I am not, so be more alert – you cannot be. This is my realization," he says. "Personality is just like a wave, or a line drawn on the water. It is a form, and form is continuously changing. The form is not truth. Only the formless can be the true. Only the unchanging can be true."

And, Buddha says, "It may take seventy years for your form to disappear, but it disappears – and that which was not one day, and again one day will not be, cannot be in the middle. I was not, one day; I will not be, one day. On two sides, nothing – and just in the middle, I am? This is not possible. How, between two nonexistences, can existence exist? How, between two emptinesses, can there be something substantial? It must be a false dream."

Why, in the morning, do you say that the dream was false? It was, but why do you say it was false? What is the criterion of its being false or true? How do you judge? In the morning everybody says, "I dreamed, and the dream was false." Dream means the false – but why? This is the criterion: in the evening it was not there, when I went to sleep it was not there, when I came out of sleep again it was not there, so how can it be in the middle? The room is real, the dream is false – because when you went into sleep the room was there, and when you came out of sleep the room was there. The room is real, the dream is false, because the dream has two nothingnesses around it, and between two nothingnesses, nothing can exist. But the room continues, so you say that the room is real, the world is real, and the dream is false.

A buddha has awakened out of this world and he sees that, just like the dream, your world is also false. He has awakened out of this great dream which we call the world, and then he says, "It was not there, now again it is not there, so how could it be in the middle?" Hence buddhas, shankaras, go on saying, "The world is illusory, it is a dream." But you cannot say it; you cannot just take the words and repeat them.

This Yamaoka must have listened, must have learned, read, studied. He is repeating like a parrot: *"There is no mind, there is no body, there is no buddha. There is no better, there is no worse"* – because they are all relative. Remember, Buddha calls anything relative false, and anything absolute true. Absoluteness is the criterion of truth, relativity is the criterion of a dream.

Try to understand this, because this is basic. You say your friend is tall. What do you mean? He can only be said to be taller, not tall – taller than somebody. He may be a pygmy next to somebody else, so tallness is not in him. Tallness is just a relationship, a relative phenomenon. In comparison to somebody he is taller, in comparison to somebody else he may be a pygmy. So who is he – is he a pygmy or a tall man? No, these two things are relativities. In himself, who is he – tall or a pygmy? In himself he is neither tall nor a pygmy. That's why Buddha says, "The better does not exist, the worse does not exist."

Who is a sinner and who is a saint? Look! – if there are only saints in the world will there be any saint? If there are only sinners in the world will there be any sinner? The sinner exists because of the saint, the saint exists because of the sinner – they are relativities. So if you want to be a saint you will create a sinner; you cannot be a saint without there being sinners. So be aware not to become a saint, because if you become a saint that means somewhere the other polarity will have to exist.

Saints are false, sinners are false. Who are you in yourself? If you are alone, are you a sinner or a saint? Then you are neither. Look into that reality which you are, unrelated to anything else; look into yourself without relation – then you will come to the absolute truth; otherwise everything is just a relative term. Relativities are dreams.

Reality is not a relativity, it is an absoluteness. Who are you?

If you go inside and you say, "I am light," you are dreaming again, because what can light mean without darkness? Light needs darkness to be there! If you say, "Inside I am blissful," again you are dreaming, because bliss needs misery to be there. You cannot use any term because all terms are relativities. That's why Buddha says that we cannot use any term – because inside there is emptiness. Also, this "emptiness" is not against "fullness"; this is just to say that all terms are empty. In absolute truth, no term applies, you cannot say anything.

Buddha will not be in agreement with Hindus and say that reality is s*at-chit-anand*, because he says that s*at* exists because of *asat*, *chit* exists because of *achit*, *anand* exists because of *dukkha*. *Sat* is existence; reality cannot be said to be existential because then nonexistence would be needed, and where will nonexistence exist? Reality cannot be said to be consciousness, because then unconsciousness would be needed, and where will unconsciousness exist? Reality cannot be said to be bliss, because then misery would be needed.

Buddha says whatsoever word you use is useless, because the opposite will be needed.

Look into yourself – then you cannot use language, only silence. Only through silence can reality be indicated. And when he says, "All terms are empty, all words are empty, all things are empty, all thoughts are empty," he means this because they are relative – relativity is a dream.

> *There is no better, there is no worse. There is no master, there is no*
> *student. There is no giving, there is no receiving. What we think we see*
> *and feel is not real. None of these seeming things really exists.*

This is the most profound teaching of Buddha, so one thing has to be remembered: you can repeat the most profound words ever uttered, and you can still be a stupid man. This Yamaoka is stupid. He's repeating exactly the same words as Buddha.

Words carry your being. When Buddha says the same words, they have a different significance, a different fragrance. The words carry something of the Buddha, something of his being: the aroma, the taste, of his inner being. The music of his inner harmony is carried by those words. When Yamaoka repeats those words they are dead, stale, they don't carry any fragrance. They will carry something: they will carry Yamaoka and his bad odor.

Remember, just by repeating the Gita, don't think anything is going to happen, although the words are the same, and Krishna said the same words you are repeating. All over the world thousands of Christian missionaries go on repeating the same words that Jesus spoke. Those words are dead. It is better not to repeat them, because the more you repeat them, the more stale they become. It is better not to touch them, because your very touch is poisonous. It is better to wait. When you attain to a Christ-consciousness, or a Krishna-consciousness, or a Buddha-consciousness, then you will begin to flower, then things will start coming out of you – never before. Don't be a gramophone record...because then you can only repeat, but that doesn't mean anything.

> *Dokuon had been sitting quietly smoking his pipe...*

A very beautiful man – he didn't even bother. He didn't interrupt, he simply continued smoking his pipe.

Remember, only Zen masters can smoke a pipe, because they are not pretenders. They don't bother what you think about them – they don't bother! They are people at ease with themselves. You cannot think of a Jaina *muni* smoking a pipe, or a Hindu sannyasin smoking a pipe, impossible. These are men of rules, regulations, they have forced themselves into disciplines. No need to smoke a pipe if you don't want to, but if you want to, then don't force something dead upon yourself, because that desire will remain hidden somewhere and will disturb. And why? If you want to smoke a pipe, why not smoke it? What is wrong in it? You are as false as the pipe and the smoke, and the smoke and the pipe are as true as you.

But why not? Deep down you want to be extraordinary, not ordinary. Smoking a pipe will make you very ordinary. This is what ordinary people are doing: smoking a pipe, drinking tea and coffee, and laughing and joking, this is what ordinary people are doing. You are a great saint – how can you do ordinary things in an ordinary way? You are very extraordinary.

To pose extraordinariness you drop many things. Nothing is bad in dropping them – if you don't like them, it's okay. There's no need to force yourself to smoke a pipe just to say that you are ordinary, no need...because this is how the mind goes! No need to do anything if you don't want to, but if you want to then don't pose, don't try to have a mask of seriousness. Then be simple. Nothing is wrong if you are simple; everything is wrong if you are not simple.

This monk Dokuon must have been a simple man:

Dokuon had been sitting quietly smoking his pipe...

very meditative, just relaxing, listening to this pretender –

and saying nothing. Suddenly, he picked up his staff and gave Yamaoka a terrible whack.

Zen masters carry a staff for such people. They are very gentle people, but very authentic, and there are people who will not listen to words, who can listen only to a whack. If you talk to them, they won't listen, they will talk still more. They need shock treatment.

Suddenly, he picked up his staff and gave Yamaoka a terrible whack.
Yamaoka jumped up in anger.
Dokuon said: "Since none of these things really exists, and all is
emptiness, where does your anger come from? Think about it."

Dokuon has created a situation, and only situations are revealing. He could have said, "Whatsoever you are saying is just borrowed information." That wouldn't have made much difference because the man sitting before him was fast asleep. Just talking would not have brought him out of it; it may have even helped him go more into it, he may have started arguing. Rather than doing that, Dokuon did the right thing; he hit hard with the staff. Suddenly, because Yamaoka was not ready for it, it came unexpectedly. It was so sudden that he could not arrange his character accordingly, he could not manage a false pose. For a moment – the whack was so sudden – the mask slipped, and the real face came out. Just by talking this would not have been possible. Dokuon must have been very compassionate.

Just for a single moment anger peeped out, the real came out – because if everything is empty, how can you be angry? Where can the anger come from? Who will be angry if even a Buddha is not, you are not, nothing is there, only emptiness exists? How, in emptiness, is anger possible?

What Dokuon is doing is bringing this Yamaoka from knowledge to being; that's what he is doing by whacking him. A situation is needed, because in a situation suddenly you become real, whatsoever you are. If words are allowed, if Dokuon talks and says, "This is wrong and that is right," he helps the continuity of the mind. Then a dialogue will be there, but of no use. He gives a shock, he brings you back to your reality. Suddenly all thinking disappears; Yamaoka is Yamaoka, not a buddha. He was talking like a buddha, and just with a hit, the buddha disappears and in comes Yamaoka – angry. Dokuon said: "Since none of these things really exists, and all is emptiness, Yamaoka, where does your anger come from? Think about it.

"Don't talk about Buddha; and don't talk about reality, and don't talk about truth – think about this anger and from where it comes. If you really think about anger, from where it comes, you will reach to emptiness."

Next time, when you feel angry…or if you cannot, then come to me, I will give you a whack. I go on giving, but my whacks are more subtle than Dokuon's. I don't need a real staff – it is not needed; you are so unreal, a real staff is not needed. I need not physically give you a whack, but spiritually I go on giving. I go on creating situations in which I try to bring you back to your Yamaokahood from your buddhahood, because that Yamaoka is real within you, buddha is just a mask. And remember, Yamaoka has to live, not the mask; Yamaoka has to breathe, not the mask; Yamaoka has to digest food, not the mask. Yamaoka will fall in love, Yamaoka will be angry, Yamaoka will have to die, not the mask – so it is better that you are freed from the mask and brought back to your Yamaokahood.

Remember, the buddha cannot be a mask. If Yamaoka goes on going deeper in himself, he will find a buddha there. And how to go deeper in yourself? Follow anything that comes from within; follow it back, regress back. Anger has come? – close your eyes; it is a beautiful moment, because anger has come from within...from the very center of your being it comes, so just look backwards, move, just see from where it is coming. From where?

What you would do ordinarily; and what this Yamaoka could have done, would be to think that the anger has been created because of this Dokuon. "Because he hit me, that's why anger is created." You would look at Dokuon as the source. Dokuon is not the source; he may have whacked you but he is not the source – if he whacked Buddha, anger would not come – it is Yamaoka.

Go back, don't look outside for the source, otherwise this beautiful moment of anger will be lost – your life has become so false that within a second you will put on your mask again, and you will smile, and you will say, "Yes, master, you did a very good thing."

The false will come in soon, so don't miss the moment. When the anger has come, it is just a split second before the false comes. And anger is true; it is truer than what you are saying – the words of Buddha are false in your mouth. Your anger is true because it belongs to you. All that belongs to you is true. So find the source of this anger, from where it is coming. Close your eyes and move inwards. Before it is lost, go backwards to the source – and you will reach emptiness. Go backwards more, go inwards more, move deeper, and a moment comes when there is no anger. Inside, at the center, there is no anger. Now, the buddha will not be just a face, a mask. Now something real has been penetrated.

From where does the anger come? It never comes from your center, it comes from the ego – and ego is a false entity. If you go deeper you will find it comes from the periphery, not from the center. It cannot come from the center: at the center is emptiness, absolute emptiness. It comes only from the ego, and ego is a false entity created by the society, it is a relativity, an identity. Suddenly you are whacked, and the ego feels hurt, anger is there.

If you help somebody, smile at somebody, bow down to somebody and he smiles, that smile is coming from the ego. If you appreciate, give compliments to somebody, if you say to a woman, "How beautiful you are!" and she smiles, that smile is coming from the ego, because at the center there is neither beauty nor ugliness. At the center there exists absolute emptiness, *anatta*, no-selfness – and that center has to be achieved.

Once you know it, you move as a nonbeing. Nobody can make you angry, nobody can make you happy, unhappy, miserable, no. In that emptiness all dualities dissolve: happy, unhappy, miserable, blissful, all dissolve. This is buddhahood. This is what happened under the bodhi tree to Gautam Siddhartha. He reached the emptiness. Then everything is silent. You have gone beyond the opposites.

A master is to help you to go to your inner emptiness, the inner silence, the inner temple; and the master has to devise methods. Only Zen masters beat you; sometimes they throw a person out of the window, or they jump on him. Because you have become so false, such drastic methods are needed – and in Japan particularly, because Japan is so false. That's why such drastic methods are needed.

In Japan, a smile is a painted smile. Everybody smiles – it is just a habit, a beautiful habit as far as the society is concerned, because in Japan, if you are driving and you hit a person on a Tokyo road, something will happen which can never happen anywhere else: the person will smile and bow down and thank you. Only in Japan can this happen, nowhere else. He will say, "This is my fault," and you will say, "This is my fault," if you are Japanese. Both will say, "This is my fault," and both will bow down and smile and go their ways. In a way it is good, because what is the use of being angry and shouting at each other and creating a crowd, what is the use?

From their very childhood the Japanese are conditioned to always smile; that's why in the West they are thought to be very sly people: you cannot rely on them because you don't know what they are feeling. You cannot know what a Japanese feels, he never allows anything to come out.

This is one extreme: everything false, painted. So Zen masters had to devise these drastic methods, because only through them would the Japanese mask fall down; otherwise it is fixed, it has almost become their skin, as if grafted on the skin. But this is happening to the whole world now, not only Japan. Degrees may differ, but now this is the whole world. Everybody laughs, smiles – neither the laugh is true, nor the smile. Everybody says good things about each other but nobody believes in them, nobody feels that way; it has become social etiquette.

Your personality is a social phenomenon. Your being is buried deep down under this personality. You need a shock, so that the personality is thrown open, or for some moments you are no longer identified with it and you reach to the center. There, everything is empty.

The whole art of meditation is how to leave the personality easily, move to the center, and be not a person. Just to be, and not be a person, is the whole art of meditation, the whole art of inner ecstasy.

Enough for today.

that which doesn't change

A Zen student came to Bankei and said: "Master, I have an ungovernable temper – how can I cure it?" "Show me this temper," said Bankei, "it sounds fascinating." "I haven't got it right now," said the student, "so I can't show it to you." "Well then," said Bankei, "bring it to me when you have it." "But I can't bring it just when I happen to have it," protested the student. "It arises unexpectedly, and I would surely lose it before I got it to you." "In that case," said Bankei, "it cannot be part of your true nature. If it were, you could show it to me at any time. When you were born you did not have it, and your parents did not give it to you – so it must come into you from the outside. I suggest that whenever it gets into you, you beat yourself with a stick until the temper can't stand it, and runs away."

The true nature is your eternal nature. You cannot have it and not have it, it is not something that comes and goes – it is you. How can it come and go? It is your being. It is your very foundation. It cannot *be* sometimes, and *not be* sometimes; it is always there.

This should be the criterion for a seeker of truth, nature, tao: that we have to come to the point in our being which remains always and always – even before you were born it was there, and even when you are dead it will be there. It is the center. The circumference changes, the center remains absolutely eternal; it is beyond time. Nothing can affect it, nothing can modify it, nothing really ever touches it; it remains beyond all reach of the outside world.

Go and watch the sea. Millions of waves are there, but deep in its depth the sea remains calm and quiet, deep in meditation; just on the surface is the turmoil, just on the surface where the sea meets the outside world, the winds. Otherwise, in itself, it always remains the same, not even a ripple; nothing changes.

It is the same with you. Just on the surface where you meet others there is turmoil, anxiety, anger, attachment, greed, lust – just on the surface where winds come and touch you. And if you remain on the surface you cannot change this changing phenomenon; it will remain there.

Many people try to change it there, on the circumference. They fight with it, they try not to let a wave arise. And through their fight even more waves arise, because when the sea fights with the wind there will be more turmoil: now not only will the wind help it, the sea will also help – there will be tremendous chaos on the surface.

All the moralists try to change a man on the periphery; the character is your periphery. You don't bring any character into the world, you come absolutely character*less*, a blank sheet, and all that you call your character is written by others. Your parents, society, teachers, teachings – all are conditionings. You come as a blank sheet, and whatsoever is written on you comes from others; so unless you become a blank sheet again you will not know what nature is, you will not know what brahman is, you will not know what tao is.

So the problem is not how to have a strong character, the problem is not how to attain no-anger, how not to be disturbed – no, that is not the problem. The problem is how to change your consciousness from the periphery to the center. Suddenly you see that you have always been calm and then you can look at the periphery from a distance, and the distance is so vast, infinite, that you can watch as if it is not happening to you. In fact, it never happens to you. Even when you are completely lost in it, it never happens to you: something in you remains undisturbed, something in you remains beyond, something in you remains a witness.

The whole problem for the seeker is how to shift his attention from the periphery to the center; how to be merged with that which is unchanging, and not to be identified with that which is just a boundary. On the boundary others are very influential, because on the boundary change is natural. The periphery will go on changing – even a Buddha's periphery changes.

The difference between a buddha and you is not a difference of character – remember it. It is not a difference of morality, it is not a difference in virtue or non-virtue. It is a difference in where you are grounded.

You are grounded on the periphery, a Buddha is grounded in the center. He can look at his own periphery from a distance; when you hit him he can see it as if you have hit somebody else, because the center is so distant...as if he is a watcher on the hills and something is happening in the valleys and he can see it. This is the first thing to be understood.

Second thing: it is very easy to control, it is very difficult to transform. It is very easy to control. You can control your anger, but what will you do? – you will suppress it. And what happens when you suppress a certain thing? The direction of its movement changes: it was going out, and if you suppress, it starts going in – just the direction changes. And for the anger to go out was good, because the poison needs to be thrown out. It is bad for the anger to move within, because that means your whole bodymind structure will be poisoned by it.

And then if you go on doing it for a long time...as everybody has been doing, because the society teaches control, not transformation. The society says, "Control yourself," and through controlling, all the negative things have been thrown deeper and deeper into the unconscious. Then they become a constant thing within you. Then it is not a question that sometimes you are angry and sometimes not – you are simply angry. Sometimes you explode, and sometimes you don't explode because there is no excuse, or you have to find an excuse. And remember, you can find an excuse anywhere!

A man, one of my friends, wanted to divorce his wife, so he went to a lawyer, an expert on marriage affairs, and he asked the lawyer, "On what grounds can I divorce my wife?"

The lawyer looked at him and said, "Are you married?" The man said, "Of course, yes." The lawyer said, "Marriage is enough grounds. There is no need to seek any other grounds. If you want a divorce, then marriage is the only thing that is needed, because it will be almost impossible to divorce a woman if you are not married. If you are married that's enough!"

And this is the situation. You are angry. Because you have suppressed so much anger, now there are no moments when you are not angry; at the most, sometimes you are less angry and sometimes more. Your whole being is poisoned by suppression. You eat with anger – and it has a different quality when a person eats without anger: it is beautiful to watch him, because he eats nonviolently. He may be eating meat, but he eats nonviolently; you may be eating just vegetables and fruits, but if anger is suppressed, you eat violently.

Just through eating, your teeth and your mouth release anger. You crush the food as if this is the enemy. And remember, whenever animals are angry, what will they do? Only two things are possible – they don't have weapons and they don't have atom bombs, what can they do? Either with their nails or with their teeth they will do violence to you.

These are the natural weapons of the body – nails and teeth. It is very difficult to do anything with your nails, because people will say, "Are you an animal?" So the only thing remaining through which you can express your anger or violence easily is the mouth – and that too you cannot use to bite anybody.

That's why we say, "a bite of bread," "a bite of food," "a few bites." You eat food violently, as if the food is the enemy. And remember, when the food is the enemy, it does not really nourish you, it nourishes all that is ill in you. People with deep, suppressed anger eat more; they go on gathering unnecessary fat in the body. And have you observed that fat people are almost always smiling? Unnecessarily, even if there is no cause, fat people always go on smiling. Why? This is their face, this is the mask: they are so much afraid of their anger and their violence that they have to keep a smiling face continuously on themselves – and they go on eating more.

Eating more is violence, anger. And then this will move in every way, in every arena of your life. You will make love, but it will be more like violence than like love, it will have much aggression in it. Because you never observe one another making love, you don't know what is happening, and you cannot know what is happening to you because you are almost always so much in aggression.

That's why deep orgasm through lovemaking becomes impossible – because you are afraid deep down that if you move totally without control, you may kill your wife or kill your beloved, or the wife may kill the husband or the lover. You become so afraid of your own anger! Next time you make love, watch: you are doing the same movements as are done when you are aggressive. Watch the face, have a mirror around so you can see what is happening to your face – all the distortions of anger and aggression will be there.

In taking food, you become angry: look at a person eating. Look at a person making love – the anger has gone so deep that even love, an activity totally opposite to anger, even that is poisoned. Eating, an absolutely neutral activity, even that is poisoned. Then you just open the door and there is anger, you put a book on the table and there is anger, you take off the shoes and there is anger, you shake hands and there is anger – because now you are anger personified.

Through suppression, mind becomes split. The part that you accept becomes the conscious, and the part that you deny becomes the unconscious. This division is not natural, the division happens because of repression. And into the unconscious you go on throwing all the rubbish that society rejects – but remember, whatsoever you throw in there becomes more and more part of you. It goes into your hands, into your bones, into your blood, into your heartbeat. Now psychologists say that almost eighty percent of diseases are caused by repressed emotions: so many heart failures means so much anger has been repressed in the heart, so much hatred that the heart is poisoned.

Why? Why does man suppress so much and become unhealthy? The society teaches you to control, not to transform, and the way of transformation is totally different. For one thing, it is not the way of control at all, it is just the opposite.

First thing: in control you repress, in transformation you express. But there is no need to express on somebody else because the "somebody else" is just irrelevant.

Next time you feel angry, go and run around the house seven times, and after it sit under a tree and watch where the anger has gone. You have not repressed it, you have not controlled it, you have not thrown it on somebody else – because if you throw it on somebody else a chain is created, because the other is as foolish as you, as unconscious as you. If you throw it on another, and if the other is an enlightened person, there will be no trouble; he will help you to throw and release it and go through a catharsis. But the other is as ignorant as you – if you throw anger on him he will react. He will throw more anger on you, he is repressed as much as you are. Then there comes a chain: you throw on him, he throws on you, and you both become enemies.

Don't throw it on anybody. It is just like when you feel like vomiting: you don't go and vomit on somebody. Anger needs a vomit; you go to the bathroom and vomit – it cleanses the whole body. If you suppress the vomit it will be dangerous, and when you have vomited you will feel fresh, you will feel unburdened, unloaded, good, healthy. Something was wrong in the food that you have taken and the body rejects it. Don't go on forcing it inside.

Anger is just a mental vomit. Something is wrong that you have taken in. Your whole psychic being wants to throw it out, but there is no need to throw it out on somebody. Because people throw it on somebody, society tells them to control.

There is no need to throw it on anybody. You can go to your bathroom, you can go on a long walk – it means that something is inside that needs fast activity so that it is released. Just do a little jogging and you will feel it is released, or take a pillow and beat it; fight and bite the pillow until your hands and teeth are relaxed. Within a five-minute catharsis you will feel unburdened, and once you know this you will never throw it on anybody, because that is absolutely foolish.

The first thing in transformation then is to express anger, but not on anybody, because if you express it on somebody you cannot express it totally. You may like to kill, but it is not possible; you may like to bite, but it is not possible. But that can be done to a pillow. A pillow means "already enlightened";

the pillow is enlightened, a buddha. The pillow will not react, and the pillow will not go to any court, and the pillow will not bring any enmity against you, and the pillow will not do anything. The pillow will be happy, and the pillow will laugh at you.

The second thing to remember: be aware. In controlling, no awareness is needed; you simply do it mechanically, like a robot. The anger comes and there is a mechanism – suddenly your whole being becomes narrow and closed. If you are watchful, control may not be so easy.

Society never teaches you to be watchful, because when somebody is watchful, one is wide open. That is part of awareness – one is open, and if you want to suppress something and you are open, it is contradictory, it may come out. The society teaches you how to close yourself in, how to cave yourself in – don't allow even a small window for anything to go out.

But remember; when nothing goes out, nothing comes in either. When the anger cannot go out, you are closed. If you touch a beautiful rock, nothing goes in; you look at a flower, nothing goes in, your eyes are dead and closed. You kiss a person, nothing goes in, because you are closed. You live an insensitive life.

Sensitivity grows with awareness. Through control you become dull and dead, that is part of the mechanism of control. If you are dull and dead then nothing will affect you, as if the body has become a citadel, a defense. Nothing will affect you, neither insult nor love.

But this control is at a very great cost, an unnecessary cost. Then it becomes the whole effort in life: how to control yourself – and then die! The whole effort of control takes all your energy, and then you simply die. And the life becomes a dull and dead thing; you somehow carry it on.

The society teaches you control and condemnation, because a child will control only when he feels something is condemned. Anger is bad; sex is bad; everything that has to be controlled has to be made to look like a sin to the child, to look like evil.

Mulla Nasruddin's son was growing up. He was ten years of age and so Mulla thought: Now, this is the time. He is old enough and the secrets of life must be revealed to him. So he called him into his study and gave him the lowdown on sex among birds and bees. And then in the end he told him, "When you feel your younger brother is old enough, you tell the whole thing to him also."

Just after a few minutes, when he was passing by the rooms of the kids, he heard the older, ten-year-old one, already at work. He was telling the younger: "Look, you know what people do, that stuff people do when they want to get a child, a baby? Well, Dad says birds and bees do the same darn thing."

A deep condemnation enters about all that is alive. And sex is the most alive thing – has to be! It is the source. Anger is also a most alive thing, because it is a protective force. If a child cannot be angry at all, he will not be able to survive. You have to be angry in certain moments. The child has to show his own being, the child has to stand in certain moments upon his own ground; otherwise he will have no backbone.

Anger is beautiful; sex is beautiful. But beautiful things can go ugly. That depends on you. If you condemn them, they become ugly; if you transform them, they become divine. Anger transformed becomes compassion – because the energy is the same. A buddha is compassionate; from where does this compassion come? This is the same energy that was moving in anger; now it is not moving in anger, the same energy is transformed into compassion. From where does love come? A Buddha is loving; a Jesus is love. The same energy that moves into sex becomes love.

So remember, if you condemn a natural phenomenon it becomes poisonous, it destroys you, it becomes destructive and suicidal. If you transform it, it becomes divine, it becomes a God-force, it becomes an elixir. You attain through it to immortality, to a deathless being. But transformation is needed.

In transformation you never control, you simply become more aware. Anger is happening – you have to be aware that anger is happening – watch it! It is a beautiful phenomenon; energy moving within you, becoming hot!

It is just like electricity in the clouds. People were always afraid of electricity. They thought in olden days, when they were ignorant, that this electricity was the god being angry, being threatening, trying to punish – creating fear so that people would become worshippers. So that people would feel that the god was there and he would punish them.

But now we have domesticated that god. Now that god runs through your fan, through your air conditioner, through the fridge: whatsoever you need, that god serves. That god has become a domestic force, it is no longer angry and no longer threatening. Through science an outer force has been transformed into a friend.

The same happens through religion for inner forces.

Anger is just like electricity in your body: you don't know what to do with it. Either you kill somebody else or you kill yourself. The society says if you kill yourself it is okay, it is your concern, but don't kill anybody else – and as far as society goes that is okay. So either you become aggressive or you become repressive.

Religion says both are wrong. The basic thing that is needed is to become aware and to know the secret of this energy, anger, this inner electricity. It is electricity because you become hot; when you are angry your temperature goes hot, and you cannot understand the coolness of a Buddha, because when anger is transformed into compassion everything is cool. A deep coolness happens. Buddha is never hot; he is always cool, centered, because he now knows how to use the inner electricity. Electricity is hot – it becomes the source of air conditioning. Anger is hot – it becomes the source of compassion.

Compassion is an inner air conditioning. Suddenly everything is cool and beautiful, and nothing can disturb you, and the whole existence is transformed into a friend. Now there is no more enemy...because when you look through the eyes of anger, somebody becomes an enemy; when you look through the eyes of compassion, everybody is a friend, a neighbor. When you love, everywhere is God; when you hate, everywhere is the Devil. It is your standpoint that is projected onto reality.

Awareness is needed, not condemnation – and through awareness, transformation happens spontaneously. If you become aware of your anger with no judgment, not saying good, not saying bad, just watching - in your inner sky there is lightning, anger, you feel hot. The whole nervous system shaking and quaking, and you feel a tremor all over the body – a beautiful moment, because when energy functions you can watch it easily; when it is not functioning you cannot watch.

Close your eyes and meditate on it. Don't fight, just look at what is happening – the whole sky is filled with electricity, so much lightning, so much beauty – just lie down on the ground and look at the sky and watch. Do the same inside.

Clouds are there, because without clouds there can be no lightning – dark clouds are there, thoughts. Somebody has insulted you, somebody has laughed at you, somebody has said this or that...many clouds, dark clouds in the inner sky and much lightning. Watch! It is a beautiful scene – terrible also, because you don't understand. It is mysterious, and if mystery is not understood it becomes terrible, you are afraid of it. And whenever a mystery is understood, it becomes a grace, a gift, because now you have the keys – and with keys you are the master.

You don't control it, you simply become a master when you are aware. And the more you become aware, the more inwards you penetrate, because awareness is a going-inwards, it always goes inwards. More aware, more in. Totally aware, perfectly in. Less aware, more out. Unconscious – you are completely out, out of your house, wandering around. Unconsciousness is a wandering outside; consciousness is a deepening of the inside.

So look! – and when anger is not, it will be difficult to look: what to look at? The sky is so vacant, and you are not yet capable of looking at emptiness.

When anger is there, look, watch, and soon you will see a change. The moment the watcher comes in, the anger has already started being cool, the heat is lost. Then you can understand that the heat is given by you; your identification with it makes it hot, and the moment you feel it is not hot, the fear is gone, and you feel unidentified with it, different, a distance.

It is there, lightning around you, but you are not it.

A hill starts rising upwards. You become a watcher: down in the valley, much lightning – distance grows more and more – and a moment comes when suddenly you are not joined to it at all. The identity is broken, and the moment the identity breaks, immediately the whole hot process becomes a cool process – anger becomes compassion.

Sex is a hot process, love is not. But all over the world people always talk about warm love. Love is not warm; love is absolutely cool, but not cold – it is not cold because it is not dead. It is cool, just like a cool breeze. But it is not hot, not warm. Because of the identification with sex, the conception has come to the mind that love should be warm.

Sex is hot. It is electricity, and you are identified with it. The more love, the more coolness – you may even feel cool love as cold; that is your misunderstanding, because you feel love has to be hot. It cannot be. The same energy, when not identified with, becomes cool. Compassion is cool, and if your compassion is still hot, understand it is not compassion.

There are people who are too hot, and they think they have much compassion. They want to transform the society, they want to change the structure, they want to do this and that, they want to bring a utopia into the world: the revolutionaries, the communists, the utopians – and they are very hot.

And they think they have compassion – no, they have only anger. The object has changed. Now their anger has an object, a very impersonal object – the society, the structure of the society, the state, the situation. They are very hot people. Lenin, or Stalin, or Trotsky – they are hot people but they are not against anybody in particular, they are against a structure.

Gandhi is a hot person – against the British Empire. The object is impersonal, that's why you cannot feel that he is angry – but he is angry. He wants to change something in the outside world, and wants to change it so immediately that he is impatient, fighting. The fighting may choose nonviolence as the means, but the fighting is violence. Fight as such is violence. You can choose nonviolent means to fight – women have always chosen them. Gandhi did nothing else, he simply used a feminine trick.

If a husband wants to fight, he will beat his wife; and if the wife wants to fight, she will beat herself. This is as old as woman – and woman is older than man! She will start beating herself; that is her way to fight. She is violent, violent against herself. And remember, beating a woman you will feel guilty, and sooner or later you will have to come down and make a compromise. But beating herself, she never feels guilty. So either you beat a woman and you feel guilty, or she beats herself and then also you feel guilty – that you created the situation in which she is beating herself. In both cases she wins.

The British Empire was defeated because it was a male aggressive force, and the British Empire could not understand this feminine fight of Gandhi's: he will fast unto death – and then the whole British mind will feel guilty. Now you cannot kill this man, because he is not fighting in any way with you, he is simply purifying his own soul – the old feminine trick, but it worked. There was only one way to defeat Gandhi, and that was impossible. It was for Churchill to go on a fast unto death, and that was impossible.

Either you are hot against someone in particular or just hot against some structure in general, but the heat remains.

Lenin is not compassion, cannot be. Buddha is compassion – not fighting at all with anything, simply being and allowing things to be as they are; they move on their own. Societies change on their own, there is no need to change them; they change as trees change in season. Societies change on their own – old societies die on their own, there is no need to destroy them! And new societies are born just like new children, new babies, on their own. There is no need to force an abortion, it goes on automatically by itself.

Things move and change. And this is the paradox: that they go on moving and changing and still in a sense they remain the same – because there will be people who are poor, and there will be people who are rich; there will be people who are helpless, powerless, there will be people who have power over them. Classes cannot disappear – that is not in the nature of things. Human society can never become classless.

Classes can change. Now in Russia, there are not the poor and the rich, but the governed and the governors – they are there now. Now a new class division has arisen: the bureaucrats and the ordinary people, the managers and the managed – the same, it makes no difference. If now Tamerlane was born in Russia, he would become the prime minister. If Ford was born in Russia, he would become the general secretary of the communist party, he would manage from there.

Situations go on changing, but in a subtle sense they remain the same. The managers, the managed; the governors, the governed; the rich, the poor – they remain. You cannot change it, because society exists through contradiction. A real man of compassion will be cool; he cannot be a revolutionary really, because revolution needs a very hot mind and heart and body.

No control, no expression on others, more awareness – and then consciousness shifts from the periphery to the center.

Now try to understand this beautiful anecdote.

> *A Zen student came to Bankei and said: "Master, I have an*
> *ungovernable temper – how can I cure it?"*

He has accepted one thing, that he has an ungovernable temper; now he
wants to cure it. Whenever there is a disease, first try to find out whether there
is really a disease or a misunderstanding, because if there is a real disease then
it can be cured, but if it is not a real disease, just a misunderstanding, then no
medicine will help. Rather, on the contrary, every medicine that is given to you
will be harmful. So first be perfectly clear about a disease, whether it is there
or not, or whether you are simply imagining it, or are you simply thinking that
it is there. It may not be there at all; it may be simply a misunderstanding. And
the way man is confused, many of his diseases don't exist at all – he simply
believes they are there.

You also are in the same boat, so try to understand this story very deeply;
it may be helpful to you.

The student said,

> *"Master, I have an ungovernable temper – how can I cure it?"*

The disease is accepted, he does not doubt it; he is asking for the cure.
Never ask for the cure. First try to find out whether the disease exists or not.
First move into the disease and diagnose it, decipher it, scrutinize it; move
into the disease first before you ask for a cure. Don't accept any disease just
on the surface, because the surface is where others meet you, and the surface
is where others reflect in you, and the surface is where others color you. It
may not be a disease at all, it may be just the reflection of others.

It is just like a silent lake, and you stand on the bank of the lake with your
orange robe, and the water near you looks orange, reflects you. The lake may
think that it has become orange. How to get rid of it? Where to find the cure?
Whom to ask?

Don't go to the experts immediately. First try to find out whether it is really
a disease or just a reflection. Just being alert will do much: many of your diseases will simply disappear without any cure, no medicine is needed.

> *"Show me this temper," said Bankei, "it sounds fascinating."*

A man like Bankei immediately starts working on the disease, not on the
cure. He is not a psychoanalyst; a psychoanalyst starts working for the cure

– and that is the difference. Now new trends in psychiatry are coming up which start working on the disease, not on the cure. New trends are developing: they are nearer to reality, and nearer to Zen, and nearer to religion. Within this century psychiatry will take on a more religious color, and then it will not be just a therapy, it will *really* become a healing force – because therapy thinks of a cure, and a healing force brings your consciousness to the disease.

Out of a hundred diseases, ninety-nine will disappear simply by bringing your consciousness to them. They are false diseases; they exist because you are standing with your back towards them. Face them, and they go, and they disappear. That is the meaning of encounter – and encounter groups can be helpful, because the whole message is how to encounter things as they are. Don't think of cure, don't think of medicine, don't think of what to do; the real thing is, first, to know what is there.

Mind has deceived you in so many ways that a disease appears on the surface and there is no disease deep down; or a disease appears on the surface, but you move within and you find there are other diseases, and that was just a trick to deceive you, that was not the real disease.

A man came to me and he said, "My mind is very much disturbed. I am continuously tense, anxiety is there, I cannot sleep. So give me some technique of meditation – how to be silent and at peace."

I asked him, "What is really the problem? Do you really want to be at peace with yourself? He said, "Yes, I am a seeker, and I have been to Sri Aurobindo's ashram, and I have been to Shree Ramana's ashram, and I have been everywhere, and nothing helps."

So I asked him, "Have you ever thought about it – that when nothing helps maybe the disease is false? Or that you have labeled it falsely? Or that the container contains something else which is not written on it? You easily accept that Sri Aurobindo failed, Sri Raman failed, and you have moved all around..." And he was feeling very victorious that everybody had failed, and nobody had been able to help, that everybody was bogus. And then I told him, "Sooner or later you will go and say the same about me also, because I don't see that you are a spiritual seeker, I don't see that you are really interested in being at peace with yourself. Just tell me, what is your anxiety? What is your tension? Just go on telling me what thoughts come continuously to you, and why you go on thinking about them."

He said, "Not many, only one thought: I had a son, he is still alive – but no more a son to me. I have thrown him out. I am a rich man, and he had fallen in love with a girl not of my caste, and economically also below my status, uneducated. And I told the boy, 'If you want to marry this girl then never come back to this house.' And he never came back." And now I am getting old. The boy lives in poverty with the girl, and I continuously think about the boy, and this is my trouble. You give me some technique of meditation."

I said: "How will this technique of meditation help? – because the technique of meditation will not bring the boy home. And this is such a simple thing, there is no need to go to Aurobindo, there is no need to go to Sri Raman or to come to me. A sword is not needed for your problem, a needle will do; you are looking for swords, and then swords prove failures because you need only a needle. This is not a spiritual problem, just ego. Why shouldn't one fall in love with a girl who is economically below one's status? Is love something economical? Something to think of in terms of finance, economics, money, wealth, status?"

I told him one story:

One marriage agent came to a young man and told him, "I have got a very beautiful girl, just exactly right for you."

The boy said, "Don't bother me. I am not interested."

The marriage agent said, "I know, but don't be worried, I have another girl who will bring five thousand rupees in dowry."

The young man said, "Stop talking nonsense. I am not interested in money either! You simply go."

The man said, "I know. You don't bother! If five thousand is not enough, I have another girl who will bring twenty-five thousand rupees in dowry."

The boy said, "You simply get out of my room, because if ever I get married, it is for me to think about, it is not a question for an agent to settle. You simply get out! Don't make me angry!"

The agent said, "Okay, now I understand. You are not interested in beauty, you are not interested in money. I have a girl who comes from a family of long tradition, a very famous family – everybody knows about it, and four prime ministers have come from that family in the past. So you are interested in family, right?"

Now by this time the boy was very very angry and he wanted to physically throw this man out. And when by physically forcing him he was just throwing him out of the door, he said, "If I ever get married it will be for love and nothing else."

The agent said, "Then why in the first place didn't you tell me? I have those kinds of girls too."

I told this man this story.

Love is not manageable, it is simply something that happens, and the moment you try to manage it everything misfires. So I told that man, "Just go and ask your son's forgiveness – that's what is needed. No meditation technique, no Aurobindo, no Raman, no Osho, nobody can help you. Simply go to your boy and ask his forgiveness! – that's what is needed. Accept and welcome him back. It is just the ego that is troubling you. And if ego is troubling you then the disease is different. You seek meditation, and you think through meditation that silence will be possible? No."

Meditation can only be a help to that person who has come to a right understanding with his inner diseases, when he has come to understand which disease is false, which disease is wrongly identified, and which disease is not there at all – the container is empty.

When one has come to an understanding, a deep understanding with all one's diseases, then ninety-nine percent of the diseases disappear – because you can do something and they disappear. Then only one thing remains, and that one thing is the spiritual search... A deep anguish, unrelated to this world, not related with anything in this world: son, father, money, prestige, power – nothing. It is not related to them, it is simply existential. Deep down, if you can pinpoint it, it is how to know oneself. Who am I? Then this anguish becomes the search. Then meditation can help, never before it. Before it, other things are needed – needles will do, why carry a sword unnecessarily? And where needles will do, swords will be failures. This is what is happening to millions of people all around the world.

This Bankei is a master. He immediately got to the point, to the business.
Show me this temper, said he, *it sounds fascinating.*

It sounds fascinating, really. Why does Bankei say it sounds fascinating? – because the whole thing is false. This boy, this student has never looked within. He is seeking for a method and he has not diagnosed what his dis-ease is.

"I haven't got it right now," said the student, "so I can't show it to you."

You cannot manage to bring about anger, can you? If I tell you: "Be angry right now," what will you do? Even if you act, even if you manage somehow to pretend, it will not be anger, because deep down you will remain cool and acting. It happens! What does it mean, "it happens"? It means it happens only when you are unconscious. If you try to bring it, you are conscious. It cannot happen when you are conscious, it can happen only when you are unconscious. Unconsciousness is a must – without it anger cannot happen. But still, the boy said:

"I haven't got it right now, said the student, so I can't show it to you."
"Well then," said Bankei, "bring it to me when you have it." "But

I can't bring it just when I happen to have it," protested the student. "It arises unexpectedly, and I would surely lose it before I got it to you."

Now, Bankei has put him on the right path. He has already moved along, he is already nearing the goal, because he is now becoming aware of things of which he was never aware. The first thing he became aware of is that he cannot produce it right now. It cannot be produced; it happens when it happens – it is an unconscious force, you cannot bring it about consciously. That means if he goes further, the next step will be that if he remains conscious it cannot happen.

Even while anger is happening, if you suddenly become conscious it drops. You try it. Just in the middle, when you are feeling very hot and would like to commit murder, suddenly become aware, and you will feel something has changed: a gear inside – you can feel the click. Something has changed, now it is no more the same thing. Your inner being has relaxed. It may take time for your outer layer to relax, but the inner being has already relaxed. The cooperation is broken; now you are not identified.

Gurdjieff used to play a very beautiful trick on his disciples. You are sitting here, and he will create a situation; he will tell you, "Somebody, A, is coming, and when he comes I will behave rudely with him, very rudely – and you all have to help me."

Then A comes and Gurdjieff laughs and he says, "You are looking a perfect fool!" – and everybody looks at the man and shows him that everybody agrees. And then he will say nasty things about this man, and everybody nods and feels in agreement. The man gets angrier and angrier, and Gurdjieff will go on and on, and everybody nods as if they are in complete agreement, and the man becomes hotter and hotter – and then he explodes. And when he explodes, suddenly Gurdjieff says "Stop and look!"

Something inside relaxes. Immediately the man understands he has been moved into a situation, he has become angry – and the moment he realizes that this is a situation, that Gurdjieff has played a trick, the gear changes: he becomes alert, aware. The body will take a little time to cool down, but deep at the center everything is cool and he can look at himself now.

The student is already on the path – Bankei has put him immediately on the path. The first thing he has become aware of is: "I cannot show it to you right now, because it is not there."

"Well then, bring it to me when you have it."

A second step has been taken.

"But I can't bring it just when I happen to have it," protested the
student. *"It arises unexpectedly."*

"I don't know when it will arise. I may be very far away, you may not be
available, and, moreover, even if I bring it to you, by the time I reach you it will
not be there." He has already arrived at a deep understanding.

You cannot bring anger to me, can you?... Because in the very effort to
bring it, you will become aware. If you are aware, the grip is lost; it starts subsiding. By the time you have reached me it will be no more.

And it was easier to reach Bankei; it is difficult to reach me, you will
have to pass through Mukta. By the time the appointment is given and by
the time you reach me, it will not be there. Hence the appointment – because
otherwise you will bring problems unnecessarily. They drop automatically by
themselves – and if they persist, then they are worth bringing to me.

By the time you come to me you will have already passed over it; and
if you understand, that means that things that come and go are not worth paying
any attention to – they come and go. You always remain, they come and go.
You are the thing to be more attentive about, not things that come and go – they
are like seasons, climate changes: in the morning it was different, in the evening it is again different. It changes. Find out that which doesn't change.

The student has already reached a beautiful understanding. He says:
Unexpectedly it arises, *"...and I would surely lose it before I got it to you."*

"In that case," said Bankei, *"it cannot be part of your true nature."*

...Because true nature is always there. It never arises and never sets, it is
always there. Anger arises, goes; hate arises, goes; your so-called love arises,
goes. Your nature is always there.

So don't be too bothered and concerned with all that comes and goes;
otherwise you can remain concerned with it for years and years, and lives and
lives, and you will never come to the point.

That's why Freudian psychoanalysis never serves much purpose. The
patient lies down on the couch for years together – three years, four years, five
years, he goes on talking; talking about things that come and go. Remember,
the whole Freudian analysis is concerned with things that come and go: what
happened in your childhood, what happened in your youth, what happened in
your sex life, what happened in your relations with others – it goes on and on!
It is concerned with what happened, not to whom it happened – and that is the
difference between Bankei and Freud.

If you are concerned with what happened then...so much has happened.

Even in twenty-four hours so much happens that if you relate it, it will take years; and you go on relating. It is just like talking about the weather for your whole life, how it has been: sometimes very hot, sometimes very cloudy, sometimes rainy, sometimes this and that. But what is the point of it all?

And what happens? How does this psychoanalysis help a patient? It helps a little. It simply gives time, that's all. For two years you are continuously talking about things that happened. These two years, or one year, or even more, just give you time; the wound heals automatically, you become readjusted again. Of course, a certain understanding also arises, the understanding that arises when you go backwards, and come forwards, moving like a shuttle in your memory. A certain understanding arises because you have to watch your memories. Because of watching...but that is not the main thing.

Freud is not concerned with your witness. He thinks that just by relating, telling your past, bringing it out through words, verbalization, something deep is changing. Nothing deep is changing. A little garbage is thrown out. Nobody listened to you, and Freud and his psychoanalysts are listening to you so attentively. Of course, you have to pay for it. They are professional listeners. They help in a way, because you would like to talk to someone intimately – even that helps. That's why people talk about their miseries; they feel a little relaxed, somebody has heard patiently, with compassion. But now nobody listens, nobody has that much time.

Bertrand Russell has written a small story. In the coming century there will be a great profession of professional listeners. In every neighborhood, every four or five houses there will be a house with a sign, "Professional Listener" – that is what psychoanalysis is – because nobody will have time, everybody will be in such a hurry. The wife will not be able to talk to the husband, the husband will not be able to talk to the wife, people will make love through phone calls, or will see each other on the television screen. That is going to happen, because what is the use of going to meet a friend when you can see him on the television screen, and he can see you? Phones will have screens also, so that you can see your friend talking to you, he can see you talking, so what is the point?...Because what will you do just sitting in front of each other in a room? The same thing is happening already: the distance is covered by the telephone and the television. Contact will be lost, so professional listeners will be needed.

You go to psychoanalysts and they listen like a friend. Of course you have to pay – and psychoanalysis is the most costly thing in the world now, only very rich people can afford it. People boast about it: "I have been in psychoanalysis for five years. How many years have you been in it?" Poor people cannot afford it.

But the Eastern methods of meditation have a different attitude: they are not concerned with what happened to you, they are concerned with to whom it happened. Find out: to whom?

Lying down on a Freudian couch you are concerned with the objects of the mind. Sitting in a Zen monastery you are concerned with to whom it happened – not with the objects but with the subject.

> *"In that case," said Bankei, "It cannot be part of your true nature. If it were, you could show it to me at any time. When you were born you did not have it, and your parents did not give it to you – so it must come into you from the outside. I suggest that whenever it gets into you, you beat yourself with a stick until the temper can't stand it, and runs away."*

He is simply joking – don't start doing it, don't take the stick literally. In Zen, awareness is called the stick with which you beat yourself. There is no other way to beat yourself, because if you take an ordinary stick the body will be beaten, not you. You can kill the body, but not you. To beat with a stick means: when you feel angry, continuously be aware; bring awareness to it, become alert, conscious, and beat with the stick of awareness continuously inside, until the temper can't stand it and runs away. The only thing that the temper can't stand is awareness. Just beating your body won't do. That's what people have been doing – beating others' bodies or their own. That's not Bankei's meaning – he is joking, and he is indicating a symbolic term Zen people use for awareness: the stick one has to beat oneself with.

In the Zen tradition, when a master dies he gives his stick, the staff, to his chief disciple, to him whom he chooses as his heir, he who is going to replace him. He gives him the stick, the staff, that he carried his whole life. The meaning is that the one to whom this stick is given has attained to the inner stick – to awareness. To receive the stick of the master is the greatest gift, because through it he accepts, agrees, recognizes, that now your inner stick is born. You have become aware of what happens to you, to *whom* it happens. The distinction is there. The gap has come in, the space is there; now the periphery and your center are not identified.

Said Bankei, "I suggest that whenever it gets into you, this anger, it must be coming from outside. You didn't have it when you were born; nobody, not your parents or anybody, presented it to you as a gift, so from where is it coming? It must be coming from outside, the periphery must be touching other peripheries. From there, you must be getting the ripples and the waves." So be conscious – because the moment you are conscious you are suddenly thrown to the center.

Be unconscious and you live on the periphery. Be conscious and you are thrown to the center. And from the center you can see what is happening on the periphery. Then if two people touch on the periphery, if two people create trouble on the periphery, it will not be any trouble for you. You can laugh, you can enjoy it, you can say, "It sounds fascinating."

It happened: Buddha was passing near a village; a few people came and they abused him very badly, saying nasty things, and using vulgar words – and he just stood there. They got a little puzzled, because he was not reacting. Then somebody from the crowd asked, "Why are you silent? Answer what we are saying!"

Buddha said, "You came a little late. You should have come ten years ago, because then I would have reacted. But now I am not there where you are doing these things to me; a distance has arisen. Now I have moved to the center where you cannot touch me. You came a little late. I am sorry for you, but I enjoy it. Now I am in a hurry, because in the other village where I am going, people will be waiting for me. If you are not yet finished, then I will pass back by the same route. You can come again. It sounds fascinating."

They were puzzled. What to do with such a man? Another from the crowd asked, "Really, are you not going to say anything?"

Buddha said, "In the other village I have come from just now, people had come with many sweets to present to me, but I take things only when I am hungry, and I was not hungry, so I gave them back their sweets. I ask you, what will they do?"

So the man said, "Of course, they will go in the village and give those sweets as *prasad* to people."

So Buddha started laughing and he said, "You are really in trouble, you are in a mess – what will you do? You brought these vulgar words to me, and I say I am not hungry – so now take them back! And I feel very sorry for your village, because people will get such vulgar things, vulgar words in their *prasad*."

When you are at the center it sounds fascinating, you can enjoy it. When you are cool you can enjoy the whole world. When you are hot you cannot enjoy it, because you get so much into it; you are lost, you get identified. You become so messed up in it, how can you enjoy it?

This may sound paradoxical, but I tell you: only a buddha enjoys this world. Then everything sounds fascinating.

Enough for today.

CHAPTER 4

the path is just in front of you

A master who lived as a hermit on a mountain was asked by a monk:
"What is the way?"

"What a fine mountain this is," the master said in reply. "I am not
asking you about the mountain," said the monk, "but the way."
The master replied: "So long as you cannot go beyond the mountain,
my son, you cannot reach the way."

The way is easy – but you are the mountain and beyond lies the way. Crossing yourself is very difficult. Once you are on the way there is no problem, but the way is very far from you. And you are such a mass of contradictions that one fragment of you goes to the east and another to the west – you are not moving in one direction. You cannot move in one direction as you are – because you need an inner unity, a crystallized being. As you are, you are a crowd with many selves, with no unity.

At the most, if you make some arrangement, as everybody has to make – if you control yourself, at the most you can become an assembly, not a crowd; and then too you will be the Indian assembly, not the British. At the most the majority of your fragments can move in one direction, but the minority will always be there, going somewhere else.

So even a very controlled man, disciplined, a man of character, of thinking, that man too never reaches to the way. He may be able to adjust to the society, but he is also unable to reach the way from where the door opens toward the divine.

You are really a mountain.

The first thing to be understood is that the crowd must go. The "polypsychic" existence must become "unipsychic"; you must be one. That means you must be thoughtless, because thoughts are a crowd; they divide you, and every thought pulls you apart. They create a chaos within you and they are always contradictory. Even when you decide, the decision is always against some part within you, it is never total.

I have heard it happened...

Mulla Nasruddin was very ill – tense, psychiatrically ill. And the illness was that he became, by and by, absolutely unable to make any decision – not big decisions at that, but small ones also: whether to take a bath or not, whether to wear this tie or that, whether to take a taxi to the office or drive the car – not big ones, small decisions, but he became unable to make them so he was put in a psychiatric hospital.

Six months of treatment and everything settled, and the doctors felt that now he was okay. They said one day, "Now, Nasruddin, you are absolutely okay. You can go back into the world, take a job, start working and functioning. We are completely satisfied. Now there is nothing wrong." But seeing a slight indecision on Nasruddin's part the doctor said, "Don't you feel that now you are ready to go into the world and start working and functioning?"

Nasruddin said, "Yes and no."

But this is the situation. Whether you are ill or healthy is not the question, the difference is only of degree – but this remains the problem deep inside: yes and no, both.

You love a person? – yes, and deep down is hidden the no. Sooner or later when you get bored and fed up with the yes, the no will come up and you will hate the person, the same person you loved. You like something but the dislike is hidden; sooner or later you will dislike the same thing.

You were mad when you loved, when you liked; and you will be mad when you hate and dislike. As you are – yes and no, both – how can you move towards the divine? The divine needs total commitment, nothing less will do. But how can you commit totally? – you are not a total being! This is the mountain.

The path is easy, but you are not on the path; and all the techniques, all the methods in the world, and all the masters, to be exact, they don't give you the path – the path already exists. Their methods and techniques simply lead you towards the path; They are not paths. They create small pathways on the mountain so you can go beyond – because the path is there; there is no need to create a path, it already exists. But you are lost in a forest. You have to be brought to the path.

So the first thing is: the more divided you are, the farther away from the way you will be; the more undivided, the nearer the path.

Thoughts divide because they are always carrying the opposite within them: love carries hate, friendship carries enmity, liking carries disliking. Sosan is right when he says: "A slight distinction between like and dislike, a slight movement in your being of like and dislike, and heaven and earth are set apart." No distinction – and you have reached, because with no distinction you are one.

So the first thing to remember is how to drop thoughts and become thoughtless – thoughtless but alert, because in deep sleep also you become thoughtless, and that won't do. It is good for the body, that is why after a deep sleep your body feels rejuvenated. But the mind remains tired even in the morning, because the mind continues its activity. The body relaxes, though it too cannot relax totally because of the mind; but still, it relaxes. So in the morning the body is okay, at least workably okay – but the mind feels tired, even in the morning. You go to bed tired, you get up in the morning more tired because the mind was continuously working, dreaming, thinking, planning, desiring; the mind was continuously working.

In deep sleep for a few moments when you are absolutely unconscious you become one. This same oneness is needed with a conscious and alert mind. As you are in deep sleep – no thought, no distinction of good and bad, heaven and hell, God and the Devil, no distinction of any sort, you simply are, but unconscious – this has to be attained while you are alert and conscious. *Samadhi*, the final, the ultimate, the utter meditation, is nothing but deep sleep with full consciousness.

In deep sleep you attain, so the only thing to be attained is to become more and more conscious. If you can add more consciousness to your deep sleep you will become enlightened. The mountain is transcended and the path opens – one thing.

Second thing: you carry the past within you – that creates multiplicity. You were a child, the child is still hidden in you, and sometimes you can still feel the child kicking; in certain moments you regress and become the child again. You were once young, now you are old; that young man is hidden there, and sometimes even an old man starts being as foolish as a young man.

You carry the whole past, every moment of it, and you have been many things! From the womb up to now you have been millions of persons, and they are all carried within you, layer by layer. You have grown, but the past has not disappeared; it may be hidden, but it is there – and it is not only in the mind, it is even in the body.

If, when you were a small child and you were angry and someone said, "Stop! Don't be angry," and you stopped, that anger is still being carried by your hand. It has to be so because energy is indestructible, and unless you relax that hand it will persist. Unless you do something consciously to complete the circle of that energy – which became anger in a certain moment fifty or sixty years back – you will carry it within you, and it will color all your actions. You can touch somebody, but the touch won't be pure: the whole past is carried by the hand; all repressed anger, all repressed hatred is there. Even if in love you touch a person, your touch is not pure, cannot be – because where will that anger go which is carried by the hand?

Wilhelm Reich worked very much on this somatic repression. The body carries the past, the mind carries the past; because of this loaded state you cannot be here and now. You have to come to terms with your past. So meditation is not only a question of doing something here and now; before that is possible you have to come to terms with your past – you have to dissolve all hangovers, and there are millions of them.

Even when one becomes old he is also a child, a young man, and all that he has ever been is there, because you don't know how to die every moment. That is the whole art of life – to die moment to moment so that there is no hangover.

A relationship has finished – you don't carry it, you simply die to it! What can you do? Something was happening and now it is not happening. You accept it and you die to it – you simply drop it with full awareness, and then you are renewed in a new moment. Now you are not carrying the past. You are a child no more, but watch yourself and you will feel the child is there – and that child creates trouble! If you were really a child there would be no trouble, but you are young or old…

I have heard:

Mulla Nasruddin was hospitalized. He was eighty – and then came his birthday, and he was waiting for his three sons to bring him some present. They came of course, but they had not brought anything – because he was eighty years old! A child feels happy with a present, but an old man, eighty years old? His eldest son was sixty. So they didn't think about it at all, but when they came and Mulla saw that they were empty-handed, he felt angry, frustrated, and he said, "What! Have you forgotten your old father, your poor old father's birthday? It is my birthday!"

The child...at that moment you could have looked into his eyes, and this eighty-year-old man was not there, just a child waiting for some toys.

One son said, "Forgive us, we forgot completely."

Mulla Nasruddin said, "I reckon I will forgive you, because it seems this forgetfulness runs in our family. Really, I forgot to marry your mother." He was really angry.

So they all three shrieked in unison, and they said, "What! Do you mean we are...?"

He said, "Yes! – and damned cheap ones at that!"

The child continues somewhere in you. When you weep you can find him, when you laugh you can find him, when somebody gives you a present you can find him, when somebody forgets to, you can find him. When somebody appreciates you, you can find him; when somebody condemns you, you can find him – it is very difficult to be really mature. One can never be mature unless the child simply dies within you, is no more a part of you – otherwise it will go on influencing your actions, your relationships.

And this is not only true for the child, every moment of the past is there and influencing your present – your present is so loaded. Millions of voices from the body and the mind go on manipulating you; how can you reach to the path? You are a mountain. This mountain has to be dissolved. What to do? It can be dissolved consciously – one thing is to live your past again, consciously.

This is the mechanism of consciousness: whenever you live something consciously it never becomes a loaded thing on you; try to understand this. It never becomes a burden on you if you live it consciously. If you go to the market to purchase something and you move consciously, walk consciously, purchase the thing consciously with full remembrance, mindfully come back home, this will never be a part of your memory. I don't mean that you will forget it – but it will not be a load. If you want to remember it, you can remember it, but it will not be constantly forcing your attention towards it, it will not be a loaded thing.

Whatsoever you do consciously is lived through and is no longer a hangover. Whatever you live unconsciously becomes a hangover, because you never live it totally – something remains incomplete. When something is incomplete it has to be carried – it waits to be completed.

You were a child, and somebody had broken your toy, and you were crying. Your mother consoled you, diverted your mind somewhere – gave you some sweets, talked about something else, told you a story, diverted you – and you were going to cry and weep, and you forgot. That has remained incomplete; it is there, and any day whenever somebody snatches a toy from you – it may be any toy, it may be a girlfriend, and somebody snatches her – you start weeping and crying. And you can find the child there, incomplete. It may be a position: you are mayor of the town and somebody snatches the position, a toy, and you are crying and weeping again.

Find out...regress into the past, move into it again, because there is no other way now; the past is no longer there, so if something has remained hanging the only way is to relive it in the mind and move backwards.

Every night for one hour make it a point to go backwards, fully alert, as if you are living the whole thing again. Many things will bubble up, many things will call your attention – so don't be in a hurry, and don't pay half-attention to anything and then move again, because that will again create incompleteness. Whatsoever comes, give total attention to it. Live it again. And when I say live it again I mean *live* it again – not just remember, because when you remember a thing you are a detached observer; that won't help. *Relive it!*

You are a child again. Don't look as if you are standing apart and look-ing at a child as his toy is being snatched. No! Be the child. Not outside the child, inside the child – be again the child. Relive the moment: somebody snatches the toy, somebody destroys it, and you start crying – and cry! Your mother is trying to console you – go through the whole thing again, but now don't be diverted by anything. Let the whole process be completed. When it is completed, suddenly you will feel your heart is less heavy; something has dropped.

You wanted to say something to your father; now he is dead, now there is no way to tell him. Or you wanted to ask his forgiveness for a certain thing you did which he didn't like, but your ego came in and you couldn't ask his forgiveness; now he is dead, now nothing can be done. What to do? – and it is there! It will go on and on and destroy all your relationships.

I am very much aware of that, because to be a master is to be in a certain sense a father – it is to be many things, but very importantly it is in a cer-tain sense to be a father. When people come to me, if they are loaded with their relationship with their father, then it becomes very difficult to be related to me because I always feel their father comes in. If they have hated their father they will hate me, if they wanted to fight with their father, they will fight. If they love their father they will love me, if they respected their father they will respect me, if they respected him just superficially and deep down they had a disrespect, it will be the same with me – and the whole thing starts working.

If you are conscious, you can watch. Go back. Now your father is no more, but for the eyes of the memory he is still there. Close your eyes; again be the child who has committed something, done something against the father, wants to be forgiven but cannot gather courage – now you can gather courage. You can say whatsoever you wanted to say, you can touch his feet again, or you can be angry and hit him – but be finished! Let the whole process be completed.

Remember one basic law: anything that is complete drops, because then there is no meaning in carrying it; anything that is incomplete clings, it waits for its completion. And this existence is really always after completion. The whole existence has a basic tendency to complete everything. It does not like incomplete things – they hang, they wait; and there is no hurry for existence, they can wait for millions of years.

Move backwards. Every night for one hour before you go to sleep, move into the past, relive. Many memories by and by will be unearthed. With many you will be surprised that you were not aware that these things are there – and with such vitality and freshness, as if they had just happened! You will be again a child, again a young man, a lover, many things will come. Move slowly, so everything is completed. Your mountain will become smaller and smaller – the load is the mountain. And the smaller it becomes, the freer you will feel. A certain quality of freedom will come to you, and a freshness, and inside you will feel you have touched a source of life.

You will be always vital – even others will feel that when you walk your step has changed, it has a quality of dance; when you touch, your touch has changed; it is not a dead hand, it has become alive again. Now life is flowing because the blocks have disappeared; now there is no anger in the hand, love can flow easily, unpoisoned, in its purity. You will become more sensitive, vulnerable, open.

If you have come to terms with the past suddenly you will be here and now in the present, because then there is no need to move to the past again and again.

Go on moving every night. By and by, memories will come up before your eyes and they will be completed. Relive them; completed, suddenly you will feel they drop. Now there is no more to be done, the thing is finished. Less and less memories will come as the time passes. There will be gaps – you would like to relive something but nothing is coming – and those gaps are beautiful. Then a day will come when you will not be able to move backwards because everything is complete. When you cannot move backwards, only then do you move forward. There is no other way. And to move forward is to reach the path, the whole consciousness moving ahead every moment into the unknown.

But your legs are being pulled back continuously by the past, the past is heavy on you; how can you move into the future, and how can you be in the present? The mountain is really big, it is a Himalaya, uncharted, unmapped; nobody knows how to pass through it – and everybody is such a different

Himalaya that you can never make a map, because it differs with everybody. You have your Himalayas to carry, others have their Himalayas to carry, and with these mountains, when you meet with people there is only clash and con-flict. The whole life becomes just a struggle, a violent struggle, and every-where you can see and feel and hear the clash. Whenever somebody comes near, you are tense and the other is also tense – both are carrying their Himalayas of tension and sooner or later they will clash. You may call it love but those who know, they say it is a clash. Now there is going to be misery.

Be finished with the past. The more you are free from the past, the more the mountain starts disappearing. And then you will attain a unison: you will become, by and by, one.

Now, try to understand this parable: What is the way?

> *A master who lived as a hermit on a mountain was asked by a monk:*
> *"What is the way?"*

Every word has to be understood because every word carries meaning:

> *A master who lived as a hermit on a mountain...*

It has been happening always, that a Buddha moves to the mountains, a Jesus moves to the mountains, a Mahavira goes into the mountains. Why do they move to the mountains, to the loneliness? Why do they become soli-taries? Just to face their inner mountains immediately and directly. In society it is difficult because the whole energy is wasted in day-to-day work and routine and relationship. You don't have enough time, you don't have enough energy to encounter yourself – you are finished in encountering others! You are so much occupied – and to come face-to-face with oneself, a very unoc-cupied life is needed, because it is such a tremendous phenomenon to face oneself. You will need all your energies. It is such an absorbing job, it cannot be done halfheartedly.

Seekers have always moved into solitary existence, just to face them-selves. Wherever they go – just to face themselves, to make it uncomplicated. In relationship it becomes complicated because the other brings his or her miseries and mountains. You are already loaded – and then comes the other! And then you clash, then things become more complex. Then it is two dis-eases meeting, and a very complicated disease is created out of it. Everything becomes entwined, it becomes a riddle. You are already a riddle – it is better to solve it first and then move in relationship, because if you are not a mountain, only then you can help somebody.

And remember, two hands are needed to make a sound, and two mountains are needed for a clash. If you are no longer a mountain, now you are capable of being related. Now the other may try to create a clash, but it cannot be created because there is no possibility of creating a sound with one hand. The other will start feeling foolish – and that is the dawn of wisdom.

You can help if you are unburdened; you cannot help if you are not unburdened. You can become a husband, you can become a father, a mother, and you will be burdening others with your burdens also. Even small children carry your mountains; they are crushed under you – it has to be so because you never bother to have a clarity about your being before you become related.

That must be the basic responsibility of every alert being: "Before I move in any relationship I must be unburdened. I should not carry a hangover; only then can I help the other to grow. Otherwise I will exploit, and the other will exploit me. Otherwise I will try to dominate and the other will try to dominate me." And it will not be a relationship, it cannot be love, it will be a subtle politics.

Your marriage is a subtle politics of domination. Your fatherhood, motherhood, is a subtle politics. Look at mothers; just simply watch and you will feel they are trying to dominate their small children. Their aggression, their anger, is thrown on them – they have become objects of catharsis, and by this they are already burdened. They will move in life carrying mountains from the very beginning, and they will never know that life is possible without carrying such loaded heads; and they will never know the freedom that comes with an unloaded being. They will never know that when you are not loaded you have wings and you can fly into the sky and into the unknown.

Truth is available only when you are unburdened. But they will never know. They will knock at the doors of temples but they will never know where the real temple exists. The real temple is freedom: dying moment to moment to the past and living the present. And freedom to move, to move into the dark, into the unknown – that is the door of the divine.

A master who lived as a hermit on a mountain...

Alone.

You must make a distinction between two words: lonely and alone. In the dictionary they carry the same meaning, but those who have been meditating, they know the distinction. They are not the same, they are as different as possible.

Loneliness is an ugly thing, loneliness is a depressive thing – it is a sadness, it is an absence of the other. Loneliness is the absence of the other – you would like the other to be there, but the other is not, and you feel that and you miss them. You are not there in loneliness, the absence of the other is there.

Alone? – it is totally different. You are there, it is your presence; it is a positive phenomenon. You don't miss the other, you meet yourself. Then you are alone, alone like a peak, tremendously beautiful. Sometimes you even feel a terror – but it has a beauty. But the presence is the basic thing: you are present to yourself. You are not lonely, you are with yourself. Alone, you are not lonely, you are with yourself. Lonely, you are simply lonely – there is no one. You are not with yourself and you are missing the other. Loneliness is negative, an absence; aloneness is positive, a presence.

If you are alone, you grow, because there is space to grow – nobody else to hamper, nobody else to obstruct, nobody else to create more complex problems. Alone you grow, and as much as you want to grow you can grow because there is no limit, and you are happy being with yourself, and a bliss arises. There is no comparison: because the other is not there, you are neither beautiful nor ugly, neither rich nor poor, neither this nor that, neither white nor black, neither man nor woman. Alone, how can you be a woman or a man? Lonely, you are a woman or a man, because the other is missing. Alone, you are no one, empty, empty of the other completely.

And remember, when the other is not, the ego cannot exist; it exists with the other. Either present or absent, the other is needed for the ego. To feel "I" the other is needed; a boundary of the other. Fenced off from the neighbors I feel "I." When there is no neighbor, no fencing, how can you feel "I"? You will be there, but without any ego. The ego is a relationship, it exists only in relationship.

Alone the master lived – a hermit means alone – on a mountain, facing himself, meeting himself at every corner. Wherever he moves he is encountering himself – not burdened with the other, so knowing well what he is, who he is.

Things start solving themselves if you can be alone, even things like madness. Just the other night I was talking to a few friends. In the West if a man goes crazy, mad, insane, neurotic, much treatment is given – too much really, for years. And the result is almost nothing; the man remains the same.

I have heard, once it happened:

A psychiatrist was treating a woman who had an obsession – the obsession is called kleptomania, stealing things. She was very rich, there was no need, just a psychological obsession. It was impossible for her not to steal: wherever she found an opportunity she would steal, even worthless things: a needle, a button. She was treated for years.

After the five-year-long treatment – thousands of dollars had gone down the drain – after five years the psychiatrist who was treating her, the Freudian psychoanalyst, asked, "Now you look normal, and now there is no need to continue the treatment. You can drop out of it. What do you feel?"

She said, "I feel perfect. I feel fine. Everything is good. Before you started treatment I always used to feel guilty about stealing things – now I steal, but I never feel guilty. Fine! Everything is good. You really did it. You helped me a lot."

This is all that happens. You simply become accustomed, attuned to your illness, that's all.

In the East, particularly in Japan – because of Zen – a totally different treatment has existed for at least one thousand years. Zen monasteries are not in any way hospitals, not meant for ill people, but in a village, if a Zen monastery exists, it is the only place; if someone goes mad or neurotic, where can they go? In the East they always bring the neurotic people to the master, because if he can treat normal people, why not neurotics? The difference is only of degree.

So they will bring the neurotic people to the Zen monastery, to the master, and they will say, "What to do? You take charge of him." And he will take charge. And the treatment is really unbelievable! The treatment is no treatment at all. The man has to be given a solitary cell somewhere at the back of the monastery, in a corner; the neurotic has to live there. He will be given food, every facility – that's all. And he has to live with himself. Within three weeks, only three weeks, with no treatment, the neurosis disappears.

Now many Western psychiatrists are studying this as a miracle. This is not a miracle. This is simply giving the man a little space to sort it out, that's all. Because he was normal a few days ago, he can be normal again. Something has become too heavy on him and he needs space, that's all. And they will not pay him much attention, because if you pay a neurotic person much attention, as happens in the West, he is never going to be back to normal again; because nobody paid him so much attention before.

He is never going to be again as he was, because then nobody bothered about him. And now great psychoanalysts are bothering – great doctors, names, world-famous names, and they talk to him or her. The patient lying on the couch resting, and a great name just sitting behind, and whatsoever he or she says is listened to carefully, every word. And with so much attention! The neurosis becomes an investment, because people need attention.

A few people start behaving foolishly because then the society gives them attention. In every old country, in every village, you will find a village fool – and he is not a mediocre man, he is very intelligent. Fools are almost always intelligent, but they have learned a trick: people pay them attention, they feed them, everybody knows them, they are already famous without holding any post – the whole village looks after them. Wherever they pass, they are like great leaders, a crowd follows them: children jumping and throwing things at them – and they enjoy it! They are great ones in the town, and they know now that this being a fool is a good investment. The village takes care of them, they are well fed, well clothed – they have learned the trick. No need to work, no need to do anything – just be a fool and it is enough.

If a neurotic person...and remember ego is neurosis and it needs attention; pay it attention, and ego feels good. Many people have murdered simply to get the attention of the newspapers, because only when they murder are they covered in the headlines. They become suddenly very, very important – their pictures are shown, their names, their biographies are covered: suddenly they are not nobodies, they have become somebodies.

Neurosis is a deep hankering after attention, and if you give it attention, you feed it – that's why psychoanalysis has been a complete failure.

In Zen monasteries they treat a person within three weeks. In Freudian psychoanalysis they cannot treat him in thirty years, because they miss the very point. But in Zen monasteries no attention is given to the neurotic person, nobody thinks that he is somebody important – they simply leave him alone, that is the only treatment. He has to sort out his own things; nobody bothers. Within three weeks he comes out absolutely normal.

Solitariness has a healing effect, it is a healing force. Whenever you feel that you are getting messed up, don't try to solve it. Move away from society for a few days, for at least three weeks, and just remain silent, just watching yourself, feeling yourself, just being with yourself, and you will have a tremendous force available which heals. Hence, in the East, many people have moved to the mountains, to the forests, somewhere alone, somewhere where there is nobody else to be bothered with. Only oneself...so one can feel oneself directly, and you can see what is happening within.

Except yourself, nobody is responsible for you, remember. If you are mad you are mad; you have to sort it out – it is your doing.

This is what Hindus say: it is your karma. The meaning is very deep. It is not a theory. They say, whatsoever you are it is your own work, so sort it out. Nobody else is responsible for you, only you are responsible.

So go into solitary confinement – to sort out things, to meditate on your own being and your problems. And this is the beauty: that if you can just be quiet, living with yourself for a few days, things settle automatically, because an unsettled state is not natural. An unsettled state is unnatural, you cannot prolong it for long; it needs effort to prolong it. Simply relax and let things be, and watch, and make no effort to change anything. Remember; if you try to make any change you will continue the same because the very effort will continue to disturb things.

It is just like sitting by the side of a river: the river flows, the mud settles, the dead leaves go to the sea; by and by the river becomes absolutely clean and pure. You need not go into it to clean it – if you go, you will muddy it more. Simply watch, and things happen. This is what the theory of karma is: you have messed yourself up, now move alone.

So you need not throw your problems on others, you need not throw your diseases on others – you simply move alone; suffer them in silence, watch them. Just sit by the bank of the river of your mind. Things settle. When things settle you have a clarity, a perception. Then move back into the world – if you feel like it. That too is not a necessity, that too should not be an obsession. Nothing should be an obsession, neither the world nor the mountain.

Whatsoever you feel is natural, whatsoever you feel is good and heals you, whatsoever you feel you are whole in, not divided – that is the path. The mountain is crossed. You have reached the path – now follow it, now flow into it. The mountain is the problem. The path is available when you have crossed the mountain. And you have accumulated this mountain in many lives – your karmas, whatsoever you have done. It is now heavy on you.

A master who lived as a hermit on a mountain was asked by a monk...

a seeker –

"What is the way?" "What a fine mountain this is," the master said in reply.

Looks absurd – because the man is asking about the way and the master is saying something about the mountain. Looks absolutely irrational, outlandish, because the man has not asked anything about the mountain.

Remember, this is my situation. You ask about A, I talk about B; you ask about the way, and I talk about the mountain. If you love me, only then can you feel; if you simply listen to me, I am absurd – because I am not talking relevantly. If I talk relevantly I cannot help you; that is the problem. If I say something which seems relevant to you it will not be of much help, because you are the problem; and if I talk relevantly that means I adjust to you. Even if to you I look relevant, it means something has gone wrong. By the nature of the phenomenon itself, I have to be irrelevant.

I will look absurd, irrational. And this gap between the question and the answer can only be bridged if you have trust. Otherwise it cannot be bridged – how to bridge it? The gap between the seeker and the master, the disciple and the master, the gap between the question and the answer – because you question about the way and the answer is given about the mountain – how to bridge it?

Hence trust becomes very, very significant. Not knowledge, not logic, not argumentative capacity, no – but a deep trust, which can bridge the irrelevant answer, which can see through the irrelevance deeply and can catch a glimpse of the relevancy.

> *"What a fine mountain this is," the master said in reply. "I am not asking you about the mountain," said the monk, "but the way."*

He sticks to his question. If you stick you will miss – because you are wrong, your question cannot be right; that's impossible. How can you ask a right question? If you can ask a right question the right answer is not very far away, it is hidden there. If you can ask a right question you are already right! And with a mind which is already right, how can the answer remain hidden? No, whatsoever you ask, whatsoever you say, carries *you*.

It happened:

Mulla Nasruddin was getting fatter and fatter, stouter and stouter. The doctor advised a diet.

After two months Mulla went to see the doctor. The doctor said, "My God! It is a miracle! You are even fatter than before – I cannot believe my eyes! Are you strictly following the diet I gave you? Are you eating only that which I prescribed and nothing else?"

Nasruddin said, "Nothing whatsoever! Of course I'm following your diet."

The doctor couldn't believe it. He said, "Tell me, Nasruddin, nothing whatsoever?"

Nasruddin said, "Of course! Except my regular meals." Regular meals plus the diet the doctor has prescribed.

But this has to be so. Your mind moves in whatsoever you do, you ask, you think – it colors everything. You cannot ask a right question. If you can ask a right question there is no need to ask, because the right is the thing, not the question and not the answer. If *you* are right, you ask the right question – suddenly the right answer is there. If you can ask a right question you simply have no need to go anywhere; just close your eyes and ask the right question and you will find the right answer there.

The problem is not with the right answer, the problem is not with the way; the problem is the mountain, the problem is the mind, the problem is you.

"What a fine mountain this is," the master said in reply. "I am not asking you about the mountain," said the monk, "but the way." The master replied, "So long as you cannot go beyond the mountain, my son, you cannot reach the way."

Many things to be understood – to be felt, rather.

The master replied, "So long as you cannot go beyond the mountain, my son, you cannot reach the way."

Why suddenly, *my son*? Up to now the master has not used a single loving word; why suddenly, *my son*? Because now the trust will be needed, and you cannot create trust in a person just by saying something, even if it is the absolute truth. A trust can be created only if the master is loving, because only love creates trust. On the side of the disciple a trust is needed, *shraddha*, a deep faith is needed. But the faith arises only when the master says "my son."

Now the thing is moving differently. It is not an intellectual relationship, it is becoming one of the heart. Now the master is becoming more a father than a master; now the master is moving towards the heart. He is now making a relationship.

If you ask head-oriented questions and the master goes on answering them, it may be a dialogue on the face of it, but it cannot be a dialogue. You can crisscross but you cannot meet that way. When people talk, listen to them: they crisscross each other but they never meet. This is not a dialogue. They both remain rooted in themselves, they never make any effort to reach the other. "My son" is an effort on the part of the master to reach the monk. He is preparing the way for the disciple to trust.

But then again a problem arises because the disciple can think, "This is too much! I have not come here in search of love, I have come here in search of knowledge." But a master cannot give you knowledge. He can give you wisdom, and wisdom comes only through the vehicle of love. Hence suddenly he says: *My son, so long as you cannot go beyond the mountain you cannot reach the way.*

One thing more he says: *What a fine mountain this is.* To an enlightened person even madness is beautiful. To an unenlightened person even enlightenment is not beautiful. The whole attitude changes. He says: *What a fine mountain.* To an enlightened person even your neurosis is a beautiful thing, he accepts that also; it has to be transcended, but not destroyed. One has to go beyond it, but it also is beautiful while it lasts. One has to reach somewhere else, but the goal is not the thing – the thing is each moment, living the goal here and now.

For an enlightened person everything is beautiful and for an unenlightened person everything is ugly. For an unenlightened person there are two catego-ries: less ugly, more ugly. No beauty exists. Whenever you say to a person, "You are beautiful," in fact you are saying, "You are less ugly." Watch when you say it again and then find out what you really mean. Do you really mean beautiful? – because that is impossible for your mind; your mind cannot see beauty, you are not so perceptive. At the most you can manage to say that this person is less ugly than others – and less ugly can become more ugly any moment, with just a change of mood.

Your friend is nothing but the person least inimical towards you. You have to be that way because your mind is so messed up, it is such a chaos; every-thing is muddled, murky, you cannot see direct. Your eyes are covered with millions of layers, it is really a miracle how you manage even to see; you are completely blind.

You cannot hear, you cannot see, you cannot touch, you cannot smell. Whatsoever you do, it is impure; many things come into it. You love, and mil-lions of things are there: immediately you start being possessive, and you never know that being possessive is part of hate, not part of love. Love can never pos-sess. Love is giving freedom to the other. Love is an unconditional gift, it is not a bargain. But to your mind love is nothing but less hate, that's all. At the most you think, "I can tolerate this person; I cannot tolerate that person so I cannot love him. This person I can tolerate." But the valuation remains negative.

When you are enlightened the valuation becomes positive. Then every-thing is beautiful; even your mountain, your neurosis is beautiful – even a madman is something beautiful. Beauty may have gone a little astray, but it is still beautiful. Existence may have gone a little astray and sinned, but it is existence.

So nothing can be wrong for an enlightened person. Everything is right – less right, more right. The difference between the Devil and God is nothing, the difference is only of less and more. God and the Devil are not two poles, enemies.

Hindus have beautiful words; no other country has been so understanding about words. Sanskrit is really something which exists nowhere else – very perceptive people! The English word devil comes from the same root as *deva*; *deva* means god. Devil and god come from the same root, *dev*. Dev means light; from the same dev comes the devil; and from the same dev comes deva, *devata*, the divine. The words divine and devil come from the same Sanskrit root dev. It is one phenomenon. Your seeing may be different, your standpoint may be different, but it is one phenomenon. An enlightened person will say even to the Devil: "How beautiful! How divine! How wonderful!"

It happened:

One Mohammedan mystic woman, Rabiya al-Adabiya, changed many lines in her Koran. Wherever it is said, "Hate the Devil," she crossed it out. Once another mystic, Hassan, was staying with Rabiya, and on the journey he had forgotten his own copy of the Koran somewhere and in the morning, for morning prayers, he needed it. So he asked for Rabiya's copy; Rabiya gave it to him. He was a little surprised in the beginning because the Koran had collected so much dust – that meant it was not used every day. It was not used at all it seemed; for many months it had not been used. But he thought it would be impolite to say something so he opened the Koran and started his morning prayer.

Then he was surprised even more, even shocked, because nobody can correct the Koran, and there were many corrections. Wherever it is said, "Hate the Devil," Rabiya had simply crossed it out completely, rejected it.

Hassan couldn't pray, he was so disturbed: this Rabiya had become a heretic, she had become an atheist, or what?…because it is impossible for a Mohammedan to conceive that you can correct the Koran. It is God's word, nobody can correct it. That's why they say that now no more prophets will be coming, because if a prophet comes again and he says something which is not in the Koran, it will create trouble. So the doors have been closed after Mohammed – he is the last prophet.

And they are very clever. They say there have been many other prophets in the past: Mohammed is not the first, but he is the last. Now no more messages will be coming from God – he has given the final message with Mohammed. So how dare this woman Rabiya…? She is correcting the Koran? Hassan couldn't pray, he was so disturbed. He finished somehow, went to Rabiya….

Rabiya was an enlightened woman. Very few women have become enlightened in the whole world; Rabiya is one of them. Looking at Hassan she said, "It seems you couldn't do your prayer. It seems the dust on the Koran disturbed you. So, you are still attached to things like dust? And it seems my corrections in the Koran must have shocked you very much."

Hassan said, "How…how could you know?"

Rabiya said, "I passed by when you were praying and I felt all around you much disturbance; it was not a prayerful prayer at all. It was so neurotic, the vibrations – so what is the matter? Tell me and be finished with it!"

Hassan said, "Now that you have started the conversation yourself... don't think I am impolite, but I couldn't believe a woman like you would correct the Koran!"

Rabiya said, "But look first at my difficulty: the moment I came to realize, the moment I came face to face with the divine, after that, in every face I can see that same face. No other face is possible. Even if the Devil comes to stand before me, I see the same face. So how can I hate the Devil now that I have realized the face of the divine that I have come to see? Now every face is the face of the divine. I had to correct it, and if ever I meet Mohammed I have to tell him frankly that these words are not good. They may be good for the ignorant because the ignorant divide; but they are not good for those who know, because they cannot divide."

Hence the master says:

"What a fine mountain this is."

Everything is beautiful and divine for a man who knows.

"I am not asking you about the mountain," said the monk, "but the way."

Have you ever observed that you never ask any question about yourself, about the mountain, you always ask about the way? People come to me and they ask, "What to do? How to reach God? How to become enlightened?" They never ask, "What to be?" They never ask anything about themselves, as if they are absolutely okay – only the path is missing. What do you think? You are absolutely okay, only the path is missing? So somebody can say, "Go to the right and then turn to the left and you are on the path"?

It's not so simple. The path is just in front of you. You are not missing the path at all. You have never missed it, nobody can miss it – but you cannot look at it because you are a mountain.

It is not a question of finding the way, it is a question of finding yourself, who you are. When you know yourself, the way is there; when you don't know yourself, the way is not there.

People go on asking about the way, and there are millions of ways proposed – but there cannot be millions. There is only one way. The same way passes before Buddha's eyes, and the same way passes before Lao Tzu, and the same way before Jesus. Millions are the travelers but the way is one, the same. That is the Tao, the Dharma, the Logos of Heraclitus – it is one.

Millions are the travelers but the way is one. There are not a million ways, and you are not missing it; but you always ask about the way, and you always get entangled in the ways – because when you ask, when foolish people ask, there are more foolish people to answer them. If you ask and insist on an answer, then somebody has to supply it. This is the law of economics: you demand, and there will be a supply. You ask a foolish question and a foolish answer will be given…because don't think that you are the ultimate fool – there are better ones. Smaller fools become disciples, and better fools become "masters." You ask, and they supply the answer.

Then there are millions of ways, and always in conflict. A Mohammedan saying is: You cannot reach through that way because it never leads anywhere, it goes into a cul-de-sac. Come to our way – and if you don't listen we will kill you. Christians are persuading: Come to our way. They are cleverer than Mohammedans; they don't kill really, they bribe, they seduce, they give you bread, they give you hospitals, they give you medicine, and they say, "Come our way! Where are you going?" They are merchants, and they know how to bribe people; they have converted millions just by giving things to them.

There are Hindus, they go on saying: We possess the whole truth. And they are so arrogant they don't bother even to convert anybody, remember: You are fools, you need not be converted. They are so arrogant, and they think: We know the way; if you want to you can come. We are not going to bribe you or kill you – you are not that important. You can come if you want, but we are not going to make any effort. And then there are three hundred religions in the world, and each religion thinking that this is the only way, *the* way, and all others are false.

But the question is not of the way, the question is not, "Which way is true?" The question is, have you crossed the mountain? The question is, have you gone beyond *you*? The question is, can you look at yourself from a distance, as a watcher? Then, the one way is yours.

Mohammed and Mahavira and Krishna and Christ – they all walked on the same way. Mohammed is different from Mahavira, Krishna is different from Christ, but they walk on the same way – because the way cannot be many. How can many lead to one? Only the one can lead you to the one.

So don't ask about the way and don't ask about the method. Don't ask about the medicine. First ask about the disease that you are. A deep diagnosis is needed first, and nobody can diagnose it for you. You have created it and only the creator knows all the nooks and corners. You have created it, so only you know how these complexities arise, and only you can solve them.

A real master simply helps you to come to yourself. Once you are there, the way opens. The way cannot be given but you can be thrown upon yourself.

And then the real conversion happens: not a Hindu becoming a Christian or a Christian becoming a Hindu, but an outward-moving energy becomes an inward-moving energy – that is conversion. You become inward-looking. The whole attention moves inwards, and then you see the whole complexity – the mountain. And if you simply watch it, it starts dissolving.

In the beginning it looks like a mountain; in the end you will feel that it was just a molehill. But you never looked at it because it was behind you, and it became so big. When you face it, it immediately decreases, becomes a mole-hill, you can laugh about it. Then it is no longer a burden. You can even enjoy it and sometimes can go in it for a morning walk.

Enough for today.

CHAPTER 5

death is no ordinary phenomenon

At the death of a parishioner, Master Dogo, accompanied by his disciple Zengen, visited the bereaved family.
Without taking time to express a word of sympathy, Zengen went up to the coffin, rapped on it, and asked Dogo: "Is he really dead?" "I won't say," said Dogo. "Well?" insisted Zengen. "I'm not saying, and that's final," said Dogo.
On their way back to the temple the furious Zengen turned on Dogo and threatened: "By God, if you don't answer my question, why I'll beat you." "All right," said Dogo, "beat away."
A man of his word, Zengen slapped his master a good one.
Some time later Dogo died, and Zengen, still anxious to have his question answered, went to the master Sekiso, and, after relating what had happened, asked the same question of him. Sekiso, as if conspiring with the dead Dogo, would not answer. "By God!" cried Zengen. "You too?" "I'm not saying," said Sekiso, "and that's final."
At that very instant Zengen experienced an awakening.

Life can be known, death also – but nothing can be said about them. No answer is true; it cannot be by the very nature of things. Life and death are the deepest mysteries. It is better to say that they are not two mysteries, but two aspects of the same mystery, two doors of the same secret. But nothing can be said about them. Whatever you say, you will miss the point.

Life can be lived, death also can be lived. They are experiences – one has to pass through them and know them. Nobody can answer your questions. How can life be answered? or death? Unless you live, unless you die, who's going to answer?

But many answers have been given – and remember, all answers are false. There is nothing to choose. It is not that one answer is correct and other answers are incorrect; all answers are incorrect. There is nothing to choose. Only experience can answer, not answers.

So this is the first thing to be remembered when you are near a real mystery, not a riddle created by man. If it is a riddle created by man it can be answered, because then it is a game, a mind game – you create the question, you create the answer. But if you are facing something which you have not created, how can you answer it, how can the human mind answer it? It is incomprehensible for the human mind. The part cannot comprehend the whole. The whole can be comprehended by becoming whole. You can jump into it and be lost – and there will be the answer.

I will tell you one anecdote Ramakrishna loved to tell. He used to say: Once it happened that there was a great festival near a sea, on the beach. Thousands of people were gathered there and suddenly they all became engrossed in a question – whether the sea is immeasurable or measurable; whether there is a bottom to it or not; fathomable or unfathomable? By chance, one man completely made of salt was also there. He said, "You wait, and you discuss, and I will go into the ocean and find out, because how can one know unless one goes into it?"

So the man of salt jumped into the ocean. Hours passed, days passed, then months passed, and people started to go to their homes. They had waited long enough, and the man of salt was not coming back.

The man of salt, the moment he entered the ocean, started melting, and by the time he reached the bottom he was not. He came to know – but he couldn't come back. And those who didn't know, they discussed it for a long time. They may have arrived at some conclusions, because the mind loves to reach conclusions.

Once a conclusion is reached, mind feels at ease – hence so many philosophies exist. All philosophies exist to fulfill a need: the mind asks and the mind cannot remain with the question, it is uneasy; to remain with the question feels inconvenient. An answer is needed – even if it is false, it will do; mind is put at rest.

To go and take a jump into the sea is dangerous. And remember, what Ramakrishna says is true: we are all men of salt as far as the ocean is concerned – the ocean of life and death. We are men of salt, we will melt into it because we come out of it. We are made by it, of it. We will melt.

So mind is always afraid of going into the ocean; it is made of salt, it is bound to dissolve. It is afraid, so it remains on the bank, discussing things, debating, arguing, creating theories – all false because they are based on fear. A courageous man will take the jump, and he will resist accepting any answer which is not known by himself.

We are cowards, that's why we accept anybody's answer: Mahavira, Buddha, Christ, we accept their answers. Their answers cannot be our answers. Nobody else's knowledge can be yours – they may have known, but their knowledge is just information for you. You will have to know. Only when it is your own is it knowledge; otherwise it will not give you wings. On the contrary, it will hang around your neck like stones, you will become a slave to it. You will not achieve liberation, you will not be set free by it.

Says Jesus, "Truth liberates." Have you seen anybody being liberated by theories? Experience liberates, yes, but theories about every experience? No, never! But the mind is afraid to take the jump, because mind is made of the same stuff as the universe; if you take the jump you will be lost. You will come to know, but you will know only when you are not.

The salt man came to know. He touched the very depth. He reached the very center but he couldn't come back. Even if he could, how would he relate…? Even if he comes back, his language will belong to the center, to the depth, and your language belongs to the bank, to the periphery.

There is no possibility of any communication. He cannot say anything meaningfully, he can only remain silent meaningfully, significantly. If he says something he himself will feel guilty, because he will immediately know that whatsoever he knows has not been transferred through the words; his experience is left behind. Only words have gone to you, dead, stale, empty. Words can be communicated but not truth. It can only be indicated.

The salt man can say to you, "You also come" – he can give you an invitation – "and take a jump with me into the ocean."

But you are very clever. You will say, "First answer the question; otherwise how do I know that you are right? Let me first consider and think and brood and ponder, then I will follow. When my mind is convinced, then I will take the jump."

But mind is never convinced, cannot be convinced. Mind is nothing but a process of doubt; it can never be convinced, it can go on arguing infinitely, because whatsoever you say it can create an argument around it.

Once I was traveling with Mulla Nasruddin. At a station, at a stop, a newcomer came into the compartment – he may have known Nasruddin. He said, "Hello." They greeted each other and then he said, "How are you, Nasruddin?"

Nasruddin said, "Fine! Absolutely fine!"

Then the man said, "And how is your wife?"

Nasruddin said, "She is also fine, thank you."

"And how are your children?"

Nasruddin said, "They are all very well, thank you."

I was surprised. When the man left at another stop, I asked Nasruddin, "What is the matter? – because I know well that you don't have a wife, you don't have any children."

Nasruddin said, "I also know – but why create an argument?"

Many times buddhas have nodded to you, just not to create any argument. They have remained silent just not to create any argument. They have not said much, but whatsoever they have said has created enough argument around it. You are like that. You will weave theories, you will spin philosophies, and you will get so engrossed in them that you will completely forget that the ocean is just near. You will completely forget that the ocean exists.

Philosophers completely forget what life is. They go on thinking and thinking and thinking and going astray, because mind is a distance from the truth. The more you are in the mind, the farther away you are from the truth; the less in the mind, the nearer. If there is no mind, even for a single moment, you have taken the jump – but then you become one with the ocean.

So the first thing to remember is, if it is a question created by you, not relating to the existential mystery of the universe, then it can be answered. Really, only mathematical questions can be answered. That's why mathematics is such a clear-cut science, because the whole thing is created by man. Mathematics does not exist in the universe, that's why mathematics is the purest science – you can be certain about it; you have created the whole game.

Trees are there, but not one tree, two, three trees, four trees – numbers don't exist there. You create the numbers, you create the very base, and then you ask, "How many? If two are added to two, what is the conclusion, what is the result?" you can answer "Four," and that answer will be true because you have created the whole game, all the rules: two and two make four. But in existence that is not true because in existence no arithmetic exists – it is a wholly man-made affair. So you can go on and on and create as many mathematics, as many arithmetics, as you like.

Once people thought that there was only one mathematics; now they know there can be many, because man can create them. Once people knew that there was only one geometry – Euclid's; now they know that you can create as many geometries as you want, because they are man-created. So now there is Euclidean geometry and non-Euclidean geometry.

Many mathematicians have played with numbers. Leibnitz worked with three digits: one, two, three. In Leibnitz' mathematics, two plus two cannot be four, because the four doesn't exist: one, two, three – only three digits are there, so in Leibnitz' mathematics two plus two will become ten, because after three comes ten. The four doesn't exist. Einstein worked with two digits: one and two, so two plus two in Einstein's mathematics will be eleven. And they are all right, because the whole game is man-made. It is up to you.

There is no inner necessity to believe in nine or ten digits, except that man has ten fingers, so people started counting on the fingers. That's why ten became the basic unit all over the world; otherwise there is no necessity.

Mathematics is a thought product: you can ask a question and a right answer can be given to you – but except for mathematics everything moves into the mysterious. If it belongs to life, no answer can be given. And whatsoever you say will be destructive because the whole cannot be said. Words are so narrow, tunnel-like; you cannot force the sky into them, it is impossible.

Second thing to remember: when you ask something of a master – a master is not a philosopher, he is not a thinker; he knows, he is a seer. When you ask something of a master, don't look for and don't wait for his answer, because *he* is the answer. When you ask something, don't be attentive towards the answer; be attentive towards the master, because he is the answer. He is not going to give you any answer; his presence is the answer. But there we miss.

You go and you ask a question; your whole mind is attentive to the question and you are waiting for the answer – but the master, his whole being, his presence is the answer. If you look at him, if you watch him, you will receive an indication – his silence, the way he looks at you in that moment, the way he walks, the way he behaves, the way he remains silent or talks. The master is the answer, because it is an indication. The master can show you the truth, but cannot say it. And your mind is always obsessed with the answer: "What is he going to say?"

If you go to a master, learn to be attentive to his presence; don't be too head-oriented – and don't insist, because every answer can be given only when the time is ripe. Don't insist, because it is not a question of your insistence; a right thing can be given only when you are ready, when you are ripe. So when you are near a master you can ask a question – but then wait. You have asked, then he knows. Even if you have not asked, he knows what is troubling you within. But he cannot give you anything right now – you may not be ready; and if you are not ready and something is given it will not reach you, because only in a certain readiness can certain things penetrate you. When you are ripe you can understand. When you are ready, you are open, receptive. The answer will be given, but not in words; the master will reveal it in many ways. He can do it. He can devise many methods to indicate it, but then you will have to be ready.

Just because you have asked a question doesn't mean that you are ready. You can ask a question – even children can raise questions so mysterious that even a buddha will be unable to answer them. But just because you have asked, just because you are articulate enough to form a question, does not mean that you are ready, because questions come out of many many sources. Sometimes you are simply curious. A master is not there to fulfill your curiosities, because they are childish. Sometimes you really never meant it. Just by the way you asked, you showed you were not concerned and you are not going to use the answer in any way. Somebody is dead and you simply ask the question, "What is death?" – and by the next moment you have forgotten it.

Curiosity is one thing – it is childish and no master is going to waste his breath on your curiosities. When you ask a certain thing it may be just intellectual, philosophic; you are interested, but intellectually – you would like an answer just to become more knowledgeable, but your being will remain unaffected. Then a master is not interested, because he is interested only in your being.

When you ask a question in such a way as if your life and death depend on it, then if you don't receive the answer you will miss. Your whole being will remain hungry for it; you are thirsty, your whole being is ready to receive it, and if the answer is given you will digest it, it will become your blood and your bones and move into the very beat of your heart. Only then will a master be ready to answer you.

You ask a question…then the master will try to help you to become ready to receive the answer. Between your question and the master's answer there may be a great gap. You ask today and he may answer you after twelve years, because you have to be ready to receive it; you have to be open, not closed, and you have to be ready to absorb it to the very depth of your being.

Now try to understand this parable:

> At the death of a parishioner, Master Dogo, accompanied by his disciple
> Zengen, visited the bereaved family.
> Without taking time to express a word of sympathy, Zengen went up to
> the coffin, rapped on it, and asked Dogo: "Is he really dead?"

The first thing: when death is there you have to be very respectful because death is no ordinary phenomenon, it is the most extraordinary phenomenon in the world. Nothing is more mysterious than death. Death reaches to the very center of existence, and when a man is dead you are moving on sacred ground: it is the holiest moment possible. No, ordinary curiosities cannot be allowed. They are disrespectful.

In the East particularly, death is respected more than life – and the East has lived long to come to this conclusion. In the West life is more respected than death; hence so much tension, so much worry and so much anguish, so much madness.

Why? If you respect life more, you will be afraid of death, and then death will look antagonistic, the enemy; and if death is the enemy you will remain tense your whole life, because death can happen any moment. You don't accept it, you reject it – but you cannot destroy it. Death cannot be destroyed. You can reject it; you can deny it; you can be afraid, scared, but it is there, just at the corner, always with you like a shadow. You will be trembling your whole life – and you are trembling. And in the fear, in all fears if searched deeply, you will find the fear of death.

Whenever you are afraid, something has given you an indication of death. If your bank goes bankrupt and you are filled with fear and trembling, anxiety, that too is anxiety about death, because your bank balance was nothing but safety against death. Now you are more open, vulnerable. Now who will protect you if death knocks at the door? If you become ill, if you become old, then who is going to take care of you? The guarantee was there in the bank, and the bank has gone bankrupt.

You cling to prestige, power, position, because when you have a position you are so significant that you are more protected by people. When you are not in power, you become so impotent that nobody will bother in any way who you are. When you are in power you have friends, family, followers; when you are not in power, everybody leaves. There was a protection, somebody was there to care; now nobody cares. Whatsoever you are afraid of, if you search deeply you will always find the shadow of death somewhere.

You cling to a husband, you are afraid he may leave; or you cling to a wife, afraid she may leave you. What is the fear? Is it really the fear of a divorce, or is it the fear of death? It is the fear of death...because in divorce you become alone. The other gives a protection, a feeling that you are not alone, somebody else is with you. In moments when somebody else will be needed, you will have somebody to look to. But the wife has left, or the husband has left, and now you are left alone, a stranger. Who will protect you? Who will care for you when you are ill?

When people are young they do not need a wife or a husband so much, but when they are old their need is more. When you are young it is a sexual relationship. The older you become the more it becomes a life relationship, because now if the other leaves you, death is immediately there. Wherever you are afraid, try to explore, and you will find death hiding somewhere behind. All fear is of death. Death is the only source of fear.

In the West people are very scared, worried, anxious, because you have to fight continuously against death. You love life, you respect life – that's why in the West old people are not respected. Young people are respected, because old people have moved further towards death than you; they are already in its grip. Youth is respected in the West – and youth is a transitory phenomenon, it is already passing from your hands.

In the East old men are respected, because in the East death is respected; and because in the East death is respected, there is no fear about death. Life is just a part; death is the culmination. Life is just the process; death is the crescendo. Life is just the moving; death is the reaching. And both are one! So what will you respect more, the way or the goal? The process or the flowering?

Death is the flower, life is nothing but the tree. And the tree is there for the flower, the flower is not there for the tree. The tree should be happy and the tree should dance when the flower comes.

Death is accepted; not only accepted, welcomed. It is a divine guest. When it knocks at the door, it means the universe is ready to receive you back.

In the East we respect death. And this young man Zengen just came in without even expressing a word of sympathy or respect. He simply became curious. Not only that, he was very disrespectful – he tapped on the coffin and asked Dogo: *Is he really dead?* His question was beautiful, but was not in the right moment. The question is right but the moment he has chosen is wrong. To be curious before death is childish; one has to be respectful, silent. That is the only way to have a rapport with the phenomenon.

When somebody dies it is really something very deep happening. If you can just sit there and meditate many things will be revealed to you. Questioning is foolish. When death is there, why not meditate? Questioning may be just a trick to avoid the thing, it may be just a safety measure so as not to look at death directly.

I have watched when people go to burn or to cremate somebody – they start talking too much there. At the cremation ground they discuss many philosophical things. In my childhood I loved very much to follow everybody. Whosoever died, I would be there. Even my parents became very much afraid; they would say, "Why do you go? We don't even know that man. There is no need to go."

I would say, "That is not the point. The man is not the concern. Death…it's such a beautiful phenomenon, and one of the most mysterious. One should not miss it." So the moment I heard that somebody had died I would be there, always watching, waiting, witnessing what was happening.

And I watched people discussing many things, philosophical problems such as: What is death? And somebody saying: "Nobody dies. The innermost self is immortal." They would discuss the Upanishads, the Gita, and quote authorities. I started feeling that they are avoiding; just becoming engaged in a discussion, they are avoiding the phenomenon that is happening. They are not looking at the dead man. And the thing is there! Death is there, and you are discussing it! What a fool!

You have to be silent. If you can be silent when death is there you will suddenly see many things, because death is not just a person stopping breathing. Many things are happening. When a person dies, his aura starts subsiding. If you are silent you can feel it – an energy force, a vital energy field, subsiding, getting back to the center.

When a child is born just the opposite happens. When a child is born the aura starts spreading; it starts near the navel. Just as if you throw a pebble into a silent lake, ripples start – they go on spreading, go on spreading. Breath, when a child is born, is like a pebble in the lake; when the child breathes the navel center is hit. The first pebble has been thrown into the silent lake, and the ripples go on spreading.

For your whole life your aura goes on spreading. Nearabout the age of thirty-five your aura is completed, at its peak. Then it starts subsiding. When a person dies it goes back to the navel. When it reaches to the navel, it becomes a concentrated energy, a concentrated light. If you are silent you can feel it, you will feel a pull. If you sit near a dead man you will feel as if a subtle breeze is blowing towards the dead man and you are being pulled. The dead man is contracting his whole life, the whole field that he was.

Many things start happening around a dead man. If he loved a person very deeply, that means he has given a part of his life energy to that person, and when a person dies, immediately that part that he had given to another person leaves that person and moves to the dead man. If you die here and your lover lives in Hong Kong, something will leave from your lover immediately – because you have given a part of your life and that part will come back to you. That's why when a loved one dies you feel that something has left you also, something in you has died also. A deep wound, a deep gap will exist now.

Whenever a lover dies, something in the beloved also dies, because they were involved into each other. And if you have loved many, many people – for example, if a person like Dogo dies, or a buddha – from all over the universe energy moves back to the center. It is a universal phenomenon because he is involved in many many lives, millions of lives, and from everywhere his energy will come back. The vibrations that he has given to many will leave, they will move to the original source, they will become again a concentration near the navel.

If you watch you will feel ripples coming back in a reverse order, and when they are totally concentrated in the navel, you can see a tremendous life energy, a tremendous light-force. And then that center leaves the body. When a man "dies," that is simply a stopping of the breath, and you think he is dead. He is not dead; it takes time. Sometimes, if the person has been involved in millions of lives, it takes many days for him to die – that's why with sages, with saints, particularly in the East, we never burn their bodies. Only saints are not burned; otherwise everybody is burned, because others' involvement is not so much. Within minutes the energy gathers, and they are no longer part of this existence.

But with saints, the energy takes time. Sometimes it goes on and on – that's why if you go to Shirdi, to Sai Baba's town, you will still feel something happening, still the energy goes on coming; he is so much involved that for many people he is still alive. Sai Baba's tomb is not dead. It is still alive. But the same thing you will not feel near many tombs – they are dead. By "dead" I mean they have accumulated all their involvement, they have disappeared.

When I am dead, don't bury my body, don't burn it, because I will be involved in you, many of you. And if you can feel, then a sage remains alive for many years, sometimes thousands of years – because life is not only of the body. Life is an energy phenomenon. It depends on the involvement, on how many persons he was involved in. And a person like Buddha is not only involved with persons, he is involved even with trees, birds, animals; his involvement is so deep that if he dies his death will take at least five hundred years.

Buddha is reported to have said, "My religion will be a live force for only five hundred years." And the meaning is here, because he will be a live force for five hundred years. It will take five hundred years for him to get out of the involvement totally.

When death happens, be silent. Watch.

All over the world, whenever you pay respect to a dead man, you become silent, you remain silent for two minutes – without knowing why. This tradition has been continued all over the world. Why silence?

The tradition is meaningful. You may not know why, you may not be aware, and your silence may be filled with inner chattering, or you may do it just like a ritual – that is up to you. But the secret is there.

Without taking time to express a word of sympathy, Zengen went up to the coffin, rapped on it, and asked Dogo: "Is he really dead?"

His question is right, but the time is not right. He has chosen the wrong opportunity. This is not the moment to talk about it, this is the moment to *be* with it. And the man who is dead must have been someone very deep; otherwise Dogo would not be going to pay his respects. Dogo is an enlightened man. The disciple who is dead must have been something. And Dogo was there to do something more for him. A master can help you when you are alive; a master can help you when you are dead even more – because in death a deep surrendering happens.

In life you are always resisting, fighting, even with your master; not surrendering, or surrendering halfheartedly – which means nothing. But when you are dying, surrender is easier, because death and surrender are the same process. When the whole body is dying, you can surrender easily. To fight is difficult, resistance is difficult. Already your resistance is being broken, your body is moving into a let-go; that is what death is.

Dogo was there for something special, and this disciple asked a question. The question is right but the time is not right.

> *"I won't say," said Dogo. "Well?" insisted Zengen. "I'm not saying, and that's final," said Dogo.*

First thing: what can be said about death? How can you say anything about death? It is not possible for any word to carry the meaning of death. What does this word "death" mean? In fact it means nothing. What do you mean when you use the word death? It is simply a door beyond which we don't know what happens. We see a man disappearing inside a door; we can see up to the door, and then the man simply disappears. Your word death can give only the meaning of the door. But what happens really, beyond the door? – because the door is not the thing.

The door is to be passed through. Then what happens to one who disappears through the door and we cannot see beyond ? And what is this door? Just a stopping of the breath? Is the breath the whole of life? Don't you have anything more than the breath? Breath stops...body deteriorates...if you are body and breath alone, then there is no problem. Then death is nothing. It is not a door to anything. It is simply a stopping, not a disappearance. It is just like a clock.

The clock was tick-ticking, working, then it stops; you don't ask where the tick-tick has gone – that would be meaningless! It has gone nowhere. It has not gone at all, it has simply stopped; it was a mechanism and something has gone wrong in the mechanism. You can repair the mechanism, then it will tick-tick again. Is death just like a clock stopping? Just like that?

If so, it is not a mystery, it is nothing really. But how can life disappear so easily? Life is not mechanical. Life is awareness. The clock is not aware – you can listen to the tick-tick, the clock has never listened to it. You can listen to your own heartbeat. Who is this listener? If only the heartbeat is life, then who is this listener? If breath is the only life, how can you be aware of your breath? That's why all Eastern techniques of meditation use breath awareness as a subtle technique – because if you become aware of the breathing, then who is this awareness? It must be something beyond breath because you can look at it and the looker cannot be the object. You can witness it; you can close your eyes and you can see your breath going in and coming out. Who is this seer, the witnessing? It must be a separate force that does not depend on breathing. When the breathing disappears it is the stopping of a clock, but where does this awareness go? Where does this awareness move into?

Death is a door, it is not a stopping. Awareness moves but your body remains at the door – just as you have come here and left your shoes at the door. The body is left outside the temple, and your awareness enters the temple. It is the most subtle phenomenon, life is nothing before it. Basically life is just a preparation for death, and only those are wise who learn in their life how to die. If you don't know how to die you have missed the whole meaning of life: it is a preparation, it is a training, it is a discipline.

Life is not the end, it is just a discipline to learn the art of dying. But you are afraid, you are scared, at the very word *death* you start trembling. That means you have not yet known life, because life never dies. Life cannot die.

Somewhere you have become identified with the body, with the mechanism. The mechanism is to die, the mechanism cannot be eternal, because the mechanism depends on many things; it is a conditioned phenomenon. Awareness is unconditional, it doesn't depend on anything. It can float like a cloud in the sky, it has no roots, it is not caused, it is never born so it can never die.

Whenever someone dies you have to be meditative near them, because a temple is just near and it is holy ground. Don't be childish, don't bring curiosities, be silent so you can watch and see. Something very, very meaningful is happening – don't miss the moment. And when death is there, why ask about it? Why not look at it? Why not watch it? Why not move with it a few steps?

> *"I won't say," said Dogo. "Well?" insisted Zengen. "I'm not saying, and that's final," said Dogo. On their way back to the temple, the furious Zengen turned on Dogo and threatened: "By God, if you don't answer my question, why I'll beat you!"*

This is possible in Zen, that even a disciple can beat the master, because

Zen is very true to life and very authentic. A Zen master does not create the phenomenon around him that, "I am holier than you." He does not say, "I am so superior." How can one who has achieved say, "I am superior and you are inferior"? The disciple can think that he is superior, but the master cannot claim any superiority, because superiority is only claimed by inferiority. Superiority is only claimed by the ego that is impotent, inferior. Strength is claimed only by weakness: when you are uncertain you claim certainty, when you are ill you claim health, when you don't know you claim knowledge. Your claims are simply to hide the truth. A master claims nothing. He cannot say, "I am superior." It is foolish. How can a wise man say, "I am superior"?

So a Zen master even allows this – a disciple to hit him – and he can enjoy the whole thing. Nobody else in the world has done that; that's why Zen masters are rare – you cannot find rarer flowers. The master is so superior, really, that he allows you even to hit him; his superiority is not challenged by it. You cannot challenge him in any way, and you cannot bring him down in any way. He is no longer there. He is an empty house.

And he knows that a disciple can only be foolish. Nothing else is expected because a disciple is ignorant; compassion is needed. And in ignorance a disciple is bound to go on doing things, things that are not proper, because how can an improper person do proper things? And if you force proper things on an improper person, he will be crippled, his freedom will be cut. And a master is to help you to be free – so hitting is allowed. In fact it is not irreverence; in fact the disciple also loves the master so much, so intimately, that he can come so close. Even hitting a person is a sort of intimacy – you cannot hit just anybody.

Sometimes it happens that even a child hits his father, or a child slaps his mother. No antagonism is meant, it is just that the child accepts the mother so deeply and so intimately that he doesn't feel that anything is improper. And the child knows he will be forgiven, so there is no fear.

A master forgives infinitely, unconditionally.

The disciple was very angry because he had asked a very meaningful question – it looked meaningful to him. He couldn't conceive why Dogo should behave so obstinately and say, "No!" – and not only that, he said, "This is final! And I am not going to say anything more."

When you ask a question you ask because of your ego, and when the answer is not given the ego feels hurt. The disciple was hurt; his ego was disturbed, he couldn't believe it – and this must have happened in front of many people. They were not alone, there were many others, there must have been – when someone dies many people gather there. And in front of all those people the master said, "No, and this is final! I am not going to say anything." They all must have thought, "This disciple is just a fool, asking irrelevant questions."

Zengen must have felt angry, he must have been boiling. When he found himself alone with the master going back to the monastery he said:

> *"By God, if you don't answer my question, why I'll beat you!" "All*
> *right," said Dogo, "beat away."*

Be finished with it! If you are angry, then be finished with it.

A master is always ready to bring out all that is in you, even your negativity. Even if you are going to hit him he will allow you to. Who knows – in hitting
the master you may become aware of your negativity; you may become aware
of your illness, your disease, your madness. Hitting the master may become a
sudden enlightenment – who knows. And a master is there to help you in every
way. So Dogo said:

All right – go ahead – *beat away.*

> *A man of his word, Zengen slapped his master a good one. Some*
> *time later Dogo died, and Zengen, still anxious to have his question*
> *answered, went to the master Sekiso, and, after relating what had*
> *happened, asked the same question of him. Sekiso, as if conspiring with*
> *the dead Dogo, would not answer.*

All masters are always in a secret conspiracy. If they are masters at all,
they are always together – even if they contradict each other, they belong to
the same conspiracy; even if sometimes they say that the other is wrong, they
are in a conspiracy.

It happened that Buddha and Mahavira were contemporaries and they
moved in the same province, Bihar. It is known as Bihar because of them: *Bihar*
means their field of movement, they walked all over that part. Sometimes they
were in the same village. Once it happened that they were staying in the same
roadside inn – half the inn was engaged by Buddha and half by Mahavira – but
they never met each other.

And continually they refuted each other. Disciples used to move from one
master to the other, and it has remained a puzzle – why? Buddha would even
laugh, he would joke about Mahavira. He would say, "That fellow! So he claims
that he is enlightened? He claims that he is all-knowing? But I have heard that
he says it once happened that he knocked at a door to beg for his food and
there was no one inside, and I have heard that he claims that he is all-knowing!
And even this much he didn't know, that the house was vacant?"

He goes on joking. He says, "Once Mahavira was walking and he stepped
on the tail of a dog. Only when the dog jumped and barked did he know that

the dog was there, because it was morning and dark. And that fellow says that he is all-knowing?" He goes on joking, he cuts many jokes against Mahavira; they are beautiful.

They are in a conspiracy and this has not been understood, neither by Jainas nor by Buddhists – they have missed the whole point. They think they are against each other, and Jainas and Buddhists have remained against each other for these two thousand years.

They are not against each other! They are playing roles, and they are trying to help people. They are two different types. Somebody can be helped by Mahavira, and somebody else can be helped by Buddha. The person who can be helped by Buddha cannot be helped by Mahavira – that person has to be taken away from Mahavira. And the person who can be helped by Mahavira cannot be helped by Buddha – that person has to be taken away from Buddha. That's why they talk against each other; it is a conspiracy. But everybody should be helped, and they are two different types, absolutely different types.

How can they be against each other? Nobody who ever became enlightened is against any other enlightened person, cannot be. He may talk as if it is so, because he knows the other will understand. Mahavira is never reported to have said anything about the jokes that Buddha was telling here and there. He kept completely silent. That was his way. By being completely silent, not even refuting, he was saying, "Leave that fool to himself!" – by being completely silent, not saying anything.

Every day reports would come, people would come and they would say, "He has said this," and Mahavira would not even talk about it. And that was fitting, because he was very old, thirty years older than Buddha; it was not good for him to come down and fight with a young man – this is how young fools are! But he was the same as Buddha, against other teachers who were older than him. He was talking about them, talking against them, arguing against them.

They are in a conspiracy. They have to be – because you cannot understand. They have to divide paths, because you cannot understand that life exists through opposites. They have to choose opposites. They have to stick to one thing, and then they have to say – for you – "Remember that all others are wrong." Because if they say everybody is right, you will be more confused. You are already confused enough. If they say, "Yes, I am right. Mahavira is also right, Buddha is also right – everybody is right," you will immediately leave them; you will think: "This man can't help, because we are already confused. We don't know what is right and what is wrong, and we have come to this man to know exactly what is right and what is wrong."

So masters stick to something and they say, "This is right and everything else is wrong," knowing all along that there are millions of ways to reach the way; knowing all along that there are millions of paths which reach to the final path. But if they say that millions of paths reach, you will be simply confused.

This disciple Zengen was in trouble, because his master Dogo died. He never expected that this was going to happen so soon. Disciples always feel in great difficulty when their masters die. When their masters are there, they fool around and waste time. When their masters are dead, then they are in a real fix and difficulty – what to do? So Zengen's question remained, the problem remained, the puzzle was as it was before. The disciple had not yet come to know what death is, and this Dogo had died.

He went to another master, Sekiso, and after relating the whole thing about what had happened, asked the same question of him.

> Sekiso, as if conspiring with the dead Dogo, would not answer. "By God!" cried Zengen. "You too?" "I'm not saying," said Sekiso, "and that's final."

They are doing something, they are creating a situation. They are saying, "Be silent before death. Don't ask questions, because when you ask you come to the surface, you become superficial. These questions are not questions to be asked. These questions are to be penetrated, lived, meditated on. You have to move into them. If you want to know death – die! That is the only way to know. If you want to know life – live!"

You are alive but not living, and you will die and you will not die...because everything is lukewarm in you. You live? – not exactly; you just drag. Somehow, somehow you pull yourself along.

Live as intensely as possible, burn your candle of life from both ends. Burn it so intensely...if it is finished in one second it is okay, but at least you will have known what it is, because only intensity penetrates. And if you can live an intense life you will have a different quality of death, because you will die intensely. As life is, so will the death be. If you live dragging, you will die dragging. You will miss life, and you will miss death also. Make life as intense as possible. Put everything at stake. Why worry? Why be worried about the future? *This* moment is there. Bring your total existence into it. Live intensely, totally, wholly, and this moment will become a revelation. And if you know life, you will know death.

This is the secret key: if you know life, you will know death. If you ask what death is, it means you have not lived – because deep down they are one. What is the secret of life? The secret of life is death. If you love, what is the secret of love? Death. If you meditate, what is the secret of meditation? Death.

Whatsoever happens that is beautiful and intense always happens through death. You die, you simply bring yourself totally in it and die to everything else. You become so intense that you are not there, because if you are there then the intensity cannot be total; then two are there. If you love and the lover is there, then love cannot be intense. Love so deeply, so totally, that the lover disappears and you are just an energy moving. Then you will know love, you will know life, you will know death.

These three words are very meaningful: love, life, and death. Their secret is the same, and if you understand them there is no need to meditate. Because you don't understand them, that's why meditation is needed. Meditation is just a spare wheel. If you really love, it becomes meditation. If you don't love, then you will have to meditate. If you really live, it becomes meditation. If you don't live, then you will have to meditate; then something else will have to be added.

But this is the problem: if you cannot love deeply, how can you meditate deeply? If you cannot live deeply, how can you meditate deeply? ...Because the problem is neither love nor meditation nor death, the problem is how to move to the depth? Deepness is the question.

If you move deeply in anything, life will be on the periphery and death will be in the center. Even if you watch a flower totally, forgetting everything, in watching the flower you will die in the flower. You will experience a merging, a melting. Suddenly you will feel you are not, only the flower is.

Live each moment as if this is the last moment. And nobody knows – it may be the last.

Both the masters were trying to bring Zengen an awareness. Sekiso, when he heard the disciple telling him the whole story, said, "No. *I'm not saying... and that's final."* He repeated the same words Dogo had said. The first time the disciple missed, but not the second time.

At that very instant, Zengen experienced an awakening.

A satori happened. Suddenly, lightning – he became aware. The first time he missed. It is almost always so. The first time you will miss, because you don't know what is happening. The first time, your old habits of the mind will not allow you to see. That's why the second master, Sekiso, simply repeated the words of Dogo – simply repeated. He did not change even a single word. The very line is the same: *"I'm not saying,"* he said, *"and that's final."* He again created the same situation.

It was easy to fight with a Dogo, it was not easy to fight with Sekiso. He was not Zengen's master. It was easy to hit Dogo, it will not be possible to hit Sekiso. It is enough that he answers, it is his compassion; he is not bound to answer.

An intimacy was there between Dogo and this disciple, and sometimes it happens when you are very intimate that you can miss – because you take things for granted. Sometimes a distance is needed; it depends on the person. A few people can learn only when a distance is there, a few people can learn only when there is no distance – there are these two types of people. Those who can learn from a distance, they will miss a master; they will miss their own master, but he prepares them. Many of you are here who have worked in many lives with many other masters. You have missed them, but they have prepared you to reach me. Many of you will miss me, but I will have prepared you to reach somebody else. So nothing is lost, no effort is wasted.

Dogo created the situation, Sekiso fulfilled it.

At that very instant Zengen experienced an awakening.

What happened? Hearing again the same words...is there a certain conspiracy? Why the same words again? Suddenly he became aware: My question is absurd, I am asking something which cannot be answered. It is not the master who is denying me the answer, it is my very question, the nature of it.

A silence is needed in the presence of death, of life, of love. If you love a person you sit silently with the person. You would not like to chatter, you would like to just hold their hand and live and be silent in that moment. If you chatter, that means you are avoiding the person – love is not really there. If you love life, chattering will drop, because every moment is so filled with life that there is no way, no space to chatter. Each moment life is flooding you so vitally – where is the time to gossip and chatter? Each moment you live totally, mind becomes silent. Eat, and eat so totally – because life is entering you through food – that mind becomes silent. Drink, and drink totally: life is entering through water, it will quench your thirst; move with it as it touches your thirst, as the thirst disappears. Be silent and watch. How can you chatter when you are drinking a cup of tea? Warm life is flowing within you. Be filled with it. Be respectful.

Hence, in Japan, tea ceremonies exist, and every house worth calling a house has a tearoom just like a temple. A very ordinary thing, tea – and they have raised it to a very holy status. When they enter the tearoom, they enter in complete silence, as if it is a temple. They sit silently in the tearoom. Then the kettle starts singing, and everybody listens silently, as you are listening to me here, the same silence. And the kettle goes on singing millions of songs, sounds, *omkar* – the very mantra of life – and they listen silently. Then the tea is poured. They touch their cups and saucers. They feel grateful that this moment is again given to them. Who knows if it will come again or not? Then they smell the tea, the aroma, and they are filled with gratitude. Then they start sipping. And the taste...and the warmth...and the flow...and the merging of their own energy with the energy of the tea...it becomes a meditation.

Everything can become a meditation if you live it totally and intensely. And then your life becomes whole.

Suddenly, listening to the same words again, Zengen came to realize, "I was wrong and my master was right. I was wrong because I thought he was not answering, he was not paying attention to my question; he was not caring about me at all, and my inquiry. My ego was hurt. But I was wrong – he was not hitting my ego. I was not at all in the question. The very nature of death is such..." Suddenly he was awakened.

This is called satori; it is a special enlightenment. In no other language does there exist a word equivalent to satori. It is a specially Zen thing. It is not *samadhi* and yet it is *samadhi*. It is not *samadhi* because it can happen in very ordinary moments: drinking tea, taking a walk, looking at a flower, listening to the frog jumping in the pond. It can happen in very ordinary moments, so it is not like the *samadhi* about which Patanjali talks. Patanjali would simply be surprised that a frog jumps into the pond and at the sound of it somebody becomes enlightened. Patanjali would not be able to believe that a dry leaf drops from the tree, zigzags, moves on the wind a little, then falls to the ground and goes fast asleep – and somebody sitting under the tree attains enlightenment? No, Patanjali would not be able to believe it: "Impossible," he will say, "because *samadhi* is something exceptional; *samadhi* comes after much effort, millions of lives. And then it happens in a particular posture, *siddhasana*. It happens in a particular state of body and mind."

Satori is *samadhi* and yet not *samadhi*. It is a glimpse, and a glimpse of the extraordinary in the very ordinary. It is *samadhi* happening in ordinary moments. A sudden thing, also – it is not gradual, you don't move in degrees. It is just like water coming to the boiling point, to one hundred degrees – and then the jump, and the water becomes vapor, merges into the sky, and you cannot trace where it has gone. Up to ninety-nine degrees it is boiling and boiling and boiling, but not evaporating. From the ninety-ninth degree it can fall back, it was only hot. But if it passes the hundredth degree, then there is a sudden jump.

The situation is the same in the story. With Dogo, Zengen became hot, but couldn't evaporate. It was not enough, he needed one more situation, or he may have been in need of many more situations. Then with Sekiso – the same situation, and suddenly something is hit. Suddenly the focus changes, the gestalt. Up to this point he had been thinking that it was his question to which Dogo had not replied. He had been egocentric. He had been thinking, "It is I who have been neglected by my master. He was not careful enough about me and my inquiries. He didn't pay enough attention to me and my inquiry."

Suddenly he realizes: "It was not me who was neglected, or that the master was indifferent, or that he didn't pay attention. No, it was not me – it is the question itself. It cannot be answered. In the presence of the mysteries of life and death, one has to be silent." The gestalt changes. He can see the whole thing. Hence, he attains a glimpse.

Whenever the gestalt changes you attain a glimpse. That glimpse is satori. It is not final, you will lose it again. You will not become a buddha with satori; that's why I say it is a *samadhi* and yet not a *samadhi*. It is an ocean in a teacup. Ocean, yes, and yet not the ocean – *samadhi* in a capsule. It gives you a glimpse, an opening…as if you are moving in a dark night, in a forest, lost; you don't know where you are moving, where the path is, whether you are moving in the right direction or not – and then suddenly there is lightning. In a moment you see everything! Then the light disappears. You cannot read in lightning, because it lasts only a moment. You cannot sit under the sky and start reading in lightning. No, it is not a constant flow.

Samadhi is such that you can read in its light. Satori is like lightning – you can see a glimpse of the whole, all that is there, and then it disappears. But you will not be the same again. It is not final enlightenment, but a great step towards it. Now you know. You have had a glimpse, now you can search for more of it. You have tasted it, now buddhas will become meaningful.

Now if Zengen meets Dogo again he will not hit him, he will fall at his feet and ask for his forgiveness. Now he will weep millions of tears, because now he will say, "What compassion Dogo had, that he allowed me to hit him; that he said, 'All right beat away!'" If he meets Dogo again, Zengen will not be the same. He has now tasted something, which has changed him. He has not attained the final – the final will be coming – but he has got the sample.

Satori is the sample of Patanjali's *samadhi*. And it is beautiful that the sample is possible, because unless you taste it how can you move towards it? Unless you smell it a little, how can you be attracted and pulled towards it? The glimpse will become a magnetic force. You will never be the same and you will know something is there and "whether I find it or not, that is up to me." But trust will arise. Satori gives trust and starts a movement, a vital movement in you, towards the final enlightenment that is *samadhi*.

Enough for today.

the perfect man is centered

Lieh-Tzu exhibited his skill in archery to Po-Hun Wu-Jen.
When the bow was drawn to its full length, a cup of water was placed on his elbow and he began to shoot.
As soon as the first arrow was let fly, a second was already on the string, and then a third one followed. In the meantime he stood, unmoving, like a statue.
Po-Hun Wu-Jen said: "The technique of shooting is fine, but it is not the technique of non-shooting. Let us go up to a high mountain and stand on a projecting rock, and then you try and shoot."
They climbed up a mountain. Standing on a rock that projected over a precipice ten thousand feet high, Po-Hun Wu-Jen moved backwards until one third of his feet were overhanging the edge. He then motioned Lieh-Tzu to come forward.
Lieh-Tzu fell down on the ground with perspiration flowing down to his heels.
Said Po-Hun Wu-Jen: "The perfect man soars up above the blue sky, or dives down to the yellow springs, or wanders all over the eight limits of the world, yet shows no sign of change in his spirit. But you betray a sign of trepidation, and your eyes are dazed. How can you expect to hit the target?"

Action needs skill. But no-action also needs skill. The skill of action is just on the surface; the skill of no-action is at the very core of your being. The skill of action can be learned easily; it can be borrowed; you can be educated in it because it is nothing but technique. It is not your being, it is just an art.

But the technique, or the skill, of no-action is not technique at all. You cannot learn it from somebody else, it cannot be taught; it grows as you grow. It grows with your inner growth, it is a flowering. From the outside, nothing can be done to it; something has to evolve from the inside.

The skill of action comes from without, goes within; the skill of no-action comes from within, flows without. Their dimensions are totally different, diametrically opposite. So first try to understand this, then we will be able to enter this story.

For example, you can be a painter just by learning the art; you can learn all that can be taught in art schools. You can be skillful, and you can paint beautiful pictures, you can even become a renowned figure in the world. Nobody will be able to know that this is just technique, unless you come across a master; but *you* will always know that this is just technique.

Your hands have become skillful, your head has the know-how, but your heart is not flowing. You paint, but you are not a painter. You create a work of art but you are not an artist. You do it, but you are not in it. You do it as you do other things – but you are not a lover. You are not involved in it totally; your inner being remains aloof, indifferent, standing by the side. Your head and your hands, they go on working, but you are not there. The painting will not carry your presence, it will not carry *you*. It may carry your signature, but not your being.

A master will immediately know, because this painting will be dead. Beautiful...you can decorate a corpse also, you can paint a corpse also, you can even put lipstick on the lips and they will look red. But lipstick, howsoever red, cannot have the warmth of flowing blood. Those lips are painted, but there is no life in them.

You can create a beautiful painting, but it will not be alive. It can be alive only if you flow in it; that's the difference between a master when he paints and an ordinary painter. The ordinary painter really always imitates because the painting is not growing within him. It is not something with which he is pregnant. He will imitate others, he will have to look for ideas; he may imitate nature – that makes no difference. He may look at a tree and paint it, but the tree has not grown within him.

Look at van Gogh's trees. They are absolutely different – you cannot find trees like that in the world of nature. They are totally different; they are van Gogh's creations, he is living through the trees. They are not like these ordinary trees around you, he has not copied them from nature, he has not copied them from anybody else. If he were a god then he would have created those trees in the world. In the painting he is the god, he is the creator. He is not even imitating the creator of the universe; he is simply being himself. His trees are so high they grow and touch the moon and stars.

Somebody asked van Gogh, "What type of trees are these? From where did you get the idea?"

Van Gogh said: "I don't go on getting ideas from anywhere – these are *my* trees! If I were the creator, my trees would touch the stars, because my trees are desires of the earth, dreams of the earth to touch the stars. My trees are the earth trying to reach, to touch the stars – the hands of the earth, dreams and desires of the earth." These trees are not imitations. These are van Gogh trees.

A creator has something to give to the world, something he is pregnant with. Of course, even for a van Gogh technique is needed, because hands are needed. Even van Gogh cannot paint without hands – if you cut off his hands what will he do? He also needs technique, but technique is just a way to communicate. Technique is just the vehicle, the medium. The technique is not the message, the medium is not the message. The medium is simply a vehicle to carry the message. He has a message; every artist is a prophet – has to be! Every artist is a creator – has to be, he has something to share. Of course, technique is needed. If I have to say something to you, words are needed. But if I am saying only words, then there is no message; then this whole thing is just a chattering. Then I am throwing garbage on others. If words carry my silence, if words carry my wordless message to you, only then is something being said.

When something is to be said, it has to be said in words, but that which has to be said is not words. When something has to be painted it has to be painted using colors and brush and canvas, and the whole technique is needed – but the technique is not the message. Through the medium the message is given, but the medium in itself is not enough.

A technician has the medium, he may have the perfect medium, but he has nothing to deliver, he has no message. His heart is not overflowing. He is doing something with the hand and with the head, because the learning is in the head, and the know-how, the skill, is in the hand. Head and hand cooperate, but the heart remains aloof, untouched. Then painting will be there, but without a heart. There will be no beat in it, there will be no pulse of life in it, no blood will flow in it; very difficult to see – you can see only if you know the difference within yourself.

Take another example, which will be easier to understand. You love a person: you kiss, you hold his or her hand in your hand, you embrace, you make love. All these things can be done to a person you don't love – exactly the same kiss, exactly the same embrace, the same way of holding hands; the same gestures in making love, the same movements – but you don't love the person. What will be the difference? – because as far as action is concerned there is no difference: you kiss, and you kiss in the same way, as perfectly the same as possible. The medium is there, but the message is not there. You are skillful, but your heart is not there. The kiss is dead. It is not like a bird on the wing, it is like a dead stone.

You can make the same movements while making love, but those movements will be more like yoga exercises. They will not be love. You go to a prostitute; she knows the technique – better than your beloved. She has to know, she is professionally skillful – but you will not get love there. If you meet the prostitute on the street the next day, she will not even recognize you. She will not even say hello, because no relationship exists. It was not a contact, the other person was not there. While making love to you, she may have been thinking about her lover. She was not there! She cannot be; prostitutes have to learn the technique of how not to be there – because the whole thing is so ugly.

You cannot sell love, you can sell the body. You cannot sell your heart, you can sell your skill. For a prostitute making love is just a professional thing. She is doing it for the money, and she has to learn how not to be there, so she will think of her lover; she will think of a thousand and one things but not about you – the person who is present there – because to think about the person who is there will create a disturbance. She will not be there…absent! She will make movements, she is skillful in that, but she is not involved.

This is the point of this anecdote. You can become so perfect that you can deceive the whole world, but how will you deceive yourself? And if you cannot deceive yourself, you cannot deceive an enlightened master. He will see through all the tricks that you have created around you. He will see that you are not there in your technique; if you are an archer you may hit the target perfectly, but that is not the point. Even a prostitute brings you to orgasm, she hits the target as perfectly as possible, sometimes even more perfectly than your own beloved; but that is not the point – because although a person remains incomplete, a technique can easily become complete.

A person remains incomplete unless he becomes enlightened. You cannot expect perfection from a person before enlightenment, but you can expect perfection in a skill. You cannot expect perfection in the being, but in the doing it can be expected, there is no problem about it. An archer can hit the target without ever missing it – and may not be in it. He has learned the technique, he has become a mechanism, a robot. It is simply done by the head and the hand.

Now, let us try to penetrate this story, The Art of Archery. In Japan and in China, meditation has been taught through many skills – that is the difference between Indian meditation and Chinese and Buddhist and Japanese meditation. In India, meditation has been taken away from all action in life. It, in itself, is the total thing. That created a difficulty – that's why in India, religion by and by died. It created a difficulty, and the difficulty is this: if you make meditation the whole thing, then you become a burden on the society. Then you cannot go to the shop, you cannot go to the office, you cannot work in the factory – meditation becomes your whole life, you simply meditate. In India, millions of people simply existed meditating; they became a burden on the society, and the burden was too much. Some way or other, the society had to stop it.

Even now, today, almost ten million sannyasins exist in India. Now they are not respected. Only a few...not even ten in those ten million are respected. They have become just beggars. Because of this attitude – that when you do meditation, when religion becomes your life, then there is only religion, then you drop all life and you renounce – Indian meditation has been, in a way, anti-life. You can tolerate a few persons but you cannot tolerate millions, and if the whole country become meditators, then what will you do? And if meditation cannot be available for each and everybody – that means even religion exists only for the few, even in religion class exists, even God is not available to all? No, that cannot be. God is available to all.

In India, Buddhism died. Buddhism died in India, the country of its source, because Buddhist monks became a heavy burden. Millions of Buddhist monks – the country could not tolerate them, it was impossible to support them, they had to disappear. Buddhism completely disappeared; the greatest flowering of Indian consciousness and it disappeared, because you cannot exist like a parasite. A few days, okay; a few years, okay. India tolerated it – it is a great tolerating country, it tolerates everything – but then there is a limit. Thousands of monasteries filled with thousands of monks – it became impossible for this poor country to continue to support them. They had to disappear. In China, in Japan, Buddhism survived, because Buddhism took a change, it passed through a mutation – it dropped the idea of renouncing life. Rather, on the contrary, it made life an object of meditation.

So whatsoever you do, you can do meditatively – there is no need to leave it. This was a new growth, this is the base of Zen Buddhism: life is not to be denied. A Zen monk goes on working; he will work in the garden, he will work on the farm, and he lives on his own labor. He is not a parasite, he is a lovely person. He need not bother about the society, and he is more free from the society than the one who has renounced. How can you be free from the society if you have renounced it? Then you become a parasite, not free – and a parasite cannot have freedom.

This is my message also: be in the society and be a sannyasin. Don't become a parasite, don't become dependent on anybody, because every sort of dependence ultimately will make you a slave. It cannot make you a *mukta*, it cannot make you an absolutely free person.

In Japan, in China, they started to use many things, skills, as an object, as a help, as a support to meditation. Archery is one of them – and archery is beautiful, because it is a very subtle skill, and you need much alertness to be skillful in it.

Lieh-Tzu exhibited his skill in archery to Po-Hun Wu-Jen.

Po-Hun Wu-Jen was an enlightened master. Lieh-Tzu himself became enlightened later on, this story belongs to the days of his seeking. Lieh-Tzu himself became a master in his own right, but this is a story from before he became enlightened.

Lieh-Tzu exhibited...

The desire to exhibit is a desire of an ignorant mind. Why do you want to exhibit? Why do you want people to know you? What's the cause of it? And why do you make it so significant in your life, the exhibition, that people should think that you are somebody very significant, important, extraordinary – why? Because you don't have a self. You have only an ego – a substitute for the self.

Ego is not substantial. Self is substantial, but that is not known to you – and a man cannot live without the feeling of "I." It is difficult to live without the feeling of "I." Then from what center will you work and function? You need an "I." Even if it is false it will be helpful. Without an "I" you will simply disintegrate! Who will be the integrator, the agent within you? Who will integrate you? From what center will you function?

Unless you know the self, you will have to live with an ego. Ego means a substitute self, a false self; you don't know the self, so you create a self of your own. It is a mental creation. And for anything that is false, you have to make supports. Exhibition gives you support.

If somebody says, "You are a beautiful person," you start feeling that you are beautiful. If nobody says so, it will be difficult for you to feel that you are beautiful; you will start suspecting, doubting. If you even say to an ugly person continuously "You are beautiful," the ugliness will drop from his mind, he will start feeling he is beautiful – because the mind depends on others' opinions, it accumulates opinions, depends on them.

The ego depends on what people say about you: the ego feels good if people feel good about you; if they feel bad, the ego feels bad. If they don't give you any attention, the supports are withdrawn; if many people give you attention, they feed your ego – that's why so much attention is asked for continuously.

Even a small child asks for attention. He may go on playing silently, but a guest comes...and the mother has said to the child that when the guest comes, he has to be silent: "Don't create any noise, and don't create any disturbance" – but when the guest comes, the child has to do something because he also wants attention. And he wants more, because he is accumulating an ego – just growing. He needs more food and he has been told to keep silent – that is impossible! He will have to do something. Even if he has to harm himself, he will fall. Harm can be tolerated, but attention must be paid to him. Everybody must pay attention, he *must* become the center of attention!

Once I stayed in a home. The child there must have been told that while I was there he was not to make any trouble, he had to remain quiet and everything. But the child could not remain quiet, he wanted my attention also, so he started creating noise, running here and there, throwing things. The mother was angry and she told him many times, admonished him: "Listen, I am going to beat you if you go on doing this." But he wouldn't listen. Then finally she said to the child, "Listen, go to that chair and sit there *now*!"

From the very gesture the child understood, "Now it is too much and she is going to beat me," so he went to the chair, sat there on the chair, glared at his mother and said, very meaningfully, "Okay! I am sitting, on the outside – but on the inside I am standing."

From childhood to the final, ultimate day of your death, you go on asking for attention. When a person is dying the only idea that is in his mind, almost always, is, "What will people say when I am dead? How many people will come to give me the last goodbye? What will be published in the newspapers? Is any newspaper going to write an editorial?" These are the thoughts. From the very beginning to the last we look at what others say. It must be a deep need.

Attention is food for the ego; only a person who has attained to the self drops that need. When you have a center, your own, you need not ask for others' attention. Then you can live alone. Even in the crowd you will be alone, even in the world you will be alone, you will move in the crowd, but alone.

Right now you cannot be alone. Right now if you go to the Himalayas and move into a dense forest, sitting under a tree, you will wait for somebody to pass by, at least somebody who can carry the message to the world that you have become a great hermit. You will wait, you will open your eyes many times to see

– has somebody come yet or not?... Because you have heard the stories that when somebody renounces the world, the whole world comes to his feet, and up to now nobody has reached – no newspaper man, no reporters, no camera-men, nobody! You cannot go to the Himalayas. When the need for attention drops you are in the Himalayas wherever you are.

Lieh-Tzu exhibited his skill in archery...

Why "exhibit"? He was still concerned with the ego, he was still looking for attention, and he showed his skill to Po-Hun Wu-Jen who was an enlightened master, a very old man. The story says he was almost ninety – very, very old – when Lieh-Tzu went to see him. Why to Po-Hun? – because he was a renowned master, and if he says, "Yes, Lieh-Tzu, you are the greatest archer in the world," it will be such a vital food that one can live on it for ever and ever.

When the bow was drawn to its full length, a cup of water was placed on his elbow and he began to shoot –

and even a single drop of water would not come out of the full cup placed on his elbow, and he was shooting!

As soon as the first arrow was let fly, a second was already on the string, and then a third one followed. In the meantime he stood unmoved like a statue.

Great skill – but Po-Hun Wu-Jen was not impressed, because the moment you want to exhibit you have missed. The very effort to exhibit shows that you have not attained to the self, and if you have not attained to the self you can stand like a statue on the outside – in the inside you will be running, following many, many motivations, desires and dreams. Outside, you may be unmoving; inside, all sorts of movements will be going on there together, simultaneously; in many directions you must be running. Outside you can become a statue – that is not the point.

It is said of Bokuju: he went to his master and for two years he sat before his master, near him, just like a statue, a marble statue of Buddha. At the beginning of the third year the master came, gave Bokuju a whack with his staff, and told him: "You stupid! We have a thousand and one Buddha statues here, we don't need any more!" – because his master lived in a temple where there were one thousand and one Buddha statues. He said, "There are enough! What are you doing here?"

Statues are not needed, but a different state of being. It is very easy to sit silently on the outside – what is difficult in it? Just a little training is needed. I have seen one man, very much respected in India, who has been standing for ten years – he even sleeps standing. His legs have become so thick and swollen that now he cannot bend his legs. People respect him very much, but when I went to see him he wanted to see me alone, and then he asked: "Tell me how to meditate. My mind is very much disturbed."

Standing ten years like a statue! – he has not sat, he has not slept, but the problem remains the same: how to meditate, how to become silent inside. Unmoving outside, many movements inside. There may be even more than there are with you, because your energy is divided; much energy is needed for body movements. But a man who stands without moving – his whole energy moves inwards in the mind, he becomes inside mad. But people respect him – and that has become an exhibition. Ego is fulfilled but the self is nowhere to be found. *Po-Hun Wu-Jen said: "The technique of shooting is fine"* – you did well, beautiful! – *"but it is not the technique of non-shooting."*

This may be a little bit difficult because in Zen they say that the technique of shooting is just the beginning. To know how to shoot is just the beginning; but to know how *not* to shoot, so that the arrow shoots by itself, is to know the end.

Try to understand: when you shoot, the ego is there, the doer. And what is the art of non-shooting? The arrow shoots in that too, it reaches the target in that too, but the target is not the point. It may even miss the target – that is not the point. The point is, inside there should be no doer. The *source* is the point. When you put an arrow on the bow, you should not be there; you should be as if nonexistent, absolutely empty, and the arrow shoots by itself. No doer inside – then there can be no ego. You are so much one with the whole process that there is no division. You are lost in it. The act and the actor are not two – not even the slight distinction of "I am the doer and this is my action." It takes many years to attain. And if you don't understand, it is very difficult to attain it; if you understand the thing, you create the possibility.

Herrigel, a German seeker, worked for three years with his master in Japan. He was an archer, when he reached Japan he was already an archer, and a perfect one, because a hundred percent of his targets were hit by the arrow; there was no question about it. When he arrived he was already an archer just like Lieh-Tzu. But the master laughed. He said, "Yes, you are skilled in shooting, but what about non-shooting?"

Herrigel said, "What is this non-shooting? – never heard of it."

The master said, "Then I will teach you."

Three years passed; he became more and more skillful and the target became nearer and nearer and nearer. He became absolutely perfect, there was nothing lacking. And he was worried because…and this is the problem for the Western mind: the East looks mysterious, illogical, and the East is. He couldn't understand this master; was he a madman? …because now he was absolutely perfect, the master could not find a single fault, and he goes on saying, "No!" This is the problem: the gulf between the Eastern and the Western approaches towards life. The master goes on saying no, goes on rejecting.

Herrigel started getting frustrated. He said, "But where is the fault? Show me the fault and I can learn how to go beyond it."

The master said, "There is no fault. *You* are faulty. There is no fault, your shooting is perfect – but that is not the point. *You* are faulty; when you shoot, *you* are there, you are too much there. The arrow reaches the target, that's right! – but that is not the point. Why are you there too much? Why the exhibition? Why the ego? Why can't you simply shoot without being there?"

Herrigel, of course, continued arguing, "How can one shoot without being there? Then who will shoot?" – a very rational approach: then who will shoot?

And the master would say, "Just look at me." And Herrigel also felt that his master had a different quality, but that quality is mysterious and you cannot catch it. He felt it many times: that when the master shoots it is really different, as if he becomes the arrow, the bow, as if the master is there no more; he is completely one, undivided.

Then he started asking how to do this. The master said, "This is not a technique. You have to understand, and you have to soak yourself into that understanding more and more, and sink into it."

Three years lost, and then Herrigel understood that this was not possible. Either this man is mad, or it is not possible for a Westerner to attain this non-shooting: I have wasted three years, now it is time to go.

So he asked the master straight; the master said, "Yes, you can go."

Herrigel asked, "Can you give me a certificate stating that for three years I learned with you?"

The master said, "No, because you have not learned anything. You have been three years with me, but you have not learned anything. All that you have learned you could have learned in Germany also. There was no need to come here."

The day he was to leave he just went to say goodbye, and the master was teaching other disciples, and demonstrating. It was just morning, and the sun was rising and there were birds singing; and Herrigel was now unworried because he had decided, and once the decision is taken the worry disappears. He was not worried. For these three years he was tense in the mind – how to attain? How to fulfill the conditions of this madman? But now there was no worry. He had decided, he was leaving, he had booked; by the evening he would leave and all this nightmare would be left behind. He was just waiting for the master so that when he was finished with his disciples he could say goodbye and a thank you and leave.

So he was sitting on a bench. For the first time, suddenly he felt something. He looked at the master. The master was pulling the string of the bow and, as if he was not walking towards the master, he suddenly found himself standing and walking from the bench. He reached the master, took the bow from his hand...the arrow left the bow, and the master said, "Good, fine, you have attained! Now I can give you a certificate."

And Herrigel says: "Yes, that day I attained. I now know the difference. That day something happened by itself – I was not the shooter, I was not there at all. I was just sitting on the bench relaxed. There was no tension, no worry, no thinking about it. I was not concerned."

Remember this, because you are also near a madman. It is very difficult to fulfill my conditions. It is almost impossible – but it is possible also. And it will happen only when you have done everything that you can do, and you come to the point to say goodbye, when you come to the point where you would like to leave me and go away. It will come to you only when you come to the point where you think, "Drop all these meditations and everything. The whole thing is nightmarish." Then there is no worry. But don't forget to come to me and say goodbye; otherwise you may leave without attaining.

Things start happening when you are finished with effort, when the effort has been done totally – of course, Herrigel was total in his effort; that's why in three years he could finish the whole thing. If you are partial, fragmentary, your effort is not total, then three lives may not be enough. If you are lukewarm in your effort then you will never come to a point when the whole effort becomes useless.

Be total in the effort. Learn the whole technique that is possible to do meditation. Do everything that you can do. Don't withhold anything. Don't try to escape from anything; do it wholeheartedly. Then there comes a point, a peak, where no more can be done. When you come to the point where no more can be done and you have done all, and I go on saying, "No, this is not enough!" – my "no" is needed to bring you to the total, to the final, to the peak from where no more doing is possible.

And you don't know how much you can do. You have tremendous energy which you are not using; you are using only a fragment. And if you are using only a fragment, then you will never come to the point where Herrigel reached – I call that the Herrigel point.

But he did well. He did whatsoever could be done; on his part he was not saving anything. Then the boiling point comes. At that boiling point is the door. The whole effort becomes so useless, so futile: you are not reaching anywhere through it, so you drop it. A sudden relaxation...and the door opens.

Now you can meditate without being a meditator. Now you can meditate without even meditating. Now you can meditate without your ego being there. Now you become the meditation – there is no meditator. The actor becomes the action, the meditator becomes meditation; the archer becomes the bow, the arrow – and the target is not there outside somewhere hanging on a tree. The target is you, inside you – the source.

This is what Po-Hun Wu-Jen said. He said:

> *"The technique of shooting is fine..."*

of course Lieh-Tzu was a good shot, a perfect archer –

> *"...but it is not the technique of non-shooting. Let us go up to a high mountain and stand on a projecting rock, and then you try and shoot."*

What is he bringing Lieh-Tzu to? The outside is perfect but the source is still trembling. The action is perfect but the being is still shaking. The fear is there, death is there; he has not known himself yet. He is not a knower; whatsoever he is doing is just from the head and the hand: the third H is still not in it. Remember always to have all the three H's together – the hand, the heart and the head. You have learned the three R's, now learn the three H's. And always remember that the head is so cunning that it can deceive you, it can give you the feeling, "Okay, all the three H's are there," because as a skill develops, as you become more and more technically perfect, the head says, "What else is needed?"

Head means the West, heart means the East. The head says, "Everything is okay." Herrigel is the head, the master is the heart – and the master looks mad. And remember: for the head, the heart always looks mad. The head always says, "You keep quiet. Don't come in, otherwise you will create a mess. Let me tackle the whole thing. I have learned everything, I know the arithmetic, and I know how to deal with this." And technically the head is always correct. The heart is technically always wrong, because the heart knows no technique, it knows only the feeling, it knows only the poetry of being. It knows no technique, it knows no grammar, it is a poetic phenomenon.

> *"Let us go to a high mountain,"*

said the old master – very very old, ninety years old –

"...and stand on a projecting rock and then you try and shoot."

Then we will see.

*They climbed up a mountain. Standing on a rock that projected over a
precipice ten thousand feet high...*

And remember, that is the difference between the head and the heart: ten
thousand feet high is the heart, on a projecting rock overlooking a ten thousand foot deep valley...

Whenever you move nearer to the heart you will feel dizzy. With the head,
everything is on level ground; it is a highway, concrete. With the heart you
move into the forest – no highways, ups and downs, everything mysterious,
unknown, hidden in a mist; nothing is clear, it is a labyrinth; it is not a highway,
it is more like a puzzle. Ten thousand feet high!

Somewhere Nietzsche has reported that once it happened that he suddenly
found himself ten thousand feet high, ten thousand feet high from time – as
if time is a valley, and he found himself ten thousand feet high and away from
time itself. The day he reported this in his diary is the day he went mad. The
day he reported this in his diary is the day his madness came in.

It is a very dizzy point; one can go mad. The nearer you move towards
the heart you will feel you are moving nearer to madness. "What am I doing?"
Things get dizzy. The known leaves you behind, the unknown enters. All maps
become useless, because no maps exist for the heart; all maps exist for the
conscious mind. It is a clear-cut thing; in it, you are secure. That's why love
gives you fear, death gives you fear, meditation gives you fear. Whenever you
are moving towards the center, fear grips you.

*They climbed up a mountain. Standing on a rock that projected over a
precipice ten thousand feet high, Po-hun Wu-jen moved backwards...*

not forwards; on this projecting rock ten thousand feet high he moved
backwards.

*Po-Hun Wu-Jen moved backwards until one third of his feet were
overhanging the edge...*

and backwards.

He then motioned Lieh-Tzu to come forward.

It is said that this ninety-year-old man was almost bent; he couldn't stand erect, he was very, very old. This bent old man, half of his feet overhanging the edge – not even looking that way, backwards.

He then motioned Lieh-Tzu to come forward.

That is where I am standing and calling you to come forward.

Lieh-Tzu fell down on the ground...

He would not come near him. Wherever he was standing, far away from the projecting precipice, Lieh-Tzu fell down on the ground.

The very idea of coming closer to this old madman who is just standing, overhanging death; any moment he will fall and will not be found ever...

...With perspiration flowing down to his heels.

Lieh-Tzu fell down on the ground with perspiration flowing down to his heels. Remember, first perspiration comes to the head. When the fear starts, first you perspire on the head; the heels are the last thing. When fear enters so deep in you that not only is the head perspiring, but the heels are perspiring, then the whole being is filled with fear and trembling. Lieh-Tzu could not stand – he could not stand even the idea of coming nearer to the old master.

Said Po-Hun Wu-Jen: "The perfect man soars up above the blue sky, or
dives down to the yellow springs, or wanders all over the eight limits of
the world, yet shows no sign of change in his spirit."

"Lieh-Tzu, so much? To the very heels? And why have you fallen there on the ground, dazed? Why this change in spirit? Why are you shaking so much? Why this trembling? What is the fear? – because a perfect man has no fear!"

Perfection is fearlessness...because a perfect man knows there is no death. Even if this old Po-Hun Wu-Jen falls, he knows he cannot really fall; even if the body shatters into millions of pieces and nobody can find it again, he knows he cannot die. He will remain as he is. Only something on the periphery will disappear; the center remains, remains always as it is.

Death is not for the center. The cyclone is only on the periphery, the cyclone never reaches the center. Nothing ever reaches the center. The perfect man is centered, he is rooted in his being. He is fearless. He is not unafraid – no! He is not a brave man – no! He is simply fearless. A brave man is one who has fear, but goes against his fear; and a coward is one who also has fear, but goes with his fear. They don't differ, the brave and cowards, they don't differ basically, they both have fears. The brave is one who goes on in spite of the fear, the coward is one who follows his fear. But a perfect man is neither; he is simply fearless. He is neither a coward, nor is he brave. He simply knows that death is a myth, death is a lie – the greatest lie; death does not exist.

Remember, for a perfect man death does not exist – only life, or godliness, exists. For you, godliness does not exist, only death exists. The moment you feel deathlessness you have felt the divine. The moment you feel deathlessness you have felt the very source of life.

> *"The perfect man soars up above the blue sky, or dives down to the yellow springs, or wanders all over the eight limits of the world, yet shows no sign of change in his spirit."*

Change may happen on the periphery but in his spirit there is no change. Inside he remains unmoving. Inside he remains eternally the same.

"But you betray a sign of trepidation, and your eyes are dazed," Lieh-Tzu. *"How can you expect to hit the target?"*

...Because if you are trembling within, howsoever exactly you hit the target, it cannot be exact because the trembling inside will make your hands tremble. It may be invisible, but it will be there. For all outward purposes you may have hit the target, but for inward purposes you have missed. How can you hit the target?

So the basic thing is not to hit the target, the basic thing is to attain a non-trembling being. Then whether you hit the target or not is secondary. That is for children to decide, and child's play.

This is the difference between the art of shooting and the art of non-shooting. It is possible that this master, old master, may miss the target, it is possible; but still, he knows the art of non-shooting. Lieh-Tzu will never miss the target, but still he has missed the real target, he has missed himself.

So there are two points: the source from where the arrow moves, and the end where the arrow reaches. Religion is always concerned with the source from where all the arrows move. It is not the point where they reach; the basic thing is from where they move – because if they move from a non-trembling being they will attain the target. They have already attained, because in the source is the end, in the beginning is the end, in the seed is the tree, in the alpha is the omega.

So the basic thing is not to be worried about the result; the essential thing is to think, to meditate, about the source. Whether my gesture is a perfect love gesture or not is not the point. Whether love is flowing or not, that is the point. If love is there it will find its own technique, if love is there it will find its own skill. But if love is not there, and you are skilled in the technique, the technique cannot find its love – remember this.

The center will always find its periphery, but the periphery cannot find the center. The being will always find its morality, its character, but the character will not find its being. You cannot move from without towards within. There is only one way: energy flows from within towards without. The river cannot move if there is no source, no originating source. Then the whole thing will be false. If you have the source, the river will move, and it will attain to the ocean – there is no problem. Wheresoever it goes, it will reach to the target. If the source is overflowing, you will attain; and if you are simply playing with techniques and toys, you will miss.

In the West particularly, technology has become so important that it has entered even in human relationship. Because you know too much about techniques, you are trying to convert everything into technology. That's why books, thousands of books, are published every year about love – the technique, how to attain orgasm, how to make love. Even love has become a technological problem and orgasm a technological thing, it has to be solved by technicians. If love has also become a technological problem then what is left? Then nothing is left, then the whole life is just a technology. Then you have to know the know-how – but you miss; you miss the real target which is the source.

Technique is good as far as it goes, but it is secondary. It is nonessential. The essential is the source and one must first look for the source – and then the technique can come. It is good that you learn the technique, it is good! People come to me and I see they are always concerned with technique. They ask how to meditate. They don't ask, "What is meditation?" "How?" – they ask how to attain peace. They never ask, "What is peace?" As if they already know.

Mulla Nasruddin killed his wife and then there was a case in the court. The judge said to Nasruddin, "Nasruddin, you go on insisting again and again that you are a peace-loving man. What type of peace-loving man are you? You killed your wife!"

Nasruddin said, "Yes, I repeat again that I am a peace-loving man. You don't know: when I killed my wife such peace descended on her face, and for the first time in my house there was peace all over. And I still insist that I am a peace-loving man."

Technique kills. It can give you a peace which belongs to death, not to life. Method is dangerous, because you may forget the source completely and you may become obsessed with the method. Methods are good if you remain alert and you remain conscious that they are not the end, they are only the means. Too much obsession with them is very harmful, because you can forget the source completely.

This is the point. This old master, Po-Hun Wu-Jen, showed Lieh-Tzu one of the secrets. Lieh-Tzu himself became an enlightened man, he himself became what this old man was at that moment: backwards, moving towards the precipice ten thousand feet high and half his feet hanging over – and a very old body, ninety years old, and still no trembling came to the old man; not a slight change, not even a tremor! Inside he must have been totally fearless. Inside he must have been rooted, grounded in himself, centered. Remember this always, because there is always a possibility of becoming a victim of techniques and methods.

The ultimate comes to you only when all techniques have been dropped. The ultimate happens to you only when there is no method, because only then are you open. The ultimate will knock at your door only when you are not there. When you are absent, you are ready, because when you are absent only then is there a space for the ultimate to enter into you. Then you become a womb. If *you* are there, you are always too much; there is not even a slight gap, space, for the ultimate to enter into you – and the ultimate is vast. You have to be so vastly empty, so infinitely empty – only then is there a possibility of the meeting.

That's why I go on saying you will never be able to meet God, because when God comes you will not be there. And as long as you are, he cannot come. You are the barrier.

Enough for today.

let the moment decide

While Tokai was a visitor at a certain temple, a fire started under the kitchen floor.
A monk rushed into Tokai's bedroom, shouting: "A fire, master, a fire!"
"Oh?" said Tokai, sitting up. "Where?"

"Where?" exclaimed the monk. "Why, under the kitchen floor – get up at once."

"The kitchen, eh?" said the master drowsily. "Well, tell you what, when it reaches the passageway, come back and let me know."
Tokai was snoring again in no time.

The whole ignorance of mind consists in not being in the present. Mind is always moving: into the future, or into the past. Mind is never here and now. It cannot be. The very nature of mind is such that it cannot be in the present, because mind has to think, and in the present moment there is no possibility to think. You have to see, you have to listen, you have to be present, but you cannot think.

The present moment is so narrow that there is no space to think about. You can be, but thoughts cannot be. How can you think? If you think, it means it is already past, the moment has gone. Or you can think if it has not come yet, it is in the future.

For thinking, space is needed, because thinking is like a walk – a walk of the mind, a journey. Space is needed. You can walk into the future, you can walk into the past, but how can you walk in the present? The present is so close, really not even close – the present is you. Past and future are parts of time; the present is *you*, it is not part of time. It is not a tense: it is not at all a part of time, it doesn't belong to time. The present is you; past and future are out of you.

The mind cannot exist in the present. If you can be here, totally present, mind will disappear. Mind can desire, can dream – dream a thousand and one thoughts. It can move to the very end of the world, it can move to the very beginning of the world, but it cannot be here and now – that is impossible for it. The whole ignorance consists in not knowing this. And then you worry about the past, which is no more – it is absolutely stupid! You cannot do anything about the past. How can you do anything about the past which is no more? Nothing can be done, it has already gone; but you worry about it, and worrying about it, you waste yourself.

Or you think about the future, and dream and desire. Have you ever observed? – the future never comes. It cannot come. Whatsoever comes is always the present, and the present is absolutely different from your desires, your dreams. That's why whatsoever you desire and dream and imagine and plan for and worry about, never happens. But it wastes you. You go on deteriorating. You go on dying. Your energies go on moving in a desert, not reaching any goal, simply dissipating. And then death knocks at your door. And remember: death never knocks in the past, and death never knocks in the future; death knocks in the present.

You cannot say to death, "Tomorrow!" Death knocks in the present. Life also knocks in the present. God also knocks in the present. Everything that is always knocks in the present, and everything that is not is always part of past or future.

Your mind is a false entity because it never knocks in the present. Let this be the criterion of reality: whatsoever is, is always here and now; whatsoever is not is never a part of the present. Drop all that which never knocks in the now. And if you move in the now, a new dimension opens – the dimension of eternity.

Past and future move in a horizontal line: Just like A moves to B, B to C, C to D, in a line. Eternity moves vertically: A moves deeper into the A, higher into the A, not to B; A goes on moving deeper and higher, both ways. It is vertical. The present moment moves vertically, time moves horizontally. Time and present never meet. And you are the present: your whole being moves vertically. The depth is open, the height is open, but you are moving horizontally with the mind. That's how you miss God.

People come to me and they ask how to meet God, how to see, how to realize. That is not the point. The point is: how are you missing him? – because he is here and now, knocking at your door. Otherwise it cannot be! If he is real, he must be here and now. Only unreality is not here and now. He is already at your door – but you are not there. You are never at home. You go on wandering into millions of words, but you are never at home. There you are never found, and God comes to meet you there, reality surrounds you there, but never finds you there. The real question is not how you should meet God; the real question is how you should be at home, so that when God knocks he finds you there. It is not a question of your finding him, it is a question of him finding you.

So it is a real meditation. A man of understanding does not bother about God or that type of matter, because he is not a philosopher. He simply tries how to be at home, how to stop worrying and thinking about the future and the past, how to settle here and now, how not to move from this moment. Once you are in this moment, the door opens. This moment is the door!

I was staying once with a Catholic priest and his family. It happened one evening that I was sitting with the family: the priest, his wife, and their young child who was playing in the corner of the room with a few blocks, making something. Then suddenly the child said, "Now everybody be quiet, because I have made a church. The church is ready, now be silent."

The father was very happy that the boy understood that in a church one has to be quiet. To encourage him he said, "Why is it one needs to be quiet in a church?" "Because," said the boy, "the people are asleep."

The people are really asleep, not only in the church, but on the whole earth, everywhere. They are asleep in the church because they come asleep from outside. They go out of the church, they move in sleep – everybody is a sleepwalker, a somnambulist. And this is the nature of sleep: that you are never here and now, because if you are here and now you will be awake!

Sleep means you are in the past, sleep means you are in the future. Mind is the sleep, mind is a deep hypnosis – fast asleep. And you try many ways, but nothing seems to help you – because anything done in your sleep will not be of much help, because if you do it in sleep it will not be more than a dream.

I have heard that once a man came to a psychoanalyst, a very absent-minded psychoanalyst – and everybody is absentminded because mind is absentmindedness, not at home; that's what absentmindedness means. A man went to this very absentminded psychoanalyst and told him. "I am in much trouble and I have knocked at the doors of all types of doctors but nobody could help me, and they say that nothing is wrong. But I am in trouble. I snore so loudly in my sleep that I wake myself up. And this happens so many times in the night: the snoring is so loud that I wake myself up!"

Without exactly listening to what this man was saying, the psychoanalyst said, "This is nothing. A simple thing can change the whole matter. You simply sleep in another room."

You understand? – this is exactly what everybody is doing. You go on changing rooms, but sleep continues, snoring continues, because you cannot leave it in another room. It is not something separate from you; it is you, it is your mind, it is your whole accumulated past, your memory, your knowledge – what Hindus call *samskaras*, all the conditionings that make your mind. You go in another room, they follow you there.

You can change your religion: you can become a Christian from a Hindu, you can become a Hindu from a Christian – you change rooms. Nothing will happen out of it. You can go on changing your masters – from one master to another, from one ashram to another: nothing will be of much help. You are changing rooms; and the basic thing is not to change rooms but to change *you*. The room is not concerned with your snoring; the room is not the cause, you are the cause. This is the first thing to be understood; then you will be able to follow this beautiful story.

Your mind, as it is, is asleep. But you cannot feel how it is asleep because you look quite awake, with open eyes. But have you ever seen anything? You look wide awake with your open ears, but have you ever heard anything?

You are listening to me and you say "Yes!" But are you listening to me or listening to your mind inside? Your mind is constantly commenting. I am here, talking to you, but you are not there listening to me. Your mind constantly comments, "Yes, it is right, I agree"; "I don't agree, this is absolutely false"; your mind is standing there, constantly commenting. Through this commentary, this fog of the mind, I cannot penetrate you. Understanding comes when you are not interpreting, when you simply listen.

In a small school the teacher found that one boy was not listening. He was very lazy and fidgety, restless. So she asked: "Why? Are you in some difficulty? Are you not able to hear me?"

The boy said, "Hearing is okay, listening is the problem."

He made a really subtle distinction. He said, "Hearing is okay, I am hearing you; but *listening* is the problem" – because listening is more than hearing; listening is hearing with full awareness. Just hearing is okay, sounds are all around you – you hear, but you are not listening. You have to hear, because the sounds will go on knocking at your eardrum; you have to hear. But you are not there to listen, because listening means a deep attention, a rapport – not a constant commentary inside, not saying yes or no, not agreeing, disagreeing, because if you agree and disagree, in that moment how can you listen to me?

When you agree, what I said is already past; when you disagree, it is already gone. And in the moment you nod your head inside, say no or yes, you are missing – and this is a constant thing inside you.

You cannot listen. And the more knowledge you have the more difficult listening becomes. Listening means innocent attention – you simply listen. There is no need to be in agreement or disagreement. I am not in search of your agreement or disagreement. I am not asking for your vote, I am not seeking your following, I am not in any way trying to convince you.

What do you do when a parrot starts screeching in a tree? Do you comment? Yes, then too you say, "Disturbing." You cannot listen even to a parrot. When the wind is blowing through the trees and there's the rustling noise, do you listen to it? Sometimes, maybe; it catches you unawares. But then too you comment, "Yes, beautiful!"

Now watch: whenever you comment, you fall asleep. The mind has come in, and with the mind the past and future enter. The vertical line is lost – and you become horizontal. The moment mind enters you become horizontal. You miss eternity.

Simply listen. There is no need to say yes or no. There is no need to be convinced or unconvinced. Simply listen, and the truth will be revealed to you – or the untruth! If somebody is talking nonsense, if you simply listen the nonsense will be revealed to you – without any commentary from the mind. If somebody is speaking the truth, it will be revealed to you. Truth or untruth is not an agreement or a disagreement of your mind, it is a feeling. When you are in total rapport, you feel, and you simply feel that it is true or it is untrue – and the thing is finished! No worrying about it, no thinking about it! What can thinking do?

If you have been brought up in a certain way, if you are a Christian, or a Hindu, or a Mohammedan, and I am saying something which happens to agree with your upbringing, you will say yes. If it doesn't happen so, you will say no. Are *you* here, or is only the upbringing here? And upbringing is just accidental.

The mind cannot find what is true, the mind cannot find what is untrue. The mind can reason about it, but all reasoning is based on conditioning. If you are a Hindu you reason in one way, if you are a Mohammedan you reason in a different way. And every type of conditioning rationalizes. It is not really reasoning: you rationalize.

Mulla Nasruddin became very aged; he attained one hundred years. A reporter came to see him, because he was the oldest citizen around those parts. The reporter said, "Nasruddin, there are a few questions I would like to ask. One is, do you think you will be able to live a hundred years more?"

Nasruddin said, "Of course, because a hundred years ago I was not as strong as I am now." A hundred years before, he was a child, just born, so he said: "A hundred years ago I was not as strong as I am now, and if that small child, helpless, weak, could survive for a hundred years, why shouldn't I?"

This is rationalization. It looks logical, but it misses something. It is a wish-fulfillment. You would like to survive longer, so you create a rationale around it: you believe in the immortality of the soul. You have been brought up in a culture which says that the soul is eternal. If somebody says, "Yes, the soul is eternal," you nod, you say, "Yes, that's right." But that's not right – or wrong. You say yes because it is a deep-rooted conditioning in you. There are others: half the world believes – Hindus, Buddhists and Jainas believe – that the soul is eternal, and there are many rebirths. And half the world – Christians, Mohammedans, Jews, – believe the soul is not eternal and there is no rebirth, only one life and then the soul dissolves into the ultimate.

Half the world believes this, half the world believes that, and they all have their own arguments, they all have their own rationalizations. Whatsoever you want to believe, you will believe, but deep down your desire will be the cause of your belief, not reason. Mind looks rational, but it is not. It is a rationalizing process: whatsoever you want to believe, the mind says yes. And where does that wanting come from? It comes from your upbringing.

Listening is a totally different affair, it has a totally different quality to it. When you *listen*, you cannot be a Hindu, or a Mohammedan, or a Jaina, or a Christian. When you listen you cannot be a theist or an atheist; when you listen you can't listen through the skin of your "isms" or scriptures – you have to put them all aside; you simply listen.

I'm not asking you to agree, don't be afraid! Simply listen, not bothered by agreement or disagreement, and then a rapport happens.

If the truth is there, suddenly you are drawn – your whole being is drawn as if by a magnet. You melt and merge into it, and your heart feels "This is true," without any reason, without any arguments, without any logic. This is why religions say reason is not the way to the divine. They say it is faith, they say it is trust.

What is trust? Is it a belief? No, because belief belongs to the mind. Trust is a rapport. You simply put aside all your defense measures, your armor; you become vulnerable. You listen to something, and you listen so totally that the feeling arises in you as to whether it is true or not. If it is untrue, you feel it. Why does this happen? If it is true, you feel it. Why does this happen?

It happens because truth resides in you. When you are totally non-thinking your inner truth can feel wherever truth is – because the same always feels the same: it fits. Suddenly everything fits, everything falls in a pattern and the chaos becomes a cosmos. The words fall in line...and a poetry arises. Then everything simply fits.

If you are in rapport, and the truth is there, your inner being simply agrees with it – but it is not an agreement. You feel a tuning. You become one. This is trust. If something is wrong, it simply falls from you – you never pay it a second thought, you never look at it a second time: there is no meaning in it. You never say, "This is untrue"; it simply doesn't fit – you move! If it fits, it becomes your home. If it doesn't fit, you move.

Through listening comes trust. But listening needs hearing plus attention. And you are fast asleep – how can you be attentive? But even fast asleep a fragment of attention remains floating in you; otherwise there would be no way. You may be in a prison, but possibilities always exist – you can come out. Difficulties may be there, but it is not impossible, because prisoners have been known to escape. A Buddha escapes, a Mahavira escapes, a Jesus escapes – they were also prisoners like you. Prisoners have escaped before – prisoners have always escaped. There remains somewhere a door, a possibility; you simply have to search for it.

If it is impossible, if there is no possibility, then there is no problem. The problem arises because the possibility is there – you are a little alert. If you were absolutely unalert, then there would be no problem. If you were in a coma, then there would be no problem. But you are not in a coma; you are asleep – but not totally. A gap, a leakage exists. You have to find within yourself that possibility of being attentive.

Sometimes you become attentive. If somebody comes to hit you, the attention comes. If you are in danger, if you are passing through a forest at night and it is dark, you walk with a different quality of attention. You are awake; thinking is not there. You are fully in rapport with the situation, with whatsoever is happening. Even if a leaf creates a sound you are fully alert. You are just like a hare, or a deer – who is always awake. Your ears are bigger, your eyes are wide open, you are feeling what is happening all around because danger is there. In danger your sleep is less, your awareness is more, the gestalt changes. If somebody puts a dagger to your heart and is just going to push it in, in that moment there is no thinking. Past disappears, future disappears: you are here and now.

The possibility is there. If you make the effort you will catch the one ray that exists in you, and once you catch the one ray, the sun is not very far; then through the ray you can reach the sun – the ray becomes the path.

So remember: find attention, let it become a continuity in you twenty-four hours a day, whatsoever you do. Eat, but try to be attentive: eat with awareness. Walk, but walk with awareness. Love, but love fully aware. Try!

It cannot become total just in one day, but even if one ray is caught, you will feel a deep fulfillment – because the quality is the same whether you attain to one ray or the whole sun. Whether you taste a drop of water from the ocean or the whole ocean, the salty taste is the same – and the taste becomes your satori, the glimpse.

Here, listening to me, be alert. Whenever you feel that you have gone again into sleep, bring yourself back: just shake a little and bring yourself back. When walking on the street, if you feel you are walking in a sleep, shake a little, give a little shake to the whole body. Be alert. This alertness will remain only for a few moments; again you will lose it, because you have lived in a sleep for so long, it has become such a habit, that you cannot see how you can go against it.

I was traveling once from Kolkata to Mumbai in a plane, and one child was creating a great nuisance, running from one corner of the aisle to the other, disturbing everybody – and then the stewardess came with tea and coffee. The boy ran into her, and everything was a mess. Then the mother of the child said, "Now listen, I have told you many times – why don't you go outside and play there?"

Just old habit. She was sitting just by my side and was not aware of what she had said. I listened as she spoke, and she never became alert to what she had said. Only the child made her alert. He said, "What do you mean? If I go out I am finished!"

A child is more attentive of course, because he has less habits. A child is more alert because he has less armor around him, he is less imprisoned. That's why all religions say that when a man becomes a sage he has some quality of a child: the innocence. Then habits drop...because habits are your prison, and sleep is the greatest habit.

Now, try to enter in this parable with me.

> *While Tokai was a visitor at a certain temple, a fire started under the kitchen floor.*
> *A monk rushed into Tokai's bedroom, shouting, "A fire, master, a fire!" "Oh?" said Tokai, sitting up. "Where?" "Where?" exclaimed the monk. "Why, under the kitchen floor – get up at once." "The kitchen, eh?" said the master drowsily. "Well, tell you what, when it reaches the passageway, come back and let me know."*
> *Tokai was snoring again in no time.*

Tokai was a great Zen master, enlightened, living in total awareness, and whenever you live in total awareness you live moment to moment. You cannot plan, even for the next moment you cannot plan – because who knows, the next moment may never come! And how can you plan it beforehand, because who knows what the situation will be in the next moment? And if you plan too much you may miss it, the freshness of it.

Life is such a flux, nothing remains the same, everything moves. Heraclitus has said that you cannot step twice in the same river – how can you plan? By the time you are stepping the second time, much water has flowed, it is not the same river. Planning is possible if the past repeats itself. But the past never repeats itself, repetition never happens – even if you see something repeating itself it is just because you cannot see the whole.

Heraclitus also says, every day the sun is new. Of course, you will say, it is the same sun – but it cannot be the same, there is no possibility of its being the same. Much has changed: the whole sky is different, the whole pattern of stars is different, the sun itself has become older. Now scientists say that within four million years the sun will die, its death is coming near – because the sun is an alive phenomenon and it is very old, it has to die.

Suns are born, they live – and they die. Four million years for us is very long; for the sun it is just nothing, it is as if the next moment it is going to die. And when the sun dies, the whole solar family will disappear, because the sun is the source. Every day the sun is dying, and becoming older and older and older – it cannot be the same. Every day energy is lost – a vast amount of energy is being thrown in the rays. The sun is less every day, exhausted. It is not the same, it cannot be the same.

And when the sun rises, it rises upon a different world, and the onlooker is also not the same. Yesterday you may have been filled with love; then your eyes were different, and the sun of course looked different. You were so filled with love that a certain quality of poetry was around you, and you looked through that poetry – the sun may have looked like a god, as it looked to the seers of the Vedas. They called the sun, "God" – they must have been filled with too much poetry. They were poets, in love with existence; they were not scientists. They were not in search of what matter was, they were in search of what the mood was. They worshipped the sun. They must have been very happy and blissful people, because you can worship only when you feel a blessing; you can worship only when you feel that your whole life is a blessing.

Yesterday you may have been a poet, today you may not be a poet at all – because every moment the river is flowing within you. You are also changing. Yesterday things were fitting into each other, today everything is a mess: you are angry, you are depressed, you are sad. How can the sun be the same when the onlooker has changed? Everything changes, so a man of understanding never exactly plans for the future, cannot – but he is more ready than you to meet the future. This is the paradox. You plan, but you are not so ready.

In fact, planning means that you feel so inadequate, that's why you plan

– otherwise, why plan? A guest is coming, and you plan what you are going to say to him. What nonsense! When the guest comes can't you be spontaneous? But you are afraid, you don't believe in yourself, you have no trust; you plan, you go through a rehearsal. Your life is an acting, it is not the real thing, because a rehearsal is needed only in acting. And remember: when you are going through a rehearsal, whatsoever happens will be an acting, not the real thing. The guest has not arrived and you are planning already what you will say, how you will garland him, how you are going to respond; you are already saying things. The guest, in the mind, has already arrived – you are talking to him. In fact, by the time the guest arrives you will be fed up with him. In fact, by the time the guest arrives he has already been with you too much – you are bored, and whatsoever you say will not be true and authentic. It will not come from you, it will come from the memory. It will not pop up from your existence, it will come from the rehearsal that you have been doing. It will be false – and a meeting will not be possible, because how can a false man meet? And it may be the same with your guest: he was also planning, he also is fed up with you already. He has talked too much and now he would like to be silent, and whatsoever he says will be out of the rehearsal.

So wherever two persons meet, there are four persons meeting – at least; more are possible. Two real ones are in the background, two false ones meeting each other and encountering. Everything is false, because it comes out of planning. Even when you love a person you plan, and go through a rehearsal – all the movements that you are going to make, how you are going to kiss, the gestures – and everything becomes false. Why don't you trust yourself? When the moment comes, why don't you trust your spontaneity? Why can't you be real?

The mind cannot trust the moment; it is always afraid, that's why it plans. Planning means fear. It is fear that plans, and by planning you miss everything – everything that is beautiful and true, everything that is divine, you miss. Nobody has ever reached God with a plan, nobody can ever reach.

While Tokai was a visitor at a certain temple, a fire started under the kitchen floor.

The first thing: fire creates fear, because it is death. And if even fire cannot create fear, nothing can create fear. But even fire cannot create fear when you have encountered death, when you know that death doesn't exist; otherwise, the moment you hear the word *Fire!* you are in a panic. No need for there to be a real fire, just somebody coming running here and saying, "Fire!" and you will be in a panic. Somebody may jump out of it, and may kill himself – and there was no fire. Just the word *fire* can give you panic.

You live with words. Somebody says "Lemon" – and juice starts flowing in your mouth. Somebody says, "Fire!" – and you are here no more, you have already escaped. You live with words, not with realities. You live with symbols, not with realities. And all symbols are artifices, they are not real.

I have heard, overheard really:

An old woman was teaching a younger one how to cook a certain thing. She was explaining, and then she said, "Six glugs of molasses." The younger woman said, "Six what?" The older woman said: "Six glugs."

The younger woman was puzzled and asked again, "I've never heard of it before. What is this 'glug'?"

The older woman said, "My God! You don't know such a simple thing? Then it's difficult to teach you cookery!"

The younger one said, "Be kind and just tell me what this 'glug' is."

The older woman said: "You tip the jug; when it sounds 'glug' that is one. Five more like it – six glugs!"

But the whole of language is just like that. No word really means anything. The meaning is given by us by mutual contract. That is why three thousand languages exist in the world, but three thousand realities are not there. The whole of language is just like "glug."

You can create your own private language, there is no problem. Lovers always create their private language: they start using words – nobody understands what they are saying, but *they* understand. Words are symbolic. The meaning is given, the meaning is not really there. When somebody says, "Fire!" there is no fire in the word, there cannot be. When somebody says God, in the word *god* there is no godliness – cannot be. The word god is not godliness. When somebody says love, the word *love* is not love.

When somebody says, "I love you," don't be deceived by the words. But you will be deceived, because nobody looks at reality; people look at words only. When somebody says, "I love you," you think: Yes, he loves me; or: Yes, she loves me. You are getting into a trap and you will be in difficulty. Just look at the reality of this man or this woman. Don't listen to the words, listen to the reality. Be in rapport with the reality of this person and understanding will arise as to whether whatsoever he is saying is only words, or whether it carries some content also. And depend on the content, never depend on the word; otherwise sooner or later you will be frustrated. So many lovers are frustrated in the world – ninety percent! The word is the cause. They believed in the word and they didn't look at the reality.

Remain unclouded by the words. Keep your eyes clean from the words.

Don't allow them to settle in your eyes and in your ears; otherwise you will live in a false world. Words are false in themselves; they become meaningful only if some truth exists in the heart from where the words are coming.

> *While Tokai was a visitor at a certain temple, a fire started under the kitchen floor.*

Fire is fear, fire is death – but not the word *fire*.

> *A monk rushed into Tokai's bedroom, shouting: "A fire, master, a fire!"*

He was excited, death was near.

> *"Oh?" said Tokai, sitting up. "Where?"*

You cannot excite a master, even if death is there, because excitement belongs to the mind. And you cannot surprise a master, even if death is there, because surprise also belongs to the mind. Why can't you surprise a master? – because he never expects anything. How can you surprise a man who never expects anything? Because you expect, and then something else happens, that's why you are surprised. If you are walking on the street and you see a man coming, and suddenly he becomes a horse, you will be surprised, amazed: what has happened? But even this will not surprise a man like Tokai, because he knows life is a flux – everything is possible: a man can even become a horse, a horse can become a man. This is what has been already happening many times: many horses have become men, and many men have become horses. Life moves on!

A master remains without any expectation, you cannot surprise him. To him everything is possible, and he is not closed to any possibility. He lives in the moment totally open; whatsoever happens, happens. He has no plan against reality, no protection. He accepts.

If you expect something, you cannot accept. If you accept everything, you cannot expect. If you accept and you don't expect, you cannot be surprised – and you cannot be excited. Excitement is a fever, it is a disease; when you get excited your whole being is feverish, you are hot. You may like it sometimes because there are two types of fever: one that comes out of pleasure and one that comes out of pain. The one that you like you call pleasure, but it is also a fever, excitement; and the one that you dislike you call pain, disease, illness – but both are excitements. And try to observe: they go on changing into each other.

You love a woman; you get excited and you feel a certain pleasure, or you interpret it as pleasure. But let that woman remain there and sooner or later the excitement goes. On the contrary, a boredom creeps in, you feel fed up, you would like to escape, you would like to be alone. And if the woman still continues, now the negative enters. You are not only bored, you are in a negative fever now; you feel ill, you feel nauseous.

Look: your life is just like a rainbow. It carries all the colors – and you go on moving from one color to another. It carries all the extremes, all the opposites: from pleasure you move to pain, from pain you move to pleasure. If the pain goes on too long, you may even start getting a certain pleasure out of it. If the pleasure lasts too long, you will certainly get pain out of it. Both are states of excitement, both are fevers. A man of understanding is without fever. You cannot excite him, you cannot surprise him. Even if death is there he will coolly ask, "Where?" And this question "Where?" is very beautiful, because a man of enlightenment is always concerned with the here. He is not concerned with there, he is not concerned with then, he is concerned only with now. Now, here, is his reality; then, there, is your reality.

"A fire, master, a fire!" "Oh?" said Tokai, sitting up, "Where?"

He wants to know: there or here.

"Where?" exclaimed the monk.

...Because he couldn't believe it, that when there is a fire somebody could ask such a stupid question. One should simply jump out of the window and get out of the house; this is no time for subtle arguments.

"Where?" exclaimed the monk. "Why, under the kitchen floor – get up at once." "The kitchen, eh?" said the master drowsily. "Well, tell you what, when it reaches the passageway, come back and let me know."

When it reaches here, then come and let me know. If it is there, it is none of my concern. The anecdote is very revealing. Anything there is not a concern; only when it is here does it become real.

A master cannot plan for the future. Of course he is ready: whatsoever happens, he will respond – but he cannot go through a rehearsal, and he cannot plan...and he cannot move before the reality has come. He will say, "Let the reality come, let the moment knock at my door, and then we will see." Unburdened with rehearsals, plans, he is always spontaneous – and whatsoever he does with his spontaneity is always right.

Remember this criterion always: whatsoever comes out of your spontaneity is right. There exists no other criterion of right and wrong. Whatsoever comes out of the moment, your alive response to it is good. Nothing else is good – there exists no other criterion for good and bad.

But you are afraid. Because of your fear you create morality. Because of your fear you create distinctions between right and wrong. But don't you see that sometimes a situation is different, and the right becomes wrong and the wrong becomes right? But you remain dead. You don't look at the situation. You simply go on following your right and wrong and the conceptions around it. That's why you become a misfit. Even trees are wiser than you – they are not misfits. Even animals are better than you – they are not misfits. Even clouds are worthier than you – they are not misfits. The whole of existence fits together; only man is a misfit. Where has he gone wrong?

He has gone wrong with his mental distinctions – this is right and that is wrong – and in life such fixed things cannot be useful. Something is wrong this moment, next moment it becomes right. Something is right this moment, next moment it is right no more. What will you do? You will be constantly in a state of fear and worry, an inner tension.

The foundational teaching of all those who have known is: be alert and spontaneous, and whatsoever happens out of your spontaneous alertness is right, and whatsoever happens out of your sleep, unconsciousness, is wrong. Whatsoever you do unconsciously is wrong – whatsoever you do with awareness is right. Right and wrong is not a distinction between objects; right and wrong is a distinction between consciousnesses.

For example, there exists a Jaina sect in India: *terapanth*. Mahavira said, "Don't interfere in anybody's karma. Let him fulfill it" – a beautiful thing. He says really the exact thing that hippies are now saying in the West: "Do your own thing". From the other side Mahavira says the same thing: "Don't interfere with anybody's thing. Let him do his karma, let him fulfill it. Don't interfere. Interference is violence; when you interfere with somebody's karma you are doing a violence, you are throwing that man from his own path. Don't interfere." A beautiful thing!

But how things can go wrong, even beautiful things! The terapanth, this one sect of the Jainas, concluded that if somebody is dying by the side of the road you simply go on, you don't touch him, you don't give him any medicine, you don't give him water if he is crying, "I am thirsty!" Don't give him water because – don't interfere with anybody's karma. Logical! – because if he is suffering because of his past karmas, then who are you to interfere? He must have accumulated a certain karma to suffer in this life from thirst and die from it. Who are you to give him water? You simply neglect him, you go on.

I was talking to one of the leaders of the terapanth monks, and I told him, "And have you ever considered the possibility that it may be your karma to give him water?"

You are not interfering with his karma, but you are interfering with your own. If the desire arises to help him, what will you do? The desire shows that it is your karma to give him water. If you resist that desire and go on because of the principle, you are not being spontaneous – so what to do? If you make dead principles heavy on your head, you will always be in trouble, because life does not believe in your principles; life has its own laws. But they are not your principles and your philosophies.

Be spontaneous. If you feel like helping, don't bother about what Mahavira has said. If you feel like helping, help. Do your thing. If you don't feel like helping, don't help. Whatsoever Jesus may have said, that by helping people you will help me – don't bother, because sometimes the help may be dangerous. A man is ready to kill somebody, and he says to you, "Give me water, because I am feeling so thirsty, and I cannot go on this long journey to kill that man" – what will you do?... Because if you give him water, you help him in murder. Decide! – but never decide before the moment because all such decisions will go false. One never knows what type of situation will be there.

In old Indian scriptures there is a story: A murderer came to a crossroads where a monk was sitting meditating. He was following a man. He had already hit the man hard but he escaped, the victim escaped, and he was following him. At the crossroads he was puzzled; he asked the monk who was meditating under a tree, "Have you seen a man with blood flowing, passing by here? If so, which direction has he gone?" – because it was a crossroads.

What should this monk do? If he tells the truth, that the man has gone to the north, he will become a part of the murder. If he says that he has not gone to the north, he has gone to the south, he will be telling a lie. What should he do? Should he tell the truth, and allow the murder, or should he become a liar and stop it? What should he do?

There have been many answers. I have none.

Jainas say that even if it is going to be an untruth, let him be untrue, because violence is the greatest sin. They have their own valuation – violence is the greatest sin, untruth comes next. But Hindus say no, untruth comes first, so let him be true; he has to tell the truth and let things happen, whatsoever happens. Gandhi said – Gandhi had his own answer about this – he said, "I cannot choose between these two because both are supreme values, and there is no choice. So I will tell him the truth, and I will stand in his way, and I will tell him, 'First kill me, and then follow that man.'"

It appeals, Gandhi's answer appeals, seems to be better than both the

Hindu's and the Jaina's – but look at the whole situation: the man is going to commit one murder and Gandhi is forcing him to commit two. So what about *his* karma?

So what to do? I have no answer. Or my answer is: don't decide beforehand, let the moment come and let the moment decide, because who knows? – the victim may be a man who is worth murdering. Who knows? – the victim may be a dangerous man, and if he survives he may murder many. Who knows what the situation will be because it will never be the same again – and you cannot know the situation beforehand.

Don't decide. But your mind will feel uneasy without a decision because the mind needs clear-cut answers. Life has none, no clear-cut answers. Only one thing is certain: be spontaneous and alert and aware, and don't follow any rule. Simply be spontaneous – and whatsoever happens, let it happen. If you feel in that moment like taking the risk of losing truth, lose it. If you feel in that moment that man is not worth it, then let the violence happen, or if you feel, "That man is worth more than me," stand in between.

Millions of possibilities will be there. Don't fix it beforehand. Just be aware and alert and let things happen. You may not wish to say anything. Why not be silent? Don't tell any untruth, don't help the man in violence, don't force the murderer to commit two murders. Why not be silent? Who is forcing you?

But let the moment decide: that is what all the awakened ones have said.

But if you listen to ordinary moralists they will tell you that life is danger-ous, so go with a decision; otherwise you may do something wrong. And I tell you whatsoever you do through a decision will be wrong, because the whole existence is not following your decisions; the whole existence moves in its own way. You are a part of it – how can you decide for the whole? You have to simply be there and feel the situation and do whatsoever you can do with humbleness, with every possibility of it being wrong.

Don't be such an egoist as to think, "Whatsoever I do will be right." Then who will do the wrong? Don't be such an egoist that you think, "I am moral, and the other is immoral." The other is also you. You are also the other. We are one. The murderer and the victim are not two.

But don't decide. Just be there; feel the whole situation, be in rapport with the whole situation, and let your inner consciousness do whatsoever comes. You should not be the doer, you should be just a witness. A doer has to decide beforehand, a witness need not.

That is the whole message of Krishna and the Gita. Krishna says: Just see the whole situation, and don't follow moralists' dead rules. See the situation and act as a witness; don't be a doer. And don't be bothered what the result will be, nobody can say what the result will be. In fact there is no result, cannot be, because it is an infinity.

For example, Hitler was born. If the mother had killed this child all the courts in the world would have found her a murderess. She would have been punished. But now we know better, that it would have been better to kill Hitler than to leave him alive, because he killed millions. So did Hitler's mother do right in not murdering this child? Was she right or was she wrong? Who is to decide? And how could that poor mother know that this boy was going to murder so many people?

Who is to decide? And how to decide?...and it is an infinite sequence. Hitler killed many, but who can decide whether those were the right persons to be killed or not killed? Who will ever decide and who will ever know? Nobody knows. Who knows, perhaps God sends Hitler-like people to kill all those who are wrong, because somehow or other God is involved in everything! He is in the right and he is in the wrong.

The man who dropped the atom bomb on Hiroshima – was he right or wrong? Because of his bomb the second world war stopped. Of course, the whole city of one hundred thousand people dropped dead immediately. But if the atom bomb had not been dropped on Hiroshima, the war would have continued, and many more hundreds of thousands of people would have died. And if Japan could have survived only one year more, she could have invented the atom bomb – and then they would have dropped it on New York, on London. Who is to decide, and how to decide, whether the man who dropped the bomb was right or wrong?

Life is so entangled, entwined, and every event leads to other events; and whatsoever you do, you will disappear, but whatsoever you did, the consequences will continue forever and forever. They cannot end. Even a small act – you smile at a person, and you have changed the whole quality of existence, because that smile will decide many things.

It happened: I was reading Greta Garbo's biography. She was an ordinary girl, working with a barber, just soaping people's faces, and she would have remained the same because she was already twenty-two, and then one American film director accidentally came to that barber's shop – there were twenty shops in that town – and when she was soaping his face he smiled, looking at the girl in the mirror, and said, "How beautiful!" And everything changed.

This was the first man to say to Greta Garbo, "How beautiful!" – nobody had ever said it before, and she never thought herself beautiful, because how can you think yourself beautiful if nobody says so?

The whole night she could not sleep. The next morning she searched out the director, where he was staying, and she asked, "Do you *really* think that I am beautiful?"

The director may have made the remark casually, who knows! But when a girl comes searching for you and asks, "Really? What you told me, you really *meant* it?"...so the director said, "Yes, you *are* beautiful!"

Then Greta Garbo said, "Then why not give me some work in a film you are making?" Now things started...and Greta Garbo became one of the most famous actresses.

Very small things move around, and they go on moving. It is just like throwing a small pebble in a lake. Such a small pebble, and then ripples go on and on and on – and they will go on to the very end. By the time they reach the shore, long before it, the pebble has settled deep into the bottom, is lost.

That pebble will change the whole quality of existence, because it is all one net; it is just like a spider's web: you touch it anywhere, shake it a little, and the whole web ripples. Everywhere it is felt. You smile at a person – and the whole world is a spider's web – and the whole existence is changed through that smile.

But how to decide? Krishna says you need not be bothered with decision, because it is such a vast thing that you will never be able to make a decision. So don't think about the result, simply respond to the situation. Be spontaneous, alert; be a witness and not a doer.

> *A monk rushed into Tokai's bedroom, shouting: "A fire, master, a fire!" "Oh?" said Tokai, sitting up. "Where?" "Where?" exclaimed the monk. "Why, under the kitchen floor – get up at once." "The kitchen, eh?" said the master drowsily. "Well, tell you what, when it reaches the passageway, come back and let me know."*

When it has become already the present, then let me know. It is still in the future – don't bother me.

> *Tokai was snoring again in no time.*

This is the quality of an enlightened person: so relaxed that although a fire is burning in the kitchen, the house is catching fire – everybody is excited and running around, nobody knows what is going to happen, everything is a mess – he can relax and go to sleep again. He was snoring in no time.

This non-tenseness must come out of, has to come out of, a deep trust that whatsoever happens is good. He is not worried – even if he dies he is not worried; even if the fire comes and burns him he is not worried, because he is no more. The ego is not there; otherwise there will be fear, there will be worry, there will be a future, there will be planning, there will be a desire to escape, to save oneself. He is not worried; he simply falls back into sleep, relaxed.

There is no possibility of relaxation if you have a mind and an ego; the ego is the center of the mind. You will be tense, you will remain tense. How to relax? Is there any way to relax? There is no way unless understanding is there. If you understand the nature of the world, the nature of the very existence, then who are you to worry, and why be in a worried state continuously?

Nobody asked you about being born, nobody is going to ask you when the time comes for you to be taken away. Then why be worried? Birth happened to you; death will happen to you; who are you to come in between?

Things are happening. You feel hunger, you feel love, you feel anger – everything happens to you, you are not a doer. Nature takes care. You eat and nature digests it; you need not bother about it, about how the stomach is functioning, how the food is going to become blood. If you become too tense about it you will have ulcers – and king-size ulcers, not ordinary ones. No need to worry.

The whole is moving. The vast, the infinite is moving. You are just a wave in it. Relax, and let things be.

Once you know how to let go, you have known all that is worth knowing. If you don't know how to let go, whatsoever you know is worthless, it is rubbish.

Enough for today.

philosophy solves nothing

The master Tozan was weighing some flax in the storeroom.
A monk came up to him and asked: "What is Buddha?"
Tozan said: "This flax weighs five pounds."

Religion is not concerned with philosophical questions and answers. Howsoever profound looking, they are stupid, and a sheer waste of life, time, energy and consciousness, because you can go on asking and answers can be given – but from answers only more questions will come. If in the beginning there was one question, in the end, through many answers, there will be a million questions.

Philosophy solves nothing. It promises, but never solves anything – all those promises remain unfulfilled. It goes on promising; but the experience which can solve the riddles of the mind cannot be attained through philosophical speculation.

Buddha was absolutely against philosophy – there has never been a man more against philosophy than Buddha. Through his own bitter experience he came to understand that all those profundities of philosophy are just superficial. Even the greatest philosopher remains as ordinary as anyone; no problem has been solved, not even touched. He carries much knowledge, many answers, but he remains the same old man – no new life has happened to him. And the crux, the core of the matter is that mind is a question-raising faculty: it can raise any sort of question, and then it can befool itself by answering them. But you are the questioner, and you are the one who solves them.

Ignorance creates questions, and ignorance creates answers – the same mind creating in both ways. How can a questioning mind come to an answer? Deep down, the mind itself is the question.

So philosophy tries to answer questions of the mind, and religion looks at the very base. The mind is the question, and unless mind is dropped the answer will not be revealed to you – mind won't allow it, mind is the barrier, the wall. When there is no mind you are an experiencing being; when the mind is there you are a verbalizing being.

In a small school it happened: there was a very stupid child; he never asked any questions and also the teacher neglected him. But one day he was very excited when the teacher was explaining a certain problem of arithmetic, writing some figures on the board. The child was very excited, raising his hand again and again; he wanted to ask something. When the teacher finished with the problem, she washed the figures from the board, and was very happy that for the first time this child was so excited as to ask something, and she said, "I am happy that you are ready to ask something. Go ahead – ask!"

The child stood, and he said, "I am very worried, and the question comes again and again to me but I couldn't gather the courage to ask. Today I have decided to ask: where do these damn figures go when you wash them off?"

The question is very philosophical; all questions are like this. Many ask where a buddha goes when he dies; the question is the same. Where is God? – the question is the same. What is truth? – the question is the same. But you cannot feel the stupidity hidden in them, because they look very profound, and they have a long tradition – people have always been asking them, and people whom you think very great have been concerned with them: theorizing, finding answers, creating systems...but the whole effort is useless because only experience can give you the answer, not thinking. And if you go on thinking you will become more and more mad, and the answer will still be far away – farther away than ever.

Buddha says: When the mind stops questioning, the answer happens. It is because you are so much concerned with questions that the answer cannot enter you. You are in such trouble, you are so disturbed, so much tense, the reality cannot enter into you – you are shaking so much inside, trembling with fear, with neurosis, with stupid questions and answers, with systems, philosophies, theories; you are so filled up.

Mulla Nasruddin was passing through a village in his car. Many crowds were gathered there at many spots, and he was worried – what is the matter? Nobody was on the streets, everybody was gathered somewhere or other. Then he saw a policeman, and he stopped him and asked, "What is the matter? Has something gone wrong? What has happened? I don't see people anywhere, working, moving, in the shops...they are gathered in many crowds!"

The policeman could not believe his ears; he said, "What are you asking? There has been an earthquake just now! Many houses have fallen, many people are dead!" Then the policeman said, "I cannot believe that you couldn't feel the earthquake!"

Nasruddin said, "Because of alcohol I am always shaking so much, my hands are so jittery, that's why I missed it."

If an earthquake is going on inside you continuously, then a real earthquake will not be capable of entering you. When you are silent and still, then the reality happens. And questioning is a trembling inside. Questioning means doubt, doubt means trembling. Questioning means you don't trust anything – everything has become a question, and when everything is a question there will be very much anxiety. Have you observed yourself? Everything becomes a question. If you are miserable, it is a question: Why? Even if you are happy, it is a question: Why? You cannot believe yourself being happy.

People come to me when meditation goes deeper and they have glimpses, they come to me very disturbed because, they say, something is happening, and they cannot believe that it is happening to *them*, that bliss can happen – there must be some deception. People have said to me, "Are you hypnotizing me? – because something is happening!" They cannot believe that they can be blissful, somebody must be hypnotizing them. They cannot believe that they can be silent – impossible! "Why? Why am I silent? Somebody is playing a trick!"

Trust is not possible for a questioning mind. Immediately experience is there, the mind creates a question: Why? The flower is there – if you trust, you will feel a beauty, a blooming of beauty; but the mind says: Why? Why is this flower called beautiful? What is beauty? – you are going astray. You are in love, the mind asks: Why, what is love?

It is reported that Saint Augustine said, "I know what time is, but when people ask me, everything is lost, I cannot answer. I know what love is, but you ask me: What is love? – and I am at a loss, I cannot answer. I know what God is, but you ask, and I am at a loss." And Augustine is right, because profundities cannot be asked, cannot be questioned. You cannot put a question mark on a mystery. If you put a question mark, the question mark becomes more important; then the question covers the whole mystery. And if you think that when you have solved the question, then you will live the mystery, you will never live it.

Questioning is irrelevant in religion. Trust is relevant. Trust means moving into the experience, into the unknown, without asking much – going through it to know it.

I tell you about a beautiful morning outside, and you start questioning me about it here, walled in a room, enclosed, and you would like your every question to be answered before you take a step outside. How can I tell you if you have never known what morning is? How can I tell you? Only that can be told through words which you already know. How can I tell you that there is light, beautiful light falling through the trees, and the whole sky is filled with light, the sun has risen, if you have always lived in darkness? If your eyes are accustomed only to the dark, how can I explain to you that the sun has risen?

You will ask, "What do you mean? Are you trying to deceive us? We have lived all our lives and we have never known anything like light. First answer our questions, and then, if we are convinced, we can come out with you; otherwise it seems you are leading us astray, astray from our sheltered life."

But how can the light be described if you don't know about it? But that's what you are asking: "Convince us about godliness, then we will meditate, then we will pray, then we will search. How can we search before the conviction is there? How can we go on a search when we don't know where we are going?"

This is distrust – and because of this distrust you cannot move into the unknown. The known clings to you, and you cling to the known – and the known is the dead past. It may feel cozy because you have lived in it, but it is dead, it is not alive. The alive is always the unknown, knocking at your door. Move with it. But how can you move without trust? And even doubting persons think that they have trust.

Once it happened:

Mulla Nasruddin told me that he was thinking of divorcing his wife. I asked, "Why? Why so suddenly?"

Nasruddin said, "I doubt her fidelity towards me."

So I told him, "Wait, I will ask your wife."

So I told his wife, "Nasruddin is talking around town and creating a rumor that you are not faithful, and he is thinking of divorce, so what is the matter?"

His wife said, "This is too much. Nobody has ever insulted me like that – and I tell you, I have been faithful to him dozens of times!"

It is not a question of dozens of times – you also trust, but dozens of times? That trust cannot be very deep, it is just utilitarian. You trust whenever you feel it pays. But whenever the unknown knocks you never trust, because you don't know whether it is going to pay or not. Faith and trust are not a question of utility – they are not utilities, you cannot use them. If you want to use them, you kill them. They are not utilitarian at all. You can enjoy them, you can be blissful about them – but they don't pay.

They don't pay in the terms of this world; on the contrary, the whole world will look at you as a fool, because the world thinks someone wise if he doubts, the world thinks someone wise if he questions, the world thinks someone wise only when he moves a step with conviction, and before he is convinced he will not move. This is the cunningness and the cleverness of the world – and the world calls such people wise!

They are fools as far as Buddha is concerned, because through their so-called wisdom they are missing the greatest, and the greatest cannot be used. You can merge with it, you cannot use it. It has no utility, it is not a commodity; it is an experience, it is an ecstasy. You cannot sell it, you cannot make a business out of it – rather, on the contrary, you are lost in it completely. You will never be the same again. In fact you can never come back – it is a point of no return: if you go, you go. You cannot go back, there is no going back. It is dangerous.

So only very courageous people can enter on the path. Religion is not for cowards. But you will find in churches, temples, mosques – cowards: they have destroyed the whole thing. Religion is only for the very very courageous, for those who can take the most dangerous step – and the most dangerous step is from the known towards the unknown; the most dangerous step is from the mind to no-mind, from questioning to no-questioning, from doubt to trust.

Before we enter this small but beautiful anecdote – it is just like a diamond, very small but very valuable – a few more things are to be understood. One: you will be able to understand it only when you can take a jump, when you can bridge, somehow, the known with the unknown, mind with no-mind. Second thing: religion is not at all a question of thinking; it is not a question of right thinking, that if you think rightly you will become religious – no! Whether you think rightly or wrongly you will remain unreligous. People think that if you think rightly you will become religious; people think that if you think wrongly you will go astray.

But I tell you, if you *think*, you will go astray – rightly or wrongly is not the point. If you don't think, only then are you on the path. Think and you miss. You have already gone off on a long journey, you are no more here, now; the present is missed – and reality is only in the present.

With mind, you go on missing. Mind has a mechanism – it moves in circles, vicious circles. Try to observe your own mind: has it been on a journey, or just moving in circles? Have you been really moving, or just moving in a circle? You repeat the same, again and again. The day before yesterday you were angry, yesterday you were angry, today you have been angry – and there is every possibility that tomorrow you are going to be angry; and do you feel that anger is different? The day before yesterday it was the same, yesterday it was the same, today it is the same – the anger is the same. Situations may differ, excuses may differ, but the anger is the same! Are you moving? Are you going somewhere? Is there any progress? Are you reaching nearer to some goal? You are moving in a circle, reaching nowhere. The circle may be very big, but how can you move if you move in a circle?

I overheard once, walking in the afternoon, I heard coming from the inside of a small house a child whining and saying, "Mum, I am fed up with moving in circles." The mother said, "Either you shut up, or I will nail your other foot to the floor also."

But you are not yet fed up. One foot is nailed to the earth, and like the child you are moving in circles. You are like a broken gramophone record – the same line repeats itself, it goes on repeating. Have you ever listened to a broken gramophone record? Listen! – it is like Maharishi Mahesh Yogi's transcendental meditation, TM. You repeat one thing, *Ram, Ram, Ram, Ram, Ram*...you go on repeating. You get bored; through boredom you feel sleepy. Sleep is good! After the sleep you feel fresh – but this is not going towards truth at all, it is just getting a good sleep, through a trick. But this TM you are doing continuously; your whole life is a TM, repeating, moving in the same groove again and again and again.

Where are you going? Whenever you become aware of this you will think simply: What has been happening? You will feel very strange, shocked, that your whole life has been a misuse. You have not moved a single inch. The sooner the better – if you realize this, the sooner the better, because through this realization something is possible.

Why this repetition? Mind is repetitive, it is a broken record; the very nature of it is just like a broken record. You cannot change it. A broken record can be repaired, mind cannot be, because the very nature of the mind is to repeat; repetition is the nature of the mind. At the most you can make bigger circles, and with bigger circles you can feel that there is some freedom; with bigger circles you can deceive yourself that things are not repeating.

Somebody's circle is just twenty-four hours. If you are clever you can make a circle of thirty days; if you are even more clever you can make a circle of one year; if you are even more clever you can make a circle of a whole life – but the circle remains the same. It makes no difference. Bigger or smaller, you move in the same groove, you come back to the same point.

Because of this understanding, Hindus have called life a wheel – your life, of course, not a buddha's life. A buddha is one who has jumped out of the wheel. You cling to the wheel, you feel very secure there – and the wheel moves on; from birth to death it completes a circle. Again birth, again death. The word *sansar*, the word Hindus use for this world, means the wheel. It moves in the same groove. You come and go, and you do much – to no avail. Where do you miss? You miss in the first step.

The nature of the mind is repetition, and the nature of life is no repetition. Life is always new, always. Newness is the nature of life, Tao; nothing is old, cannot be. Life never repeats, it simply becomes every day new, every moment new – and mind is old; hence mind and life never meet. Mind simply repeats, life never repeats – how can mind and life meet? That's why philosophy never understands life.

The whole effort of religion is: how to drop the mind and move into life, how to drop the repetitive mechanism and how to enter the ever-new, evergreen phenomenon of existence. This is the whole point of this beautiful story, Tozan's Five Pounds.

> The master Tozan was weighing some flax in the storeroom. A monk
> came up to him and asked: "What is Buddha?"
> Tozan said: "This flax weighs five pounds."

Many things: first, a Zen master is not a recluse, he has not renounced life; rather, on the contrary, he has renounced the mind and entered life.

There are two types of sannyasins in the world: one type renounces life and enters the life of the mind completely – these are the anti-life people, escaping from the world towards the Himalayas, Tibet. They renounce life to be completely absorbed in the mind – and they are in the majority, because to renounce life is easy; to renounce mind is difficult.

What is the difficulty? If you want to escape from here, you can escape! You can leave the wife, the children, the house, the job – really you will feel unburdened, because the wife has become a burden, the children have become a burden, and this whole thing, working every day, earning…you are fed up! You will feel unburdened.

And what will you do in the Himalayas? The whole energy will become mind: you will repeat Ram, Ram, Ram, you will read the Upanishads and the Vedas, and you will think profound truths. You will think about where the world came from, where the world is going, who created the world, why he created the world, what is good and what is evil. You will contemplate and think great things! Your whole life energy which was engaged in other things will be freed from them now and will be absorbed in the mind. You will become a mind.

And people will pay you respect because you renounced life. You are a great man! Fools will recognize you as a great man: fools can recognize you only if you are the greatest of them and they will pay respect, they will prostrate themselves at your feet – you have done a great miracle!

But what has happened? You renounced life just to be the mind. You renounced the whole body just to be the head – and the head was the problem! You saved the disease, and you renounced everything. Now the mind will become a cancerous growth. It will do *japa*, mantra, austerities – it will do everything, and then it will become a ritual. That's why religious people move in rituals: ritual means a repetitive phenomenon. Every day in the morning they have to do their prayer: a Mohammedan does five prayers in the day – wherever he is, he is to do the prayer five times; a Hindu goes on doing the same ritual every day for his whole life; Christians have to go to the church every Sunday… just a ritual! Because mind likes repetition, mind creates a ritual.

In your ordinary life also, mind creates a ritual. You love, you meet friends, you go to parties…everything is a ritual, has to be done, repeated. You have a program for all the seven days, and the program is fixed – and this has been so always. You have become a robot, not alive. Mind is a robot. If you give too much attention to the mind it will absorb all your energy; it is a cancer, it will grow, it will spread all over.

But a Zen master belongs to the other category of sannyasins. He belongs to my category of sannyasins. A Zen master has always been a neo-sannyasin – hence I love to talk about them; I have a deep affinity with them. They renounce mind and they live life; they don't renounce life and live mind – just the contrary. They simply renounce mind because it is repetitive – and they live life. They may be living the life of a householder; they may have a wife, they may have children; they will work on the farm, they will work in the garden, they will dig holes, they will weigh flax in the storeroom…

A Hindu cannot think why an enlightened man should weigh flax – why? Why such an ordinary activity? But a Zen master renounces mind, lives life in its totality. He drops mind and becomes simple existence.

So the first thing to remember: if you renounce mind and live life you are a true sannyasin; if you renounce life and live mind you are an untrue sannyasin, you are a pseudo-sannyasin. And remember well, to be pseudo is always easier; to be real is always difficult. To live with a wife and to be happy is really difficult; to live with children and to be blissful is really difficult. To work in a shop, in an office, in a factory and to be ecstatic is the real difficulty.

To leave everything and just sit under a tree and feel happy is not difficult – anybody will feel that way. Nothing to do, you can be detached; everything to do, you become attached. But when you do everything and remain unattached, when you move with the crowd, in the world and yet alone, then something real is happening.

If you don't feel anger when you are alone, that is not the point. When you are alone you will not feel anger because anger is a relationship, it needs somebody to be angry towards. Alone, unless you are mad you will not feel anger, it will be inside but it will not find any way to come out. When the other is there, then not to be angry is the point. When you don't have any money, any things, any house – if you are unattached, what is the difficulty in it? But when you have everything and you remain unattached – a beggar in the palace – then something very deep has been attained.

So remember, and always keep it in your heart: truth, love, life, meditation, ecstasy, bliss, all that is true and beautiful and good, always exists as a paradox: in the world, and not of it; with people, yet alone; doing everything, and being inactive; moving and not moving; living an ordinary life, and yet not being identified with it; working as everybody else is working, yet remaining aloof deep down. Being in the world and not of the world, that is the paradox. And when you attain this paradox, the greatest peak happens to you: the peak experience.

It is very easy to move into a simple existence either in the world and attached or out of the world and detached – both are simple. But the greater comes only when it is a complex phenomenon. If you move to the Himalayas and are unattached, you are a single note of the music; if you live in the world and are attached, again you are a single note of the music. But when you are in the world and beyond it, and you carry your Himalaya in the heart, you are a harmony not a single note. An accord happens, including all discordant notes, a synthesis of the opposites, a bridge between two banks. And the highest is possible only when life is most complex; only in complexity the highest happens.

If you want to be simple you can choose one of the alternatives – but you will miss the complexity. If you cannot be simple in complexity, you will be like an animal, an animal or someone in the Himalayas living a renounced life – they don't go to a shop, they don't work in a factory, they don't have wives, they don't have children...

I have observed many people who have renounced life. I have lived with them, observed them deeply; they become like animals. I don't see in them something of the supreme happening; rather, on the contrary, they have fallen back. Their life is less tense of course because an animal's life is less tense, they don't have worries because no animal has worries. In fact they go on falling, they regress; they become like vegetables – they vegetate. If you go to them you will see that they are simple, no complexity exists – but bring them back to the world and you will find them more complex than you, because when the situation arises they will be in difficulty. Then everything that is suppressed will come out. This is a sort of suppression. Don't regress, don't move backwards – go ahead.

A child *is* simple, but don't become a child – become mature. Of course when you become absolutely mature, a childhood happens again, but that is qualitatively different. A sage is again a child, but not childish. A sage has again the flower, the fragrance, the newness of a child, but a deep difference is also there: a child has many repressed things in him and whenever the opportunity is given they will come out . Sex will come out, anger will come out – he will move into the world and become attached and lost. He has those seeds within him. A sage has no seeds, he cannot be lost. He cannot be lost because he is no more. He carries nothing within him.

Zen masters have lived a very ordinary life – very otherworldly, but in the world. They are more beautiful persons than any Hindu sannyasin, they are more beautiful persons than any Catholic monk. In fact, nothing like Zen exists on the earth, because they have attained to the highest paradox.

The master Tozan was weighing some flax in the storeroom.

An enlightened person, a buddha, weighing flax? You would have simply turned away. Why ask any question of this man? – if he knew anything he would not be weighing flax. Because you have a concept of a saint, a sage, as something extraordinary, beyond you, somewhere in the sky sitting on a golden throne, you cannot reach him. He is very different – whatsoever you are, he is just the opposite.

A Zen master is not that way. He is in no way extraordinary – and yet he is extraordinary. He lives the very ordinary life just like you, and yet he is not you. He is not somewhere in the sky, he is here, but still beyond you. Weighing flax – but just the same as Buddha under a bodhi tree. In India nobody can conceive of Mahavira weighing flax or Buddha weighing flax – impossible! It would look almost profane. What is Buddha doing in a storeroom? Then what is the difference between you and him? You also weigh flax, he is also weighing flax, so what is the difference?

The difference is not outward – and outward differences don't make any change. You can go and sit under a bodhi tree – nothing will happen. And when the inside changes, why be bothered with the outside? Carry on whatsoever you were doing. Carry on whatsoever is given to you. Carry on whatsoever the whole wills.

The master Tozan was weighing some flax in the storeroom.
A monk came up to him and asked: "What is Buddha?"

In Buddhism that is the greatest question to be asked – just like what is truth? or what is God? – because in Buddhism God is not a concept, Buddha is God; no other god exists. Buddha is the highest reality, the highest peak; nothing is beyond it. The truth, God, the absolute, brahman – whatsoever name you give to it, Buddha is that.

So when a monk asks, "What is Buddha?" he is asking what is truth? what is Tao? what is brahman? what is that one among the many? what is the basic reality? what is the very central core of existence? – he is asking all that.

Tozan said: "This flax weighs five pounds."

Absurd. Irrelevant. It seems to be completely pointless because the man was asking, "What is Buddha?" And this Tozan seems to be a madman. He is not talking about Buddha at all, he has not answered the question at all – and yet he has answered. This is the paradox. If you start living this paradox your life will become a symphony; it will become a higher and higher synthesis of all the opposites. In you, then, all opposites will dissolve.

Tozan said: "This flax weighs five pounds."

One thing he said: that this very ordinary life is Buddha, this very ordinary life is truth, this very ordinary life is brahman, the kingdom of God. There is no other life except this; there is no *that*, only *this* exists. Hindus say, "*That* exists, *this* is illusion"; Tozan said, "This is true, that is illusion. This very moment is truth, and don't ask for any extraordinary thing."

Seekers always ask for something extraordinary, because ego feels fulfilled only when something extraordinary is given. You come to a master and you ask questions, and if he says such things you will think he is mad, or joking, or not a man worthy to be asked. You will simply escape. Why? – because he shatters your ego completely. You were asking Buddha, you were desiring Buddha, you would like to be a buddha yourself; hence the question. And this man says: What nonsense you are asking! Not even worth answering! This flax weighs five pounds. This is more important than any buddha. This moment, this flax, is the whole of existence. In this five pounds of flax is centered the whole being of the world – here and now. Don't go astray; don't ask philosophical questions. Look at this moment.

Tozan did a wonderful thing. Tozan is a buddha. Tozan weighing flax is Buddha weighing flax – and reality is one! Tozan is Buddha, and the flax is also Buddha; and in that moment it weighed five pounds. That was the truth, the facticity of the moment. But if you are filled with philosophy you will think this man is mad and you will go away.

This happened to Arthur Koestler, one of the keenest intellects in the West. He missed the whole point completely. When he went to Japan to study Zen he thought: These people are simply mad – or else they are joking, not serious at all. He wrote a book, Against Zen. It looks absurd. It is. He is wrong, and yet right. It *is* absurd. If you don't know the language of Zen it is absurd; if you are identified too much with logical thinking, it is absurd. It is illogical – what more illogical thing can you find: somebody asking, "What is Buddha?" and somebody answering, "This flax weighs five pounds"?

You ask about the sky and I answer about the earth; you ask about God and I talk about a rock – no meeting. And yet there is a meeting – but very perceptive eyes are needed, not intellectually keen but feeling fully perceptive; not identified with reasoning but waiting to look, watching, witnessing what is happening; not already prejudiced, but open. Koestler is prejudiced...a very keen intellect, can work things out very logically in the tradition of Aristotle, but does not know anything, does not know at all that there exists an absolutely non-Aristotelian world of Zen, where two plus two are not necessarily four; sometimes they are five, sometimes they are three – anything is possible. No possibility is destroyed, all possibilities remain open, infinitely open. And every time two and two meet, something else happens. The world remains open, unknown; you cannot exhaust it.

Look: superficially this man is mad, but deeply, you cannot find a saner man than this Tozan. But Koestler will miss, and Koestler is a keen intellect, very logical; only a few people can compete with him in keen intelligence, but he misses. In this world intelligence is a means, in that world intelligence becomes a barrier. Don't be too wise, otherwise you will miss the real wisdom. Look at this Tozan without any prejudice, without any mind of your own. Simply look at the phenomenon, what is happening?

A disciple monk asks, "What is Buddha?" – and a Zen master lives in the moment, he is always here and now, he is always at home – whenever you come you will find him there, he is never absent from there – he remains in this moment. The trees, the sky, the sun, the rocks, the birds, the people – the whole world is concentrated in this moment! This moment is vast. It is not just a tick of your clock; this moment is infinite, because in this moment, everything is. Millions of stars, many new stars being born, many old stars going to die, this whole infinite expanse of time and space meets in this moment. So how to indicate this moment? – and Tozan was weighing flax – how to indicate this moment, how to bring this monk here and now? How to put his philosophic inquiry aside? How to shock him and awaken him to this moment, and in this moment?

This is a shock – because he must have been inquiring about Buddha in his mind, thinking: "What is the reality of a buddha? What is truth?" And he must have been expecting some profound answer, something very superb: "This master is enlightened, so he must say something very valuable." He never expected that this is going to be such an ordinary thing, such an ordinary and absurd answer. He must have been shocked.

In that shock you can be awake for a moment, a fraction of a moment. When you are shocked thinking cannot continue. If the answer is anything relevant, thinking can continue, because that is what mind asks for – relevancy. If something is said which is relevant to the question, thinking can continue; if something is said which is absolutely absurd, discontinuous, is not to the point at all, the mind cannot continue. Suddenly the mind is shocked, and the continuity broken. Soon it will start again, because the mind will say: "This is absurd!"

Mulla Nasruddin was being analyzed by a psychiatrist. After many months of analysis, many meetings, the psychiatrist said, as Mulla lay on the couch: "This is what I feel, this is what I conclude: you need to fall in love, you need a beautiful feminine object. Love is your need."

Mulla said, "Between me and you, don't you think love is silly?"

The psychiatrist said, "Between me and you? – it would be absurd!"

For a moment he must have been shocked, but only for a moment. If you cannot find relevancy, immediately the mind will say: "This is absurd!" If you find relevancy, the continuity continues. If there is something absurd, for a split second there is a discontinuity, the mind is not able to cope with what has been said. But immediately it recovers, it will say it is absurd; continuity restarts.

But the shock, and the assertion of the mind that it is absurd, are not simultaneous; there is a gap. In that gap, satori is possible. In that gap, you can be awakened, you can have a glimpse. It would have been wonderful if the opportunity could have been used; wonderful is this man Tozan, incomparable. You cannot find such a man anywhere else. And what a spontaneous answer! Not prefabricated, not in any way ready-made; nobody had said that ever before, and there is no point in saying it now. Nobody has ever said, *"This flax weighs five pounds"* in answer to a question about buddhahood: "What is Buddha?"

Tozan is spontaneous, he's not answering from the memory; otherwise he knows the scriptures, he was a great scholar before he became enlightened... He knows by heart and has chanted all Buddha's words, he has discussed philosophy for many years; he knows what the monk is asking, he knows what he is expecting – but he is simply spontaneous, weighing flax.

Just try to imagine and see Tozan weighing flax. In that moment what can be more spontaneous to indicate the reality of the moment, the facticity of existence? He simply said, *"This flax weighs five pounds"* – and finished! He doesn't say anything about Buddha; there is no need. This is buddhahood. This being spontaneous is buddhahood. This being true to the moment is buddhahood.

What he says is just part of it; what he leaves unsaid is the whole. If you awaken in that moment you will see Buddha weighing flax – and the flax weighs five pounds. What is he indicating? He is not saying much, but he is showing much, and by not saying much he is creating a possibility: you may, for a single moment, be aware of the whole existence that is there concentrated in this Tozan.

Whenever a buddha happens in the world, the whole existence finds a center there. Then all the rivers fall in him, and all the mountains bow down to him, and all the stars move around him. Whenever there is an enlightened man, the whole existence converges on his being. He becomes the center.

Tozan weighing flax in that moment was the buddha: the whole existence converging, flowing into Tozan, and Tozan weighing flax – and the flax weighed five pounds. This moment is so real: if you awaken, if you open your eyes, satori is possible. Tozan is spontaneous; he has no ready-made answers; he responds to the moment.

Next time if you come to Tozan the same answer cannot be given, will not be given, because Tozan may not be weighing, or may be weighing something else, or may be even weighing flax, but the flax may not weigh five pounds. Next time the answer will be different. If you come again and again, each time the answer will be different. This is the difference between a scholar and a man of knowledge. A scholar has fixed answers, whenever you come, he has a ready-made answer for you. You ask, and he will give you the answer, and the answer will always be the same – and you will feel he is very consistent. He is.

There was once a case against Mulla Nasruddin in the court, and the judge asked his age. He said, "Forty years."

The judge looked surprised and he said, "Nasruddin, four years ago you were here, and I asked that time also what is your age, and you told me forty years. Now this is absolutely inconsistent – how can you still be forty?"

Nasruddin said, "I am a man of consistency. Once forty, I remain forty always. When I have answered once, I have answered for ever! You cannot lead me astray. I am forty, and whenever you ask you will get the same answer. I am a man who is always consistent."

A consistent man is dead. If you are dead, only then can you remain forty. Then there is no need to change. A dead man never grows – and you cannot find persons more dead than pundits, scholars, men of information.

An enlightened man lives in the moment: you ask, he replies – but he has got no fixed replies. He *is* the reply. So whatsoever happens in that moment happens; he does not manipulate it, he does not think about it, about what you are asking. You simply ask, and his whole being responds. In this moment it happened that Tozan was weighing flax, and in this moment it happened that the flax weighed five pounds, and when this monk asked, "What is Buddha?" in Tozan's being five pounds was the reality. He was weighing; in Tozan's being five pounds was the fact. He simply said: Five pounds of flax.

Looks absurd on the surface. If you go deeper, deeper, you find a relevancy which is not a logical relevancy, and you find a consistency which is not that of the mind, but of the being. Understand, try to understand the difference. If next time you come and Tozan is digging a hole in the garden, and you ask, "What is Buddha?" – he will give you the answer. He will say, "Look at this hole," he will say, "It is ready; now the tree can be planted." Next time, if you come again, and if he is going for a walk with his walking stick, he may say, "This walking stick."

Whatsoever is in the moment will be the reply, because a buddha lives moment to moment – and if you start living moment to moment, you become a buddha. This is the answer: live moment to moment and you become a buddha. A buddha is one who lives moment to moment, who does not live in the past, who does not live in the future, who lives here now. Buddhahood is a quality of being present here and now – and buddhahood is not a goal, you need not wait, you can become just here and now.

Talking, I am a buddha, because only talk is happening. If only listening is happening there at the other end with you, you are a buddha in listening. Try to catch a glimpse of the moment, this moment. This moment Tozan is not weighing flax; Tozan is talking to you. This moment you have not asked, "What is Buddha?" but the question is there whether you ask it or not. The question goes around and around in the mind: What is truth? what is Buddha? what is Tao? Whether you ask it or not it is the question. *You* are the question.

In this moment you can awake. You can look, you can shake the mind a little, create a discontinuity, and suddenly you understand...what Arthur Koestler misses. If you are also too intelligent, you will miss. Don't be too intelligent, don't try to be too clever, because there is a wisdom which is attained by those who become fools; there is a wisdom which is attained by those who become like madmen; there is a wisdom which is attained only when you lose your mind.

Tozan is beautiful. If you can see, and if you can see that the answer is not absurd, you have seen it, you have understood it. But if the understanding remains intellectual it will not be of much use. I have explained it to you, you have understood it, but if the understanding remains intellectual

– you understand with the mind – again you miss. Koestler may be against Zen and you may be for it, but you both miss. It is not a question of being for or against; it is a question of a non-mental understanding. If it arises from your heart, if you feel it, not think it, if it touches your whole being, if it penetrates, is not just a verbal thing, not a philosophy, but becomes an experience, it will transform you.

I am talking about these stories just to shock you out of your mind, just to bring you down a little towards the heart – and if you are ready, then still further down towards the navel.

The further down you go, the deeper you reach...and, ultimately, depth and height are the same thing.

Enough for today.

a different way of being

Gensha complained to his followers one day: "Other masters are always carrying on about the necessity of saving everyone – but suppose you meet up with someone who is deaf, dumb and blind: he couldn't see your gestures, hear your preaching, or, for that matter, ask questions. Unable to save him, you'd prove yourself a worthless Buddhist."

Troubled by these words, one of Gensha's disciples went to consult the master Ummon who, like Gensha, was a disciple of Seppo. "Bow please," said Ummon.

The monk, though taken by surprise, obeyed the master's command – then straightened up in expectation of having his query answered. But instead of an answer, he got a staff thrust at him. He leapt back. "Well," said Ummon, "you're not blind. Now approach."

The monk did as he was bidden. "Good," said Ummon, "you're not deaf either. Well, understand?" "Understand what, sir?' said the monk. "Ah, you're not dumb either," said Ummon.

On hearing these words the monk awoke as from a deep sleep.

Jesus used to say to his disciples, and not only once but many times, "If you have eyes – look! If you have ears, then hear me!" They had eyes just like you and they had ears just like you. Then Jesus must have meant something else – not these ears, not these eyes.

There is a different way of seeing the world and a different way of hearing – a different way of being. When you have that different quality of seeing, God is seen; when you have that different way of hearing, God is heard; and when you have that different quality of being, you become God yourself. As you are, you are deaf, dumb, blind – almost dead. Deaf to God, dumb to God, blind to God, dead to God.

Nietzsche has declared that God is dead. In fact, when *you* are dead, how can God be alive to you? God is dead because you are dead. You can know God only when you live abundantly, when your life becomes an overflowing, when it is a flood. In that overflowing moment of bliss, life and vitality, for the first time you know what God is, because God is the most luxurious overflowing phenomenon.

God is not a necessity in this world. Scientific laws are a necessity – without them the world cannot be. God is not a necessity that way. Without him the world can be, but it will be worthless. Without him you can exist, but your existence will be just a vegetable existence. Without him you can vegetate, you cannot be really alive.

God is not a necessity – you can be there, but your being there will not be of any meaning, it will not carry any meaning at all. It will have no poetry, it will have no song, it will have no dance to it. It will not be a mystery. It may be an arithmetic, it may be a business, but it cannot be a love affair.

Without God all that is beautiful disappears, because the beautiful comes only as an overflowing – it is a luxury. Watch a tree: if you have not watered it well, if the tree is not getting nourishment from the soil, the tree can exist but flowers will not come. Existence will be there, but futile! It would have been better not to be, because it will be a constant frustration. Flowers come to the tree only when the tree has so much that it can share, and the tree has so much nourishment that it can flower – flowering is a luxury! The tree has so much that it can afford it.

And I tell you that God is the most luxurious thing in the world. God is not necessary – you can live without him. You can live very well, but you will miss something, you will feel an emptiness in the heart. You will be more like a wound than like an alive force. You will suffer; there cannot be any ecstasy in your life.

But how to find this meaning, this ecstasy? You will need a different way of looking. Right now you are blind. Of course you can see matter, but matter is a necessity. You can see the tree very well but you miss the flowers; and even if you can see the flowers, you miss the fragrance. Your eyes can see only the surface – you miss the center, the very core. Hence Jesus goes on saying that you are a blind man, you are deaf – and you have to be dumb, because if you have not seen him what is there to say? If you have not heard him what is there to convey and communicate? If that poetry has not happened what is there to sing? You may make gestures from your mouth, but nothing will come out of it because nothing is there in the first place.

When a man like Jesus speaks he is possessed; something greater than him speaks through him. When a man like Buddha speaks he is not Gautam Siddhartha who was born a son to a king; no, he is no longer that. He is no longer the body you can see and touch, he is not even the mind that you can comprehend and understand. Something of the beyond has entered, something which is not of time and space has come into time and space. A miracle has happened. *He* is not speaking to you, he is just a vehicle; something else is flowing through him, he is just a medium. He carries to you something from the unknown shore. Only then can you sing – when ecstasy has happened. Otherwise you can go on singing, but it will be superficial. You may make much noise, but noise is not speaking. You may use many words, but they will be empty. You may talk too much, but in fact how can you *talk*?

When it happened to Mohammed, the first day when he came in contact with the divine, he fell on the ground, started shivering and shaking and perspiring – and the morning was as cold as this morning. He was alone, and from the very pores of the soles of his feet he started perspiring; he was afraid. Something unknown had touched him and he was scared to death. He came running home and went to bed. His wife was very afraid. Many blankets were put on him but still he continued shivering and his wife asked, "What has happened? Your eyes look dazed – and why don't you speak? Why have you gone dumb?"

And Mohammed is reported to have said, "For the first time something is there to say. Up to now I have been a dumb man; there was nothing to say, I was making gestures from the mouth. I was talking but only my lips were moving, there was nothing to say. Now there is something I have to say – that's why I am trembling so much. I am pregnant with the unknown, with the divine. Something is going to take birth."

And this brings suffering, as every mother knows. If you have to give birth to a child you have to pass through many painful days, and when the birth happens there is much suffering. When life enters, it is a struggle.

For three days, it is said, Mohammed remained in his bed, absolutely dumb. Then, by and by, just as a small child starts talking, he started talking. And then the Koran was born.

You are dumb. You may be saying too many things, but remember – you talk too much just to hide that dumbness. You talk not to communicate, you talk just to hide – to hide the fact that you are dumb. Next time you start talking with someone, watch: why are you talking? Why are you so verbal? What is the need? Suddenly you will become aware that: "If I remain quiet the other will think 'Are you dumb'". So you talk just to hide this fact – and you know there is nothing to say, yet you go on talking.

I once stayed with a family and I was sitting with the man of the house, my host, when the son came, a small child, and he asked his father if he would answer a few questions. The father said, "I am engaged; you go and ask your mother."

The child said, "But I don't want to know that much! Because if she starts talking there is no end to it, and I have to do my homework – and I don't want to know that much!"

People go on talking and talking and talking and without knowing why they are talking – for what? What is there to convey? It is just to hide their dumbness. People go on moving from here to there, from this town to that; they go on traveling, and go for holidays to the Himalayas and to Switzerland – why all this traveling, moving? They want to feel they are alive.

But movement is not life. Of course life has a very deep movement, but movement is not life. You can go on moving from one town to another, and you can cover the whole earth, but that movement is not life. Life is, of course, a very subtle movement – the movement from one state of consciousness to another.

When people get stuck they start moving outwardly. Now the American has become the bona fide traveler; he travels all over the world from this corner to that – because American consciousness is stuck somewhere so badly that if you remain in one place you will feel you have gone dead. So move! Move from one wife to another, move from one job to another, move from one neighborhood to another, move from one town to another – never in the history of man has it happened. In America the average time for a person to stay in a town is three years; people move on within three years – and this is just the average, there are people who are moving every month. They go on changing – dresses, cars, houses, wives, husbands – everything.

I have heard that once one Hollywood actress was introducing her child to a new husband. She said, "Now, meet your new father."

The child said, "Hello, I am happy to meet you! Would you like to give me your signature in my visitors' book?" – because he had met so many new fathers.

Everything has to be changed just to feel that you are alive. A hectic search for life. Of course, life *is* a movement, but not from one place to another; it is a movement from one state to another. It is a deep inward movement from one consciousness to another consciousness, to the higher realms of being. Otherwise you are dead. As you are, you are dead. Hence Jesus goes on saying, "Listen! – if you have ears. See! – if you have eyes." This has to be understood first, then this story will become easier.

Then the second thing: why are you so dead? Why are you so dumb, blind, deaf? There must be something, there must be some investment in it – otherwise so many people, millions of them, could not be in such a state. It must be paying you something, you must be getting something out of it, otherwise how is it possible that Buddhas and Krishnas and Christs go on saying, "Don't be blind, don't be deaf, don't be dumb, don't be dead! Be alive! Be alert, awake!" – and nobody listens to them? Even if they appeal intellectually, you never listen to them. Even if you feel in certain sublime moments of life that they are right, you never follow them. Even if sometimes you decide to follow, you always postpone it for tomorrow – and then tomorrow never comes. What is the deep investment in it?

Just the other night I was talking to a friend. He is a very educated man, cultured – has moved all over the world, has lived in the Soviet Union and the UK and the United States, has been to China, and this and that. Listening to him I felt he is completely dead! And then he asked me, "What solution would you suggest? – because life has so many sufferings and miseries, so many injustices, so many things that hurt you. How to live life so that you don't feel hurt, so that life cannot create so many wounds in your being – what to do?"

So I told him there are two ways: one – which is easier but at a very great cost and that is to become dead, to become as insensitive as possible. ... Because if you are insensitive, if you grow a thick skin around you, an armor, then you don't bother much, nobody can hurt you. Somebody insults you and you have such a thick skin that it never enters. There is injustice, but you simply never become aware of it.

This is the mechanism of your deadness. If you are more sensitive, you will be hurt more. Then every small thing will become a pain, a misery, and it will be impossible to live – and one has to live. There *are* problems, and there are millions of people – there is violence all around, there is misery all around. You pass through the street and beggars are there; you have to be insensitive otherwise it will become a misery, a heavy weight on you. Why these beggars? What have they done to suffer this? And somehow deep down you will feel: "I am also responsible." You simply pass by the beggar as if you are deaf, dumb, blind – you don't look.

Have you ever *looked* at a beggar? You may have seen a beggar, but you have never looked at him. You have never encountered him, you have never sat with him, you have never taken his hand in your hand – it would be too much. So open – there is danger. And you have to think about your wife, not about this beggar; you have to think about your children – and you are not concerned! So whenever there is a beggar, watch: your speed increases, you walk faster and don't look that way. If you really look at a beggar you will feel the whole injustice of life; you will feel the whole misery – and it will be too much. It will be impossible to tolerate it, you will have to do something and what can you do? You feel so helpless; you have your own problems too, and you have to solve them.

You see a dying man, what can you do? You see a crippled child, what can you do? Just the other day one sannyasin came to me and he said he was very much disturbed, because on the road when he was passing a truck almost killed a dog. The dog was already not in good shape; two legs must have been crushed before. With only two legs the dog was trying to live, and then this truck again crushed him. The sannyasin took pity, felt compassion, he took the dog in his hands – and then he saw there was a hole in its back and millions of worms. He wanted to help, but how to help? And he became so disturbed that he couldn't sleep; he had nightmares and continuously the dog was haunting him: "I have not done anything – I have to do something. But what to do?" The idea came to his mind to kill the dog because that was the only thing that could be done now. With so many worms, maggots, the dog could not live. And its life would be misery, so it was better to kill it. But to kill – wouldn't that be violence? Wouldn't that be murder? Wouldn't that be a karma? So what to do? You cannot help. Then the best way is to be insensitive.

There are dogs and there are trucks, and things go on happening, you go on your way, you don't look around. It is dangerous to look, so you never use your eyes one hundred percent – scientists say only two percent. Ninety-eight percent, you close your eyes. Ninety-eight percent, you close your ears – you don't listen to everything that is happening all around. Ninety-eight percent you don't live.

Have you ever observed how you always feel fear whenever you are in a love relationship, or whenever love stays? Suddenly a fear takes over, because whenever you love a person you surrender to the person. And surrendering to a person is dangerous because the other may hurt you. Your protection is down. You don't have any armor. Whenever you love you are open and vulnerable, and who knows, how to believe in the other?...because the other is a stranger. You may have known the other for many years but that makes no difference. You don't even know yourself, how can you know the other? The other is a stranger. And to allow the other to enter into your intimate life means to allow him to hurt you.

People have become afraid of love; it is better to go to a prostitute than to have a beloved. It is better to have a wife than to have a beloved, because a wife is an institution. Your wife cannot hurt you more because you never loved her. It was arranged: your father and mother and the astrologer...everybody was involved except you. It is an arrangement, a social arrangement. Not much is involved. You take care of her, you arrange for her food and shelter. She takes care; she arranges the house, the food, she looks after the children – it is an arrangement, a business-like thing. Love is dangerous, it is not a business, it is not a bargain. You give power to the other person in love, complete power over you. The fear... the other is a stranger and who knows? Whenever you trust anybody, fear grips you.

People come to me and they say, "We surrender to you," but I know they cannot. It is almost impossible. They have never loved, how can they surrender? They are speaking without knowing what they are saying. They are almost asleep. They are talking in their sleep, they don't mean it, because surrender means that if I say, "Go on top of the hill and jump!" you cannot say no. Surrender means total power has been given to the other: how can you give that?

Surrender is just like love. That's why I say only lovers can become sannyasins – because they know a little of how to surrender. Love is the first step towards the divine, surrender is the last. And two steps is the whole journey.

But you are afraid. You would like to have your own control on your life – not only that, you would like to control the other's life also. Hence the continuous quarrel between husbands and wives and lovers, constant quarrel, conflict. What is the conflict? The conflict is: Who will dominate whom? Who will possess whom? It has to be settled first. This is not a surrender but a domination – just the opposite. Whenever you dominate a person there is no fear. Whenever you love a person there is fear, because in love you surrender and you give total power to the other. Now the other can hurt, the other can reject, the other can say *no*. That's why you live only two percent, not one hundred percent. Ninety-eight percent you are dead, insensitive. And insensitivity, deadness, is very much respected by the society. The more you are insensitive, the more society will respect you.

It is said, it happened in Lokmanya Tilak's life – one of the great Indian leaders. He lived in Pune, just this town, and before Gandhi took over and dominated the scene he was the topmost man in India – it is said about him that he was a man of discipline, and men of discipline are always dead because discipline is nothing but how to deaden yourself. His wife died, and he was sitting in his office where he published a newspaper, *Kesari,* – it is still published – when somebody reported, "Your wife has died, come home!" Hearing this, he looked at the clock at the back and he said, "But it is not yet time. I only leave my office at five."

Look at the whole thing. What type of intimacy, what type of love, what type of caring and sharing was there? This man cares about his work, this man cares about time, but not about love. It seems almost impossible that when somebody says your wife is dead, to look at the clock and then to say, "It is not yet time. I leave my office only at five." And the wonder of wonders is that all his biographers appreciate this incident very much. They say, "This is devotion to the country! This is how a disciplined man should be." They think this is non-attachment. This is not non-attachment, this is not devotion to anything. This is simply deadness, an insensitivity. And one who is insensitive towards his wife, how can he be sensitive to the whole country? Impossible.

Remember, if you cannot love a person you cannot love humanity. That may be a trick. Those who cannot love persons – because it is very dangerous to love a person –always think they love humanity. Where is humanity? Can you find it anywhere? It is just a word. Humanity exists nowhere. Wherever you go you will find a person existing. Life is persons, not humanity. Life is always personified, it exists as an individual. Society, country, humanity, are just words. Where is society? Where is the country, the motherland? You cannot love a mother, and you love a motherland? You must be deceiving somewhere. But the word is good, beautiful: motherland. You need not bother about the motherland, because the motherland is not a person, it is a fiction in your mind. It is your own ego.

You can love humanity, you can love the motherland, you can love society, and you are not capable of loving a person – because a person creates difficulties. Society will never create a difficulty because it is just a word. You need not surrender to it. You can dominate the word, the fiction, but you cannot dominate a person. Even with a small child it is impossible, you cannot dominate him because he has his own ego, he has his own mind, he has his own ways. It is almost impossible to dominate life but words can be easily dominated – because you are alone there.

People who cannot love a person start loving God. They don't know what they are doing. To talk to a person, to communicate to a person, is a difficult matter. It needs skill, it needs a very loving heart, it needs a very knowing heart, understanding heart. Only then can you touch a person, because to touch a person is to move in a dangerous arena – life is throbbing there also. And each person is so unique that you cannot be mechanical about it. You have to be very alert and watchful. You have to become more sensitive if you love a person; only then does understanding arise.

But to love a god who is somewhere sitting in the sky, it is a monologue. Go to the churches – people are talking to no one. They are as crazy as people you will find in the madhouses, but that madness is accepted by the society and this madness is not accepted, that is the only difference. Go to a madhouse; you will find people talking alone, nobody is there. They talk, and not only do they say something, they answer also. They make it look like a dialogue; it is a monologue. Then go to the churches and the temples; there people are talking to God. That too is a monologue, and if they really go mad they start doing both things: they say something and they answer also, and they feel that God has answered.

You cannot do that unless you have learned how to love a person. If you love a person, by and by the person becomes the door to the whole. But one has to start with the person, with the small, with the atomic. You cannot take the jump. The Ganges cannot simply jump into the ocean, it has to start in the Gangotri, just a small stream; then wider and wider and bigger and bigger it goes, and then finally it merges with the ocean.

The Ganga, the Ganges of love, also has to start just like a small stream, with persons, then it goes on becoming bigger and bigger. Once you know the beauty of it, the beauty of surrender, the beauty of insecurity, the beauty of being open to all that life gives – bliss and suffering both – then you get bigger and bigger and bigger and expand, and the consciousness finally becomes an ocean. Then you fall into godliness, into existence. But because of fear you create insensitivity – and the society respects it. Society does not want you to be very alive because alive people are rebellious.

Look at a small child: if he is really alive he will be rebellious, he will try to have his own way. But if he is a dumb imbecile, an idiot, somehow stuck somewhere and not growing, he will sit in the corner perfectly obedient. You tell him to go, he goes; you tell him to come, he comes. You tell him to sit down, he sits; you tell him to stand, he stands. He is perfectly obedient because he has no personality of his own. The society, the family, the parents, will like this child. They will say, "Look, he is so obedient."

I heard once...

Mulla Nasruddin was talking to his son; he had come with a report card from his school. Mulla was expecting that he would receive an A, and he had received a D; in fact he was the last in the class. So Nasruddin said, "Look, you never obey me, whatsoever I say you disobey; now this has resulted. And look at the neighbors' child – he always receives an A, always stands first in the class." The child looked at Nasruddin and said, "But that's a different matter – he has got talented parents." This child is very alive, but he has his own ways.

Obedience has a certain dumbness about it, disobedience a sharp intelligence about it. But obedience is respected because obedience gives less inconvenience. Of course that's right – disobedience creates inconvenience.

You would like a dead child because he will not create any inconvenience. You would not like an alive child – the more alive, the more danger there is.

Parents, societies, schools, they all force obedience, they dull you; and then they respect those people. That's why in life you never see people who stand first in schools, universities; in life they are simply lost. You never find them in life, where they go...they prove themselves very talented in school, but somehow in life they are lost. It seems that the ways of school are different from the ways of life. Somehow life loves lively people – the more lively, the more rebellious: people with their own consciousness, being, and personality; people who have their own ways to fulfill; people who are not dead. Schools prefer just the opposite. The whole society helps you to become dumb, deaf, blind, dead.

In the monasteries you will find dead people worshipped as saints. Go to Varanasi: you will find people lying down on beds of thorns, nails – and they are worshipped like gods. And what have they achieved? If you look at their faces you will not find more stupid faces anywhere. A person lying on a bed of nails or thorns has to be stupid. In the first place to choose this way of life one has to be stupid. And then what will he do, what can he do by lying on the nails? He has to make his whole body insensitive. That's the only way he has to not feel it. By and by he becomes thicker-skinned, then it doesn't matter. Then he becomes a rock, completely dead. And the whole society worships him: he is a sage, he has attained something. What has he attained? He has attained more deadness than you. Now the nails do not matter because the body has become dead.

You may not know, but if you ask physiologists they say there are already many spots in the body which are not alive; they call them dead spots. On your back there are many dead spots. Just give a needle to one of your friends, or your wife or your husband, and tell him to push the needle in your back on many spots. You will feel some spots and some you will not feel. Some spots are already dead, so when the needle is pushed in you don't feel it. Those people, they have done one thing: they have made their whole body a dead spot. But this is not growing, this is regression. They are becoming more material rather than more divine, because to be divine means to be perfectly sensitive, to be perfectly alive.

So I told that man that there is one way, and that is to be dead: that is easier, that is what everyone is doing. People differ in degrees, but in their own ways they are doing that.

You return to your home afraid of your wife; you become deaf, you don't hear what she says. You start reading your newspaper, and you put your newspaper in such a way that you don't see her. What she says you simply become deaf to, otherwise you feel, "How can I live if I listen to her?" You don't see that she is crying or weeping. Only when she makes it almost impossible for you, then you look – and that look is so angry.

You go to the office, you move through the traffic, everywhere you have to create a certain deadness around you. You think it protects – it does not protect, it only kills. Of course you will suffer less, but less blessings will come to you, less bliss also. When you become dead, suffering is less because you cannot feel it; blissfulness is less because you cannot feel it. A person who is in search of a higher blissfulness has to be ready to suffer.

This may look a paradox to you: that a man of the status of a buddha, a man who is awakened, is blissful – absolutely – and also suffers absolutely. Of course he is blissful inside, the flowers go on showering there, but he suffers for everybody all around. He has to, because if you have sensitivity for blessings to become available to you, suffering will also become available to you. One has to choose. If you choose not to suffer, that you don't want to suffer, then you will not attain to blissfulness either – because they both come by the same door; this is the problem. You can close your door in fear of the enemy, but the friend also comes by the same door. And if you lock it completely and block it completely, so afraid of the enemy, then the friend cannot come either. God has not been coming to you, your doors are closed. You may have closed them against the Devil, but when doors are closed they are closed. And one who needs, feels the hunger, the thirst to meet truth, has to meet the Devil also. You cannot choose one, you have to meet both.

If you are alive, death will be a great phenomenon to you. If you live totally you will die totally; if you live two percent you will die two percent. As life, so will be death. If the door is open for God it is open for the Devil also.

You have heard many stories but I don't feel that you have understood: whenever God happens the Devil happens just before him, because whenever the door is open the Devil rushes in first. He is always in a hurry. God is not in a hurry.

So with Jesus – before he attained to the final enlightenment the Devil tempted him for forty days. When he was meditating, fasting in his aloneness, when Jesus was disappearing and he was creating a place for Christ to come, the Devil tempted him. Those forty days the Devil was continuously by his side. And he tempted very beautifully and very politically; he is the greatest politician, all other politicians are his disciples. Very diplomatically he said, "Right, so now you have become the prophet, and you know that in the scriptures it is said that whenever God chooses a man, and a man becomes a messiah, a prophet, he becomes infinitely powerful. Now you are powerful. If you want you can jump from this hill and angels will be standing in the valley. And if you are really a messiah, fulfill whatever is said in the scriptures – jump!"

The temptation was great and he was quoting scriptures. Devils always quote, because to convince you a scripture has to be brought in. Devils know all the scriptures by heart.

Jesus laughed and said, "You are right but in the same scripture it is said that you should not test God."

Then one day when he was feeling very hungry...thirty days of fasting, the Devil always sitting by his side...before God comes, the Devil comes; the moment you open the door he is just standing there, and he is always first in the queue. God always lags behind because he is not in a hurry, remember: God has eternity to work, the Devil has not eternity to work – moments only. If he loses, he loses, and once a man becomes divine, he will not be hurt any more...so he has to find weak moments when Jesus is disappearing and Christ has not entered. That gap is the moment where he can enter. Then the Devil said, "But it is said in the scriptures that when a man is chosen by God he can turn even stones into bread. So why are you suffering? And *prove* this, because the world will be benefited by this." This is diplomacy. He said, "The world will be benefited by this."

It seems that's how the Devil has convinced your Satya Sai Baba. The world will be benefited by this because when you turn stones into bread, people will know that you are the man of God. They will come running, then you can help them. Otherwise who will come and who will listen to you?

Jesus said, "You are right. I can turn – but not I, God can turn stones into bread. But whenever he needs to he will tell me, you need not bother. Why are you taking so much trouble?"

Whenever you enter into meditation the first man you will find on the gate, the moment you open the door, will be the Devil, because it is in fear of him you have closed the door. And remember...but first I will tell you an anecdote, then you will understand:

In a shop they had declared a special discount for Christmas, particularly for ladies' clothes and dresses, so there was a crowd of ladies. One man had come because his wife was ill, and she forced him to go because this was not a chance to be lost. So he stood, gentlemanly, for one hour, but he couldn't reach the counter. You know ladies, their way – screaming, shouting at each other, moving from anywhere, no queue; and the man was thinking of a queue, so he stood. When one hour passed and he was nowhere near the counter, then he started shoving and shouting and screaming, and he started forcibly to enter the crowd and reach the counter.

One old lady shouted, "What! What are you doing? Be a gentleman!"

The man said, "For one hour I have been a gentleman. Now I must behave like a lady! Enough!"

Remember, the Devil never behaves like a gentleman, he behaves like a lady. He is always first in the queue. And God is a gentleman. It is difficult for him to be first in the queue and the moment you open the door, the Devil enters. And because of your fear of him, you remain closed. But if the Devil cannot enter, God also cannot. When you become vulnerable, you become vulnerable for both God and the Devil – light and dark, life and death, love and hate – you become available for both opposites.

You have chosen not to suffer, so you are closed. You may not be suffering but your life is a boredom, because although you don't suffer as much as you will suffer if you are open, there is no blessing either. The door is closed – no morning, no sun, no moon enters, no sky enters, no fresh air, everything has gone stale. And in fear you are hiding there. It is not a house where you are living; you have already converted it into a grave. Your cities are graveyards, your houses are graves. Your whole way of life is that of a dead man.

Courage is needed to be open – courage to suffer, because blessing only becomes possible then.

Now we should try to understand this beautiful anecdote: Deaf, Dumb and Blind.

> Gensha complained to his followers one day: "Other masters are always carrying on about the necessity of saving everyone – but suppose you meet up with someone who is deaf, dumb and blind? He couldn't see your gestures, hear your preaching, or, for that matter, ask questions. Unable to save him, you'd prove yourself a worthless Buddhist."

Masters generally don't complain, but when they complain it means something. This is not only Gensha complaining, it is all the masters complaining. But this is their experience, and wherever you move you find deaf, dumb and blind people, because the whole society is that way. And how to save them? They cannot see, they cannot hear, they cannot feel, they cannot understand any gesture. If you try too much to save them they will escape. They will think: This man is after something, he wants to exploit me, or he must have some scheme. If you don't do very much for them they feel: This man is not for me because he is not caring enough. And whatsoever is done they cannot understand.

This is not Gensha's complaint, because enlightened persons never complain for themselves. This complaint is general, it is how it happens. A Jesus feels the same way, a Buddha feels the same way. Wherever you go, you have to meet people who are deaf, dumb and blind. You make gestures – they cannot see; or even worse, they see something else. You talk to them – they cannot understand, and even worse, they misunderstand. You say something else, they understand something else again, because meaning cannot be given through words. Only words can be communicated, meaning has to be supplied by the listener.

I say a word; I mean one thing. But if ten thousand people are listening there will be ten thousand meanings, because each will listen from his own mind, from his prejudice, from his concept and philosophy and religion. He will listen from his conditioning and his conditioning will supply the meaning. It is very difficult, almost impossible. It is just as if you go to a madhouse and talk to people. How will you feel? That's what Gensha feels, that's the complaint.

That's my complaint also. Working with you, I always feel a block comes. Either your eyes are blocked, or your ears are blocked, or your nose is blocked, or your heart is blocked; somewhere or other, something is blocked, a stone-like thing comes. And it is difficult to penetrate because if I do too much to penetrate it, you become afraid – why am I interested so much? If I don't do too much, you feel neglected. This is how an ignorant mind works. Do this and he will misunderstand, do that and he will misunderstand. One thing is certain: he will misunderstand.

> Gensha complained to his followers one day: "Other masters are always carrying on about the necessity of saving everyone."

Buddha has said that when you are saved, the only thing to do is save others. When you have attained, the only thing to do is to spread it to others, because everybody is struggling. Everybody is on the path stumbling, everybody is moving knowingly, unknowingly, and you have attained. Help others.

And that is a necessity also, an inner necessity of energies, because a man who has become enlightened will have to live a few years, because enlightenment is not a destiny; it is not fixed, it is not caused. When it happens it is not necessarily at the moment when the body dies. There is no necessity for these two happenings to be together. Really, it is almost impossible, because enlightenment is a sudden uncaused phenomenon. You work for it but it never happens through your work. Your work helps to create the situation but it happens through something else – that something else is called grace. It is a gift from existence, it is not a by-product of your efforts; they don't cause it. Of course they create a situation: I open the door and the light enters. But the light is a gift from the sun. I cannot create light just by opening the door. Opening of the door is not a cause to it. Non-opening of the door was a hindrance but opening of the door is not a cause – I cannot cause. If you open the door and it is night, light will not enter. Opening the door is not creating light, but by closing the door you hinder.

So all the efforts that you make towards realization are just to open the door. Light comes when it comes. You have to remain with an open door so whenever it comes, whenever it knocks at your door, it finds you there and the door is open so it can enter. It is always a gift – and it has to be so, because if you can attain the ultimate through your efforts it will be an absurdity. A limited mind making efforts – how can it find the infinite? A finite mind making efforts – all efforts will be finite. How can the infinite happen through finite efforts? The ignorant mind is making efforts – those efforts are made in ignorance; how can they change, transform into enlightenment? No, it is not possible.

You make efforts; they are necessary, they prepare you, they open the door – but the happening happens when it happens. You remain available. God knocks many times at your door, the sun rises every day. And remember, nowhere else is it said what I would like to say to you, although it will be a help. It is not said because if you misunderstand it can become a hindrance. There is a day for God and there is a night also. If you open the door in the night, the door will remain open but God will not come. There is a day – if you open the door in the right moment, immediately God comes.

And it has to be so, because the whole of existence has opposites. God is also in a rest period when he sleeps. If you open the door then he will not come. There is a moment when he is awake, when he is moving – it has to be so because every energy moves through two opposites, rest and movement, and God is infinite energy! He has movements and he has a rest. That's why a master is needed.

If you do it on your own you may be working hard and nothing is happening, because you are not working at the right moment. You are working in the night; you open the door and only darkness enters. Afraid, you close it again. You open the door and there is nothing but vast emptiness all around. You become afraid, you close it again, and once you see that emptiness, you will never forget it – and you will be so afraid that it will take many years for you to gather courage again to open it. ...Because once you see the infinite abyss, when God is asleep, when God is in rest, if you see that moment of infinite negativity and abyss and darkness, you will be scared – so much so that for many years you will not make another attempt.

And I feel that many people are afraid of going into meditation – and I know that somewhere in their past life they have made some effort and they had a glimpse of the abyss at the wrong moment. They may not know it but unconsciously it is there, so whenever they come near the door and they put their hand on the knob and it becomes possible to open the door, they become afraid. They come back exactly from that moment, run back – they don't open it. An unconscious fear grips. It has to be so, because for many lives you have been struggling and striving.

Hence the necessity of the master who knows, who has attained, and who knows the right moment. He will tell you to make all the efforts when it is the night of God. And he will not tell you to open the door. He will tell you to pre-pare in the night, prepare as much as you can, be ready, and when the morning strikes and the first rays have entered he will tell you to open the door. Sudden illumination! Then it is totally different because when the light is there it is totally different.

When God is awake then the emptiness is not there. It is a fulfillment; it is perfect fulfillment. Everything is full, more than full, it is ever-flowing perfec-tion. It is the peak, not the abyss. If you open the door in the wrong moment, it is the abyss. You will get dizzy, so dizzy that for many lives together you will never attempt it. But only one who knows, only one who has become one with God, only one who knows when it is the night and when the day, can help, because now they happen in him also – he has a night, he has a day.

Hindus had a glimpse of this and they have a beautiful hypothesis: they call it Brahma's day, God's day. When the creation is there they call it God's day – but the creation has a time limit, and the creation dissolves and Brahma's night, God's night, starts. Twelve hours of Brahma's day is the whole creation. Then, tired, the whole existence disappears into nonexistence. Then for twelve hours it is Brahma's night. For us it is millions and millions of years, for God it is twelve hours – his day.

Christians also had a theory, or a hypothesis – because I call all religious theories hypotheses, for nothing is proved, nothing can be proved by the very nature of the thing. They say God created the world in six days, then on the seventh day he rested. That's why Sunday is a rest day, a holiday. Six days he created, and on the seventh day he rested. They had a glimpse that even God must rest.

These are both hypotheses, both beautiful, but you have to find the essence of it. The essence is that every day God also has a night and a day. And every day there is a right moment to enter and a wrong moment; in the wrong moment you will be against the wall, in the right moment you simply enter. Because of this, those who have knocked at the wrong moment say that to attain enlightenment is a gradual thing, you attain it by degrees; and those who have come to the door in the right moment say enlightenment is sudden, it happens in a moment. A master is needed to decide when is the right moment.

It is reported that Vivekananda started his disciplehood and then one day he attained the first glimpse. You can call it satori, the Zen word for *samadhi*, because it is a glimpse, not a permanent thing. It is just as if clouds are not there in the sky – the sky is clear and from a distance of one thousand miles you have a glimpse of Everest in all its glory, but then the sky becomes cloudy and the glimpse is again lost. It is not attainment, you have not reached Everest, you have not reached the top; from thousands of miles you had a glimpse – that is satori. Satori is a glimpse of *samadhi*. Vivekananda had a satori.

In Ramakrishna's ashram there were many people, many people were working. One man, his name was Kalu, a very simple man, a very innocent man, was also working in his own way – and Ramakrishna accepted *every* way. He was a rare man; he accepted every technique, every method, and he said everybody has to find his own way, there is no super highway. And this is good, otherwise there would be such a traffic jam! So it is good, you can walk on your own path. Nobody else is there to create any trouble or make it crowded.

That Kalu was a very simple man. He had at least one hundred gods – as Hindus are lovers of many gods, one is not enough for them. So they will put in their worship place this god, that god, whatsoever they can find; they will even put calendars there. There is nothing wrong in it; if you love it, it is okay. But Vivekananda was a logician, a very keen intellect. He always argued with this innocent man and he could not answer. Vivekananda said, "Why this nonsense? One is enough, and the scriptures say that he is one, so why these one hundred and one gods?" And they were all sorts of shapes, and Kalu had to work with these gods at least three hours in the morning and three in the evening – the whole day was gone, because with every god he had to work, and however fast he worked it took three hours in the morning and three in the evening. But he was a very, very silent man and Ramakrishna loved him.

Vivekananda always argued, "Throw these gods!" When he had a glimpse of satori he felt very powerful. Suddenly the idea came to him that in this power, if he simply sent a telepathic message to Kalu – he was worshipping in his room, this was time for worship – to take all his gods to the Ganges and throw them, it would happen.

He simply sent a message. Kalu was really a simple man. He gathered all his gods into a bed sheet and carried them towards the Ganges.

From the Ganges Ramakrishna was coming, and he said, "Wait! This is not you who is going to throw them. Go back to your room and put them in their place." But Kalu said, "Enough! Finished!"

Ramakrishna said, "Wait and come with me!"

He knocked at Vivekananda's door. Vivekananda opened the door and Ramakrishna said, "What have you done? This is not good and this is not the right moment for you. So I will take your key of meditation and will keep it with me. When the right moment comes I will give it to you." And for his whole life Vivekananda tried in millions of ways to attain, but he couldn't get that glimpse again.

Just before he died, three days before, Ramakrishna appeared in a dream and he gave him the key. He said, "Now you can take the key. Now the right moment is here and you can open the door."

And the next day in the morning he had the second glimpse.

A master knows when it is the right time. He helps you, prepares you for the right moment, and he will give you the key when the right moment is there; then you simply open the door and the divine enters – because if you open the door and darkness enters it will look like death, not like life. Nothing is wrong in this but you will get scared, and you can get so scared that you may carry that fear for ever and ever.

Buddha says that whenever you attain, start helping others, because all your energies that were moving into desire...now that door is finished, that travel is no more, that trip is no more; now let all your energies which were moving in desiring, *vasana*, become compassion, let them become *karuna*. And there is only one compassion – how to help the other to attain the ultimate, because there is nothing else to be attained. All else is rubbish. Only the divine is worth attaining. If you attain that you have attained all; if you miss that you have missed all.

When one becomes enlightened he lives for a few years before the body completes its circle. Buddha lived on for forty years because the body had got a momentum: from the parents the body had got chromosomes, from his own past karma the body had got a life circle. He was to live eighty years, enlightened or not. If enlightenment became possible or if it happened, then too he had to live eighty years. It happened nearabout when he was forty; he lived forty years more. What to do with the energies now? Now there is no desire, no ambition. And you have infinite energies flowing. What to do with those energies? They can be moved into compassion. Now there is no need for meditation either; you have attained, you are overflowing – now you can share. Now you can share with millions, you can give it to them.

So Buddha has made this a part of his basic teaching. He calls the first part *dhyana*, meditation, and the second part *pragya*, wisdom attainment. Through meditation you reach to pragya. These are your inward phenomena, two parts: you meditated, now you have attained. Now to balance it with the outer – because a man of enlightenment is always balanced. Outside, when there was no meditation inside, there was desire. Now there is wisdom inside, there should be compassion. The outer energies should become compassion; the inner energies have become wisdom, enlightenment. Enlightenment inside, compassion outside. The perfect man is always balanced. So Buddha says go on and on and help to save people.

Gensha complained: how to do it if you come to somebody who is deaf, dumb and blind? – and you almost always come across such people because only they are there. You don't come across a buddha, and a buddha doesn't need you. You come across an ignorant person, not knowing what to do, not knowing where to move. How to help him?

> *Troubled by these words, one of Gensha's disciples went to consult the master Ummon.*

Ummon was a brother disciple to Gensha – they were disciples to the same teacher, Seppo. So what to do? Gensha has said such a troubling thing to this man: how to help people? He went to Ummon.

Ummon is a very famous master. Gensha was a very silent one. But Ummon had thousands of disciples and he had many devices to work with them. And he was a man like Gurdjieff – he would create situations, because only situations can help. If words can't help because you are dumb, you are deaf – words can't help. If you are blind, gestures are useless. Then what to do? Only situations can help.

If you are blind, I cannot show you the door just by gesture because you can't see. I cannot tell you about the door because you are deaf and you cannot listen. Really, you cannot even ask the question, "Where is the door?" – because you are dumb. What to do? I have to create a situation.

I can take hold of your hand, I can take you by my hand towards the door. No gesture, no word. I have to *do* something; I have to create a situation in which the dumb, the deaf and the blind can move.

> *Troubled by these words, one of Gensha's disciples went to consult the master Ummon.*

…Because he knew well that Gensha wouldn't say much; he was not a man of many words and he never created any situation; he would say things and he would keep quiet. People had to go to other masters to ask what he meant. He was a different type, a silent type of man, like Ramana Maharshi;

he would not say much. Ummon was like Gurdjieff. He was also not a man of words, but he would create situations, and he would use words only to create situations.

He went to consult the master Ummon who, like Gensha, was a disciple of Seppo.

And Seppo was totally different from both. It is said he never spoke. He remained completely silent. So there was no problem for him – he never came across a deaf, dumb and blind man because he never moved. Only people who were in search, only people whose eyes were slightly opening, only people who were deaf but if you spoke loudly they could hear something...so that's why many people became enlightened near Seppo because only those who were just borderline cases reached him.

This Ummon and this Gensha, these two disciples became enlightened with Seppo, a totally silent man – he would simply sit and sit and do nothing. If you wanted to learn you could be with him, if you didn't want to you could go. He would not say anything. You had to learn, he would not teach. He was not a teacher, but many people learned.

The disciple went to Ummon.

"Bow please," said Ummon.

He started immediately, because people who are enlightened don't waste time, they simply jump to the point immediately.

"Bow please," said Ummon.

The monk, though taken by surprise....

...Because this is no way! You don't order anybody to bow. And there is no need – if somebody wants to bow he will bow, if he wants to pay you respect, he will pay it. If not, then not. What type of man is this Ummon? He says "Bow please" before the monk has asked anything; he has just entered his room, and Ummon says "Bow please."

*The monk, though taken by surprise, obeyed the master's command –
then straightened up in expectation of having his query answered.
But instead of an answer, he got a staff thrust at him. He leapt back.
"well," said Ummon, "you're not blind. Now approach."*

He said: You can see my staff, so one thing is certain, you are not blind. Now approach.

The monk did as he was bidden. "Good," said Ummon, "so you're not deaf either."

You can listen: I say approach and you approach.

"Well, understand?" "Understand what, sir?" said the monk.

What is he saying? He says:

"Well, understand?" "Understand what, sir? said the monk." Ah, you're not dumb either," said Ummon. On hearing these words the monk awoke as from a deep sleep.

What happened? What is Ummon pointing to? First, he is saying that if it is not a problem to you why be worried? There are people who come to me...

A very rich man came, one of the richest in India, and he said, "What about poor people, how will you help poor people?" So I told him, "If you are a poor person, then ask; otherwise let the poor ask. How is it a problem to you? You are not poor, so why create a problem out of it?"

Once Mulla Nasruddin's child asked him – I was present, and the child was working very strenuously, grumbling of course, on his homework, and then suddenly he looked at Nasruddin and said, "Gee Dad, what is this education stuff? Of what use is all this education stuff anyway?"

Nasruddin said, "Well, there is nothing like education. It makes you capable of worrying about everybody else in the world except you."

There is nothing like education. All your education simply makes you capable of worrying about situations everywhere in the world, about everyone except you – about all the troubles that are in the world. They have always been there, they will always be there. It is not because you are here that troubles are there. You were not and they were there; you will not be soon and they will remain there. They change their colors but they remain. The very scheme of the universe is such that it seems that through trouble and misery something is growing. It seems to be a step, it seems to be a necessary schooling, a discipline.

The first thing Ummon is pointing out is: You are neither blind, nor dumb, nor deaf, so why are you concerned and why are you troubled? You have eyes – why waste time thinking about blind men? Why not look at your master? – because blind men will be there always, your master will not be there always. And you can think and worry about blind and deaf people, how to save them, but the man who can save you will not be there for ever. So you be concerned about yourself.

My experience is also that people are concerned about others. Once one man brought to me even exactly the same question. He said, "We can listen to you but what about those who can't come to listen, what to do? We can read you," he said, "but what about those who cannot read?"

They appear relevant, but they are absolutely irrelevant. Because why are you worried? And if you are worried in such a way then you can never become enlightened, because a person who goes on wasting and dissipating his energy on others never looks at himself. This is a trick of the mind to escape from one-self – you go on thinking about others and you feel very good because you are worrying about others. You are a great social reformer or a revolutionary or a utopian, a great servant of the society – but what are you doing? You are simply avoiding the basic question: it is with *you* that something has to be done.

Forget the whole society, and only then can something be done to you; and when you are saved you can start saving others. But before that, please don't think – it is impossible. Before you are healed, you cannot heal anyone. Before you are filled with light, you cannot help anyone to enkindle his own heart. Impossible – only a lighted flame can help somebody. First become a lighted flame – this is the first point.

And the second point is, Ummon created a situation. He could have said this but he is not saying it; he is creating a situation, because only in a situation are you totally involved. If I say something only intellect is involved. You listen from the head; but your legs, your heart, your kidneys, your liver, your totality is not involved. But when the monk got a staff thrust at him he jumped totally. Then it was total action; then not only the head and the legs, the kidneys, the liver, but the whole of him jumped.

That's the whole point of my meditation techniques: the whole of you has to shake, jump, the whole of you has to dance, the whole of you has to move. If you simply sit with closed eyes only the head is involved. You can go on and on inside the head – and there are many people who go on sitting for years together, just with closed eyes, repeating a mantra. But a mantra moves in the head, your totality is not involved – and your totality is involved in existence. Your head is only as much in God as your liver and kidneys and your feet. You are totally in him, and just the head cannot realize this.

Anything intensely active will be helpful. Inactive, you can simply go on rambling inside the mind. And they have no end, the dreams, the thoughts, they have no end. They go on infinitely.

Kabir has said: There are two infinities in the world – one is ignorance and another is God. Two things are endless – God is endless, and ignorance. You can go on repeating a mantra, but it will not help unless your whole life becomes a mantra, unless you are completely involved it – no holding back, no division. That's what Ummon did. The monk got a staff thrust at him.

> He leapt back. "Well," said Ummon, "you're not blind. Now approach."
> The monk did as he was bidden. "Good, you're not deaf either."

What is he pointing at? He is pointing at this: "You can understand, so why waste time?" Then he asks, *"Well, understand?"* Ummon was finished. The situation was complete. But the disciple was not yet ready, had not yet got the point. He asked, *"Understand what, sir?"* The whole thing was there now. Ummon had said whatsoever was to be said. And he had created a situation where thoughts were not: when somebody pushes a staff at you, you jump without thought. If you think you cannot jump, by the time you have decided to jump, the staff would have hit you. There is no time.

Mind needs time, thinking needs time. When somebody pushes a staff at you, or suddenly you find a snake on a path, you jump! You don't think about it, you don't make a logical syllogism, you don't say: Here is a snake; a snake is dangerous; death is possible; I must jump. You don't follow Aristotle there. You simply put aside all Aristotle – you jump! You don't care what Aristotle says, you are illogical. But whenever you are illogical you are total.

That's what Ummon has said. You jump totally. If you can jump totally, why not meditate totally? When a staff is thrust at you, you jump without caring about the world. You don't ask, "That's okay, but what about a blind man? If you push a staff, how will it help a blind man?" You don't ask a question – you simply jump; you simply avoid. In that moment the whole world disappears, only you are the problem. And the problem is there – you have to solve it and come out of it.

"Understand?" – that's what Ummon asked. The point is complete.

> *"Understand what sir?"* said the monk.

He has still not got it.

> *"Ah, you're not dumb either"* – you can speak also.

> *On hearing these words the monk awoke as from a deep sleep.*

A whole situation – nonverbal, illogical, total. As if someone has shaken him out of his sleep. He awoke; for a moment everything became clear. For a moment there was lightning, there was no darkness. Satori happened. Now the taste is there. Now this disciple can follow the taste. Now he has known, he cannot forget it ever. Now the search will be totally different. Before this it was a search for something unknown – and how can you search for an unknown? And how can you put down your total life for it? But now it will be total, now it is not something unknown – a glimpse has been given to him. He has tasted the ocean, maybe out of a teacup but the taste is the same. Now he knows. It was really a small experience – a window opened, but the whole sky was there. Now he can move out of the house, come out under the sky and live in it. Now he knows that the question is individual.

Don't make it social. The question is you, and when I say you I mean *you*, each individually; not you as a group, not you as a society. When I mean you, I mean simply you, the individual – and the trick of the mind is to make it social. The mind wants to worry about others – then there is no problem. You can post-pone your own problem; that's how you have been wasting your lives for many lives. Don't waste it any more.

I have been pushing these talks, subtler ones than with Ummon, but if you don't listen to me I may have to find grosser things.

Don't think about others. First solve *your* problem, then you will have the clarity to help others also. And nobody can help unless he is enlightened himself.

Enough for today.

it is right before your eyes

A master was asked by a curious monk: "What is the way?" "It is right before your eyes," said the master. "Why do I not see it for myself?" asked the monk. "Because you are thinking of yourself," said the master. "What about you," said the monk, "do you see it?"
The master said: "So long as you see double, saying I don't, and you do, and so on, your eyes are clouded." "When there is neither I nor you, can one see it?" said the monk. "When there is neither I nor you, who is the one who wants to see it?" replied the master.

Yes, the way is right before your eyes. But your eyes are not right before the way – they are closed, closed in a very subtle manner. They are clouded. Millions of thoughts are closing them, millions of dreams are floating on them; whatsoever you have seen is all there, whatsoever you have thought is all there. And you have lived long – many lives, and you have thought much, and it is all gathered there in your eyes. But because thoughts cannot be seen you see your eyes as clear. The clarity is not there. Millions of layers of thought and dreams are there in your eyes. The way is right before you. All that is, is right before you. But you are not here. You are not in that still moment where eyes are totally empty, unclouded, and you *see*, and you see that which is.

So the first thing to be understood is: how to attain unclouded eyes, how to make eyes empty so that they can reflect truth, how not to be continuously in a mad rush within; how not to be continuously thinking and thinking and thinking, how to relax thought. When thought is not, seeing happens; when thought is, you go on interpreting and you go on missing.

Don't be an interpreter of reality, be a visionary. Don't think about it, see it!

What to do? One thing: Whenever you look, just be the look. Try. It is going to be difficult, difficult just because of old habit. But try. It happens. It has happened to many, why not you? You are no exception. The universal law is as available to you as to a buddha or to anybody. Just make a little effort.

You see a flower: then just see, don't say anything. The river is flowing: sit on the bank and see the river, but don't say anything. Clouds are moving in the sky: lie down on the ground and see, and don't say anything. Just don't verbalize!

This is the deepest habit, to verbalize; this is your whole training – to jump immediately to words from reality, to immediately start making words: "beautiful flower," "lovely sunset." If it is lovely, let it be lovely! – why bring in this word? If it is beautiful, do you think your word "beautiful" will make it more beautiful? On the contrary, you missed an ecstatic moment. The verbalization came in. Before you could have seen you moved, moved in an inner wandering. If you go too far away in this wandering you become mad.

What is a madman? He who never comes to reality, who always wanders in his own world of words – and he has wandered so far that you cannot bring him back. He is not with the reality, but are you with the reality? You are not either. The difference is only of degree. A madman has wandered very far, you never wandered that far – just in the neighborhood – and you come again and again and touch reality and go again.

You have a small touch, a small contact somewhere, uprooted, but still one root seems to be there in the reality. But that root is very fragile; any moment it can be broken, any accident – the wife dies, the husband escapes, you become bankrupt in the market – and that fragile root is broken. Then you go on wandering and wandering; then there is no coming back, then you never touch reality. This is the state of the madman, and the normal man is different only in degree.

And what is the state of a buddha, an enlightened man, a man of Tao, of understanding, awareness? He is deeply rooted in reality, he never wanders from it – just the opposite of a madman.

You are in the middle. From that middle either you can move towards being a madman or you can move towards being a buddha. It is up to you. Don't give much energy to thoughts, that's suicidal; you are poisoning yourself. Whenever thinking starts, if it is unnecessary – and ninety-nine percent of it is unnecessary – immediately bring yourself back to reality. Anything will help: even the touch of the chair you are sitting on, or the touch of the bed you are lying on. Feel the touch – it is more real than your thoughts about God, it is more godly than your thoughts about God because it is a real thing.

Touch it, feel the touch, be the touch, be here and now. You are eating? – taste the food well, the flavor. Smell it well, chew it well – you are chewing reality! Don't go wandering in thoughts. You are taking a bath? – enjoy it! The shower is falling on you? – feel it! Become more and more a feeling center rather than a thinking center.

And yes, the way is right before your eyes. But feeling is not allowed much. The society brings you up as a thinking being not as a feeling being, because feeling is unpredictable; no one knows where it will lead, and society cannot leave you on your own. It gives you thoughts: all the schools, colleges and universities exist as centers to train you for thinking, to verbalize more. The more words you have, the more talented you are thought of; the more articulate you are with words and words, the more educated you are thought. It will be difficult, because thirty, forty, fifty, sixty years of training...but the sooner you begin the better. Bring yourself back to reality.

That is the meaning of all sensitivity groups. In the West they have become a focal point and all those who are interested in consciousness, extension of consciousness, have to be interested in sensitivity groups, in training to be more sensitive. And you need not go anywhere to learn it, the whole of life is sensitivity. Twenty-four hours a day the reality is just before you, around you – it surrounds you; you breathe it in, you eat it. Whatsoever you do you have to do with reality.

But the mind moves far away. There exists a gap between your being and your mind – they are not together, the mind is somewhere else. You have to be here in reality because when you eat you have to eat real bread; thinking about bread won't help. When you take a bath you have to take a real bath; thinking about it is of no use. When you breathe you have to breathe real air; just thinking about it won't do. Reality surrounds you from everywhere, is bumping you from all sides – wherever you go you encounter it.

That is the meaning of: "The way is right in front of your eyes." It is everywhere because nothing else can be – only the real is.

Then what is the problem? Why then do people go on seeking and seeking and seeking and never find it? Where does the problem exist? What is the basic core of the whole trouble? The trouble is, mind can be in thoughts. The possibility for mind being in thoughts is there. The body is in reality, but the mind can be in thoughts – and that is the duality. And all your religions have been in favor of the mind and not in favor of the body. That has been the greatest block that has ever existed in this world. They poison the whole mind of humanity; they are for the mind, not for the reality.

If I tell you: When you are eating, eat with taste, and eat so deeply that the eater is forgotten, simply become the process of eating – you will be surprised because no religious man will say a thing like that. Religious people have been teaching: eat without taste – *aswad*; they have made a great thing out of it, the training for no-taste.

In Gandhi's ashram they had eleven rules. One of them was *aswad*, no taste – eat, but without taste, kill the taste completely. Drink – but without taste. Make your life as insensitive as possible. Deaden your body completely, so that you become a pure mind…you will become so – but this is how people go towards madness.

I teach you just the contrary, just the opposite. I am not against life – and life is the way. I affirm life in its totality. I am not a negator, I am not a denier – and I want you to bring your mind back to reality. Your body is more real than your mind. You can befool the mind, you cannot befool the body. The body is more rooted in the world; the body is more existential than your mind. Your mind is just mental. It thinks, it spins words, it creates systems – and all systems are foolish.

Once it happened:

Mulla Nasruddin was gambling in a horse race. First race he lost; second, he lost; third – he went on losing, and two ladies just by his side sitting in a box were continuously winning every race.

Then at the seventh he could not contain his curiosity. What system were they following? Every race, and it was now the seventh, they had been winners and he had been a loser, and he had been working so hard at it. So he gathered courage, leaned over, and asked the ladies: "You are doing well?"

They said, "Yes," very happily, they were beaming with happiness.

So he whispered: "Can you tell me about your system? Just a hint."

One lady said laughingly, "We have a lot of systems! But today we have decided for long tails."

But all systems and all philosophies are just like that – long tails. No system is true to reality because no system can be true to reality. I am not saying that some system can be – no. No system can be true to reality because all systems are fabrications of the mind, verbalizations, your interpretations, your projections – mind working on reality. That's how a system is born; all systems are false.

Reality needs no system. Reality needs a clarity of vision. It needs no philosophy to look at, it is right here and now. Before you started moving into a philosophy it was there; when you will come back it will be there and will have always been there with you – and you were thinking about it. Thinking about it is the way to miss it.

If you are a Hindu you will miss, if you are a Christian you will miss, if you are a Mohammedan you will miss; every "ism" is a way to miss. If you have the Koran in your head you will miss, if you have the Gita in your head you will miss; whatsoever scripture you carry – scripture is mind, and reality doesn't fall in line with the mind, reality does not bother about your mind and your fabrications.

Beautiful theories you spin, beautiful arguments you give, logical rationalizations you find. You work hard. You go on refining your theories, polishing them, but they are just like bricks – you go on rubbing, polishing, but they can never become a mirror. I say maybe bricks can become a mirror, but the mind can never become a mirror to reality. The mind is a destroyer. The moment it enters, everything becomes cloudy.

Please don't be a philosopher, and don't be an addict of any system. It is easy to bring an alcoholic back, it is easy to bring back a person who has gone too deep into drugs; it is difficult to bring a system-addict back. Organizations exist like Alcoholics Anonymous for alcoholics and other organizations for drug addicts, but there exists no organization for people who have become system-addicts – and there cannot be, because whenever there is an organization, it itself is a system.

I am not giving you a system. My whole effort is to bring you out of your systematizing mind. If you can become again a child, if you can look at reality without any preconceptions about it, you will attain. It is simple, it is ordinary, nothing is special about it. Reality is nothing special and extraordinary – it is there, it is everywhere. Only your mind is an unreal thing. Mind creates illusion, *maya*, mind creates dreams – and then you are clouded in them. And you are trying to do the impossible, that which cannot be done: you are trying to find the real through the mind. You lose the real through the mind, you cannot find it through the mind. You have to drop the mind completely.

Yes, the way is right before your eyes – but you are not there.

First thing: mind won't help. Try to understand it: mind won't help, it is the barrier. And the second thing: your over-concern about yourself is the greatest barrier. It has been my constant observation that people who meditate miss because they are concerned too much in themselves. They are too egocentric. They may pretend humbleness and they may even want to know how to be egoless, but they are the most egocentric people; they are only worried about themselves, they are only concerned with themselves.

To be worried about others is stupid; to be worried about oneself is even more stupid – because to be worried is stupidity; it makes no difference about whom you are worried. And people who are worried about others, you will feel they are always more healthy.

So in the West psychoanalysts help people to think about others and drop thinking about themselves. Psychologists go on teaching people how to be extroverts and not to be introverts, because an introvert becomes ill, an introvert becomes in reality perverted. He thinks continuously about himself, he becomes enclosed. He remains with his frustrations, worries, anxieties, anguish, depressions, anger, jealousy, hate, this and that – and he only worries. Think what type of anguish he lives in, continuously worried about things: Why am I angry? How should I become non-angry? Why do I hate? How should I transcend it? Why am I depressed? How to attain bliss? – he is continuously worried, and through this worry he creates the very same things he is worried about. It becomes a vicious circle.

Have you ever observed that whenever you want to go beyond a depression the depression deepens? Whenever you want not to be angry you become more angry. Whenever you are sad and you don't want to be sad any more, more sadness descends on you – have you not observed it? It happens because of the Law of the Reverse Effect. If you are sad and you want not to be sad, what will you do? You will look at sadness, you will try to suppress it, you will be attentive to it – and attention is food.

Psychoanalysts have found a clue. That clue is not very meaningful in the end; it cannot lead you to reality, it can at the most make you normally unhealthy. It can make you adjusted – it is a sort of adjustment to the people around you. They say: Be concerned with others' worries, help people, serve people.

Rotarians, members of Lions Clubs and others, they always say: We serve. Those are the extroverts. But you will feel that people who are in social service, those who are concerned with others and are less concerned with themselves are happier than people who are concerned too much with themselves.

Too much concern with oneself is a sort of disease. And then the deeper you move within – you are opening a Pandora's Box: many things bubble up and there seems to be no end to it. You are surrounded by your own anxieties and you go on playing with your wounds, you go on touching them again and again to see whether they are healed or not. You have become a pervert.

What to do? There seem to be only two ways: either be an extrovert – but by being an extrovert you can never become a buddha, because if you are worried about others, this worrying about others may be an escape. It is. You cannot look at your own worries when you are worried about others. Your focus is others, you are in a shadow. But how will your inner being grow this way? You will look more happy, you may look as if you are enjoying life more, but how are you going to grow? How will your inner being come to that point where it becomes light? If you are not concerned with it at all, it is not going to grow. To be an extrovert is good in the sense that you remain healthy – you don't become a pervert. To be an introvert is dangerous. If you move wrongly, you will become a pervert and the wrong movement is that you become too concerned. Then what to do? Treat yourself as if you also are the other; don't be too concerned.

And you *are* the other. Your body is other, why not my own body also? Your mind is other, why not my own mind? The question is only distance: your body is five feet away from me, my body is a little closer, that's all. Your mind is there, my mind is here – the difference is of distance. But my mind is as other as your mind, and my body is as far away from me as your body. And if this whole world is not a concern to me, why make myself a concern? Why not leave both and be neither extrovert nor introvert? – this is my message.

If you cannot follow this then it is better to follow the psychoanalysts. Be an extrovert, be unconcerned; you will not grow but at least you will not suffer so much as an introvert suffers. But don't be an introvert and don't play with your wounds. Don't be concerned too much. Don't be so selfish and don't be so self-centered. Look at yourself from a distance; the distance is there, you only have to try it once and you will feel it. You are also the other.

When your body is ill it is as if somebody else's body is ill: do whatsoever is needed but don't be too concerned, because too much concern is a greater illness than the body's illness. If you have a fever go to the doctor, take the medicine, take care of the body, and that's all. Why be concerned too much? Why create another fever – which no doctor can treat? This fever in the body can be treated, but if you become too concerned another fever is created. That fever is deeper, no doctor can help with it.

And this is the problem: the body may become well soon, but the other fever may continue; and the other fever may go on continuing, and you may feel that the body is still ill. This happens every day: the disease disappears from the body but not from the mind and the mind carries it on. It has happened many times.

Once somebody was telling me about his friend who is a drunkard – he walks on crutches, he cannot walk without them. For many years he has been walking on crutches – an accident some twenty years before. Then one day he had taken too much drink; he forgot the crutches and went out for a walk. After one hour he came running back in a panic; he said, "Where are my crutches? I cannot walk without them! I must have taken too much." But if while you are drunk you can walk, why not when you are not drunk?

All over the world many cases are reported about paralysis. Somebody is paralyzed and then the house catches fire and everybody runs out, and the man who was paralyzed and who couldn't get out of his bed – and everything was done in the bed – he also runs out, because he forgets. The house is on fire, he forgets completely that he is paralyzed. In that forgetfulness he is not paralyzed. And outside the house the family looks at him and says, "What are you doing? How can you run?" – and he falls down; remembering comes back.

You may be creating many diseases, not because the body is ill but because the mind carries the seed. So once a disease happens the mind carries the seed and goes on projecting it again and again and again. Many diseases, ninety percent, have their origin in the mind.

Too much concern about yourself is the greatest disease possible. You cannot be happy, you cannot enjoy yourself. How can you enjoy? So many problems inside! Problems and problems and problems and nothing else! – and there seems to be no solution. What to do? You go crazy. Everybody, inside, is crazy.

I have heard – it happened in Washington – one man suddenly climbed up a pole, a flagpole. A crowd gathered, policemen came, and the man shouted as loudly as he could, uttered profane words, then came down.

Immediately he was caught by the police and they asked the person, "What are you doing here?"

The man said, "Don't disturb me. If now and then I don't do such a crazy thing I will go mad, I will go nuts. I tell you, don't stop me. Now and then if I do such a thing then everything runs smoothly. And I was not thinking that anybody will be able to know, because where so much craziness is going on all around, who will bother?"

Now and then you also need to become mad – that's how anger happens: anger is a temporary madness. If you don't allow a leakage now and then you will gather so much you will explode, you will go nuts. But if you are continuously concerned with this you are already nuts.

This has been my observation, that people who meditate, pray, seek and search for the truth are more prone to neurosis than other people. And the reason is: they are concerned with themselves too much, too egocentric, just continuously thinking of this and that, this block, that block, this anger, that sadness, headache, backache, stomach, legs…they are continuously moving inside. They are never okay, they cannot be, because the body is a vast phenomenon and many things go on.

And if nothing is happening then too they are worried: why is nothing happening? And immediately they have to create something because that has become their constant business, occupation; otherwise they feel lost. What to do? Nothing is happening! How is it possible that nothing is happening to me?

They feel their ego only when something is happening – maybe it is depression, sadness, anger, an illness, but if something is they are okay, they can feel themselves.

Have you seen children? They pinch themselves to feel that they are. That child remains in you – you would like to pinch and see whether you are or not.

It is said about Mark Twain that once at a dinner party he was suddenly in a panic and he said, "Sorry, I will have to leave, and you will have to call a doctor. It seems my right leg has become paralyzed."

The lady sitting by his side started laughing and said, "Don't be worried, you have been pinching *my* leg."

Then Mark Twain said, "Once twenty years ago a doctor said to me, 'Some day or other your right side will get paralyzed,' so since then I have been pinching myself; I always feel, twenty or thirty times a day, whether it has gone. Just now I was pinching and"...he was pinching somebody else's leg.

But why go on pinching? Why be concerned with paralysis? It is more of a disease if you have to pinch your leg thirty times counted a day for twenty years. This is worse than paralysis! Paralysis happens once; this is happening thirty times a day for twenty years. They say a brave man dies once and cowards die millions of times – because they go on pinching and feeling whether they are dead yet or not.

Your diseases help you to retain your ego. You feel that something is happening – of course not bliss, not ecstasy, but sadness and "Nobody is as sad as I am," and "Nobody is as blocked as I am," and "Nobody has such a migraine as I have got." You feel superior there, everybody else is inferior.

If you are concerned too much with yourself remember, you will not attain. This over-concern will enclose you, and the way is right before your eyes. You have to open your eyes, not close them.

Now try to understand this parable.

A master was asked by a curious monk: "What is the way?"

The first thing is to understand that the monk is curious, not a seeker. If you are a seeker you inquire in a different way. You inquire with your being, you put yourself at stake, you become a gambler. If you are simply curious it is just like an itch; you feel a subtle itch in the mind but it is nothing, you are not really concerned with it, not sincere about it – whatsoever the answer you will not bother. It will not change you. And a curious man is a superficial man. You cannot ask such questions out of curiosity, you have to ask them out of a very authentic search. And when you go to a master you feel you have to ask something; otherwise you will be thought foolish.

Many people come to me and I know from where they are asking. Sometimes they are simply curious: because they have come, now they have to ask; otherwise they will be thought foolish. And by asking they prove they *are* foolish, because if the question has not really arisen in you, if the question has not become a deep inquiry, if the question does not put everything at stake, if the question is not a problem of life and death to decide, if you are not ready to be transformed by the answer, you are foolish if you ask. And if you are not questioning it from the heart, it is difficult to give any answer, and even if an answer is given you will misunderstand it.

The monk was a curious monk, that's why in this parable he does not awake. Otherwise...we have been studying many parables; when the search is true, in the end, satori happens, a certain enlightenment comes. Suddenly a disciple becomes alert, as if someone has shaken him out of his sleep. A clarity comes. Maybe only for a split second, but clouds disperse and the vast sky is seen. The clouds will come again – that's not the problem, but now you know what real sky is and you will carry this seed within you. Rightly taken care of, this seed will become a tree, and thousands will be able to find rest and shelter under you. But if you are curious, nothing will happen. If you are curious, the question has not come out of the heart. It is an intellectual itch – and in mind, seeds cannot be sown.

Jesus has a parable – he was continuously talking about it. A farmer went to sow seeds. He just threw them here and there. Some fell on the road; they never sprouted because the road was hard and the seeds could not penetrate the soil, they could not move in the deeper, darker realm of the soil...because only there does birth happen, only in the deep dark does God start working. The work is secret work, it is hidden.

Some fell by the side of the road; they sprouted, but animals destroyed them. Only some fell on the right soil; they not only sprouted, they grew to their full height, they flowered, they came to fulfillment, and one seed came to be millions of seeds.

If you ask from curiosity, you are asking from the road. The head is just a road – it has to be, it has such a constant traffic. It has to be very hard, almost concrete. Even on your roads the traffic is not so much as in your head. So many thoughts going here and there at fast speed! We have not yet been able to invent a faster vehicle than thought – our fastest vehicles are nothing before thought. Your astronauts may reach the moon, but they cannot reach it with the speed of thought, they will take time; you can simply immediately reach the moon in thought. For thought, it is as if space does not exist: one moment you can be here, next moment in London and the next in New York, and hop around the world many times within a second. So much traffic...the road is almost concrete; throw something there, it will never sprout.

Curiosity comes from the head. It is like asking a master something just as if you have encountered him in the market and you ask him. I know such people. I was traveling so much it was a problem to avoid such people. Even on the platform – I am going to catch a train and they will accompany me and they will ask, "What about God? Does God exist or not?" These people are curious and they are foolish! Never ask a question out of curiosity, because it is useless, wasting your time and others."

If somebody has asked a question to this master right from the heart, the end would have been different. The man would have flowered into satori, there would have been a fulfillment. But there is no end like that because the very beginning was wrong. A master gives you an answer out of compassion, knowing well that you are curious – but maybe, who knows, even accidents happen; sometimes curious people also become authentically interested, nobody knows.

A master was asked by a curious monk: "What is the way?" "It is right before your eyes," said the master.

This is absurd because if it is really right before the eyes then why do people seek, why do people inquire? And why can't they see for themselves?

A few things to be understood. One: the closer a thing, the more difficult it is to see it – the closest almost impossible, because eyes need a certain space, perspective, to see. I can see you, but if I go on coming closer and closer and closer everything will be blurred; your face will be blurred, lines will lose their shape. And if I go on coming and coming and just put my eyes on your face, nothing will be seen – your face will become a wall. But still I can see a little because a little distance will be there.

Not even that much distance exists between you and the real. It is just touching your eyes. It is just touching your skin – not only that, it is penetrating the skin. It is moving in your blood. It is beating in your heartbeat. It is you. The way is not only in front of your eyes, the way is you. You are one with it. The traveler is not different from the way, not in reality; they are one.

So how to see it? No perspective, no space...? Unless you attain to a clear intelligence, to a clarity of understanding, you will not be able to see it. Unless you become so intensely aware, you will not be able to see it. The distance is not there, so ordinary ways of looking *at* will not do; you need an extraordinary awareness, to be so extraordinarily alert that nothing is asleep in you. Suddenly the door opens. The way is there – you are the way. But you miss because it is there already. It has always been there – before you were born.

You were born on the way, in the way, for the way, of the way – because the way is the reality.

Remember, this way doesn't go to a goal; this way is the goal. In fact there is no traveling, just staying alert, just being still, silent, not doing anything. Just becoming a clarity, an awareness, a silent cool understanding.

> *"It is right before your eyes," said the master. "Why do I not see it for myself?" asked the monk.*

When you are curious, every answer will create another question, because curiosity can never be satisfied. Inquiry can be satisfied, inquiry can come to an end, to a conclusion; never curiosity, because you bring again the same curious mind to the answer, again a new question comes out of it. You can satisfy one who is really in inquiry, you cannot satisfy one who is simply asking, *"Why do I not see it for myself?"*

Another thing: a curious person deep down is not concerned with reality, is concerned only with himself. He says, *"Why do I not see it for myself?* Why can you see it and why can't I see it? I cannot believe you, I cannot trust, and if it is right in front of my eyes then why can't I see it?"

> *"Because you are thinking of yourself," said the master.*

The way is there, and you are thinking about yourself: "Why can't I see?" Nobody can see who is filled so much with the ego. Put it aside, because the ego means your whole past, all that you have experienced, all that you have been conditioned for, all that you have known, studied, collected, gathered – information, scripture, knowledge – all that is your ego, the whole lot, and if you are concerned with it, you cannot see it.

> *"What about you?" said the monk.*

Whatsoever a master says, every answer can become a satori – if the person is right. Just the first thing, when he said, *"It is right before your eyes"* would have become an enlightenment if the right person had been there. He missed; the next answer would have become the understanding.

> *"Why do I not see it for myself?" he asked. "Because you are thinking of yourself."*

But no. Curiosity cannot be satisfied, it never comes to an end. Suddenly, whenever you touch somebody's "I," he suddenly jumps on you. He said:

"And what about you...Do you see it?"

Ego always feels: If I cannot see it, how can anybody else see it? The ego can never feel that anybody else can be egoless: impossible. And if you can feel this your ego has already started dying. If you can feel that somebody can be egoless, already the grip is loosening. The ego won't allow you to feel that anybody has ever been without an ego. And because of your ego you go on projecting egos on others.

Many books have been written about Jesus – more than about anybody else – and many books try to prove that Jesus must have been a very deep egoist because he goes on saying, "I am the son of God; I and my father are one." He is saying: I am God. Many psychoanalysts have tried to explain that he was neurotic. How can you say you are God? You must be an egoist.

And that's how Jews felt when Jesus was alive. They also felt: this man is just mad with his ego! What is he saying – that he is God, or the only son of God? Claiming so much for himself! And they mocked. They mocked, they laughed.

And when they crucified Jesus their behavior with him is simply incomprehensible. They put a crown of thorns on his head and said, "You, King of the Jews, son of God, you and your father are one – remember us when we also come to your Kingdom of God." They forced him to carry his cross. He was weak, the cross was very heavy – they had made it very heavy knowingly, and they forced him just like an ordinary criminal to carry his own cross. And he was feeling thirsty, because it was a hill where he was crucified; the hill is known as Golgotha. It was uphill, he was carrying his big heavy cross; he was perspiring, feeling thirsty, and people were mocking all around and making jokes about him, and they said, "Look – the King of the Jews! Look! The man who claims that he is the son of God."

Many had gathered there just to enjoy it – it was a sort of amusement, a merriment. The whole town had gathered there just to throw stones at this man. Why were they taking such a revenge? – because they felt that this man had hurt their egos. He claims that he is God himself. They couldn't understand that this man had no ego at all; hence the claim. The claim was not coming from the ego, the claim was simply a reality. When your ego drops you are also a god.

But one can claim from the ego. All our claims are from the ego, so we cannot see how a person can claim without the ego. Krishna in the Gita says to Arjuna, "Come to my feet. Leave all, and surrender to me." Hindus are not so bold, and they are very mannerly; they have not written that this man is an egoist. But in the West many have felt the same as with Jesus: What manner of man is this who says, "Come to my feet!" Our egos cannot feel that when Krishna is saying to Arjuna, "Come to my feet," there is no one inside. It is coming to nobody's feet. But egos cannot see this. You can see only that which you are, you cannot see that which you are not.

Immediately the monk said, "And what about you?" He feels hurt because the master has said, "Because you are thinking of yourself, that's why you are missing the way – and it is right in front of you." Now this man is reacting. He would like to hurt the master also. He says,

"What about you...Do you see it?"

He wanted, he expected – because of his own ego – that this man would say, "Yes, I see it," and then everything would have been easy. He could have said, "Then you are also concerned with your I; how can you see it? You also assert your ego – how can you see it? We are just the same." And he would have gone away happy, because the account would have been closed with this man.

But you cannot close your account with a master. He never fulfills your expectation. He is simply unpredictable. You cannot get him caught in your trap because his ways always change. Your mind cannot give you the answer which he is going to give.

> The master said: "So long as you see double, saying I don't, and you do, and so on, your eyes are clouded."

The master has not said anything about himself. If there had been an Arjuna there the master would have said, "Yes, I know it – and please, don't you go around and around, come to my feet." But this man was no Arjuna – just a curious man, not really interested. It was just a problem, not a question. He is not going to change himself in any way. At the most he will have a little more information, he will become a little more knowledgeable.

That's why the master says, *"So long as you see double, saying I don't, and you do, and so on, your eyes are clouded"* – because the monk's eyes are clouded by "I" and "you." They are one phenomenon, try to understand this. "I" and "you" are two aspects of the same coin: this side "I," that side "you." If "I" drops, "you" drop. If "I" is there no more, "you" are there no more, because when the coin drops both the aspects drop together. I – that is one pole, thou – that is another pole; they both drop or they both remain. If you are, then all around you is a crowd, a milling crowd of "I's," "you's"; if you are not, the whole crowd has disappeared as if it was just a nightmare – it was – and simply silence exists, in which there is no division, not even this one of I and thou.

That's why Zen people never talk about God, because, they say, "if we talk about God we will have to say thou." Buddha never talked about God, and he said, "Don't pray, because your prayer will continue the division, the duality, the dual vision – I and thou."

At the very peak also you will carry the same disease, in subtle ways: you will say I, you will say thou. Howsoever lovingly you say it, the division exists, and with the division the love is not possible. That is the difference between Jewish thinking and Jesus' way of thinking.

Martin Buber has written a book, *I and Thou*. He is one of the most profound Jewish thinkers – but he remains a thinker. He may talk about mysticism, but that talk is also one of a thinker and philosopher, because at the very end he retains the old division, I and thou. Now the thou is not here, in this world, but God has become the thou, but the old division persists.

Jews, Mohammedans have always denied that you can become one with God. Just because of that fear that the I may claim that it has become God. They have retained the division. They say that you can come closer and closer and closer, but you will remain you and he will remain he. You will remain an I and he has to be addressed as thou.

And that is the trouble that Jesus created, because he said, "I and my father in heaven are one." He dropped the division of I and thou. That has been the trouble with Mohammedans in India – they couldn't understand the Upanishads, they couldn't understand the Hindu teaching that you are the same as him. Drop the I and he is no more a thou. In fact, suddenly the poles disappear and the energy is one. Here I disappear, there you disappear, and the energy is one.

Sometimes in deep love glimpses happen when neither you are an I nor is your lover or beloved a thou – but sometimes only, it is very rare, when two energies simply meet and you cannot find the division, where they are divided. They mingle and meet and merge and become one; you cannot feel where the boundary is, suddenly the boundary has disappeared. That's why love creates fear.

Deep love creates deep fear. It looks like death because the I disappears, the you disappears – and it is a sort of death. And when you die, only then do you enter into the divine. But then the divine is no longer a god, you cannot address him; hence no prayer exists in Buddhism. So Christians can't believe what type of religion Buddhism is: no prayer?

"How can you pray?" Buddha said. "Because the prayer can be possible only with a division – I praying, thou listening – how can you pray?"

In Buddhism only meditation exists. Try to understand the difference: prayer continues with the old division of I and thou, meditation drops the division. Prayer has to lead finally to meditation. Prayer cannot be the final thing. It is beautiful, but it is not the ultimate. The ultimate can only be this: when both have disappeared and only oneness exists. Tremendous...vast! You become afraid of it! All the cozy divisions of I and thou disappear. All relationship disappears – that is the fear; that's what Buber is afraid of. He's afraid that if there is no I and no thou, the whole phenomenon will be so tremendous and so terrible and fear-creating...because no relationship is possible.

Relationship gives you a home; relationship gives you a feeling of coziness; relationship gives you something which does not look like a *tremendum*, which is not fear-creating. Meditation has to be the ultimate, because prayer can never lead to the non-dual – and this is what the master is saying. He says:

> *"So long as you see double, saying I don't, and you do, and so on, your eyes are clouded."*

Division is the clouding. Through division is the mist in the eyes, through division is the dust in the eyes, through division your eyes are murky, cloudy, distorted. Drop the division and the way is there.

But a curious mind goes on and on and on. The monk could have become enlightened at that moment, because enlightenment is nothing but a clarity, an understanding. Such profound truths – and the seeds go on missing, because the man is just a highway, the man is not a right soil. He said again:

> *"When there is neither I nor you, can one see it?"*

Look: avoid this tendency of being curious. He is not listening at all, he has not understood a single word, he has not felt anything – he goes on and on, and on the same surface, at the same level, not even an inch deeper. His questioning is not an inquiry now, rather a reaction: whatsoever the master says, he reacts. Whenever this happens it means that when the master is speaking he is thinking at that moment also, preparing the next question. He is not listening.

> *"When there is neither I nor you, can one see it?"*

He will again be expecting. Whenever you ask a question of someone you already have an expected answer. If it fits with your expected answer, then the man is right; if it doesn't fit, then this man is talking nonsense.

Never come to me with your expected answers, because if you already have the answer then there is no need to ask. And this is the difference – if you ask a question without any expected answer, you will be able to hear the answer; if you have a subtle expectation that *this* is going to be the answer, if your mind has already given you an answer, you will not be able to listen. You will simply be listening either to be confirmed that your answer is right, or to be confirmed that this man is wrong – but in either case you are right.

Never ask a question with the feeling that you are right. If you are right there is no need to ask. Always ask the question from the position of a man who is ignorant, knowing well that "I don't know," so how can you expect, how can you create an answer? Knowing perfectly that "I don't know," ask – and you are a right soil, and the seeds will fall in it, and a large crop will be possible.

Asked the man again:

"When there is neither I nor you, can one see it?"

He's trying to put this master in a corner, as mind always tries – because now he must say yes. If he says yes then the curious mind can ask again, "Then who will see it if there is neither I nor you?" And if you say, "Yes, then the way can be seen," then the question will arise automatically, "Then who will see it? When I am not there and you are not there, then who will see it?"

But you cannot put an enlightened man into a corner. You can put another mind into a corner, then you can play a game of chess, but a man who has no mind – you cannot put him in a corner and you cannot defeat him, because he is not there. His victory is absolute. With him, either you are defeated or you escape. His victory is absolute because he is no longer there – who can be defeated? Who can be forced into a corner?

This is a beautiful corner. This man must have been a professor or a logician or a pundit. He has really brought the master to a corner within three questions – if a man were there he would have been put in a corner. But because a master is not, how can you force him into a corner? He is the whole sky. How can you force the whole sky into a corner? All corners exist in him, but you cannot force him into a corner.

The master said, "When there is neither I nor you, who is the one who wants to see it?"

Really, when you see...you see only when you are not. When you are not, there is no question of trying to see, wanting to see, desiring to see. Who will desire? When you are not, who bothers about the way? The way has already happened. Who bothers about God? – it is already the case!

Here you disappear and there everything is ready, everything that you ever sought, everything that you were seeking, every inquiry fulfilled. Here you dissolve and all answers disappear and all queries dissolve. Suddenly the truth is there.

Your dissolution is the truth. Your "not being there" is the way. Your absence is the presence of God.

Enough for today.

not mind, not buddha, not things

A monk asked Nansen: "Is there a teaching no master ever preached before?"
Nansen said: "Yes there is." "What is it?" asked the monk.
Nansen replied: "It is not mind, it is not Buddha, it is not things."

The "teachings" of the awakened ones are not teachings at all because they cannot be taught – so how to call them teachings? A teaching is that which can be taught. But nobody can teach you the truth. It is impossible. You can learn it, but it cannot be taught. It has to be learned. You can absorb it, you can imbibe it, you can live with a master and allow it to happen but it cannot be taught. It is a very indirect process.

Teaching is direct: something is said. Learning is indirect: something is indicated, not said – rather, something is shown. A finger is raised towards the sun, but the finger is not the point; you have to leave the finger and look at the sun, or at the moon. A master teaches but the teaching is just like the finger: you have to leave it and look where it indicates – the dimension, the direction, the beyond.

A teacher teaches, a master *lives* – you can learn from his life, the way he moves, the way he looks at you, the way he touches you, the way he is. You can imbibe it, you can allow it to happen, you can remain available, you can remain open and vulnerable. There is no way to say it directly, that's why those who are very intellectual miss it – because they know only one way of learning and that is direct. They ask, What is truth? – and they expect an answer.

This is what happened when Pontius Pilate asked Jesus, "What is truth?" and Jesus remained silent – not even a flicker, as if the question had not been asked, as if there was no Pontius Pilate standing before him and asking. Jesus remained the same as he was before the question was raised, nothing changed. Pontius Pilate must have thought this man a little mad, because he had asked a direct question: "What is truth?" and this man remained silent as if he had not heard.

Pontius Pilate was a viceroy, a well-educated, cultured, cultivated man; Jesus was a son of a carpenter, uneducated, uncultivated. It was as if two poles were meeting, two opposite poles. Pontius Pilate knew all philosophy – he had learned it, he knew all the scriptures. This man Jesus was absolutely uneducated, in fact he knew nothing – or, he knew *only* nothing. Standing before Pontius Pilate, totally silent, he replied – but the reply was indirect: he raised a finger. That total silence was the finger raised towards truth. But Pontius Pilate missed. He thought, This man is crazy. Either he is deaf, cannot hear, or he does not know, is ignorant – that's why he is silent. But silence can be a finger raised towards truth – that is incomprehensible to the intellectual Pontius Pilate.

He missed. The greatest opportunity! He may be still wandering somewhere in search of "What is truth?" On that day truth was standing before him. Could he be silent for a moment? Could he be in the presence of Jesus, not asking? just looking, watching, waiting? Could he imbibe Jesus a little? Could he allow Jesus to work upon him? The opportunity was there – and Jesus indicated it. But Pontius Pilate missed.

Intellect will always miss the teaching of the awakened ones, because intellect believes in the direct way, and you cannot hit truth in such a direct way. It is a very subtle phenomenon, delicate, the most delicate possible; you have to move very cautiously, you have to move very indirectly. You have to feel it – it comes through the heart, it never comes through the head. Teaching comes through the head, learning happens through the heart.

Remember my emphasis. It is not the master who teaches, it is the disciple who learns. It is up to you – to learn or not to learn; it is not up to me to teach or not to teach. A master, because of the way he is, goes on teaching. His every moment, his every breath is a teaching, his whole being is a teaching, a message. The message is not different from the master. If it is different then the master is simply a teacher, not a master; then he is repeating words of others. Then he is not awakened himself, then he has a borrowed knowledge; inside he remains as ignorant as the student. There is no difference in their being, they differ in their knowledge.

A teacher and a student are on the same level as far as their being is concerned; as far as their knowledge is concerned they are different: the teacher knows more, the student knows less. Some day the student will know more, he himself will become a teacher, he can even come to know more than the teacher – because it is the horizontal line of accumulation. If you accumulate more knowledge, information, you can become a teacher, but not a master.

A master is truth. He does not know *about* truth, he has become it, so he cannot help himself. It is not a question of to teach or not to teach, it is not a choice. Even if he is fast asleep, he goes on teaching. Buddha fast asleep – you simply sit near him, you can learn much; you can even become enlightened, because the way he sleeps is totally different. The quality differs because the being differs. Buddha eating – you just watch, and he is giving a message. The message is not separate, that's why I say he cannot help himself. He *is* the message.

You cannot ask the question, "What is truth?" Anyway, he will not answer you directly. He may laugh or he may offer you a cup of tea, or he may hold your hand and sit silently, or he may take you for a morning walk into the woods, or he may say, "Look! This mountain is beautiful!" But whatsoever he is doing is an indirect way of indicating, indicating towards his being.

All that is beautiful, true, good, is like happiness – I say "like happiness" because you may be able to understand that. You have known a little of happiness. Maybe you have lived very miserably, as people live. But sometimes, even in spite of yourself, moments happen when happiness enters you – you are filled with an unknown silence, an unknown bliss; suddenly those moments come. You cannot find a man who has not had a few moments of happiness in his life.

But have you observed one thing? – whenever they come they come indirectly. Suddenly they happen, unexpectedly they happen. You were not waiting for them, you were doing something else, and suddenly you become aware. If you are waiting for them, expecting them, they never come; if you are directly in search, you will miss.

Somebody says, "When I go swimming in the river I feel much happiness." You are also in search of it; you say, "Then I will come also," and you follow. You are seeking happiness – you are not concerned with swimming directly, you are concerned directly with happiness. Swimming is just a means. You swim for hours; you are tired, you wait, you expect – and you are frustrated. Nothing is happening, the bliss is not there, and you tell your friend: "You deceived me. I have been swimming for hours, feel completely tired, and not a single moment of happiness has happened."

No, it cannot happen. When you are lost in swimming so completely that there is nobody, the boat is empty, there is nobody in the house, the host is silent, swimming is so deep that the swimmer is lost in it and you simply swim, you play with the river, and the rays of the sun and the morning breeze, and you are simply lost in it...and there is happiness! Swimming by the bank, swimming all over the river, spreading all over existence, jumping from one ray to another ray of light – every breeze brings it. But if you expect you miss, because expectation leads you into the future and happiness is in the present. It is not a result of any activity; it is a consequence, it is a byproduct. You are so deeply involved, it happens.

It is a consequence, remember, it is not a result; a result can be expected. If you put two plus two, then four, the result, can be expected; it is already there in the two plus two, it will come out. The result can be expected if things are mechanical, mathematical. But a consequence is not a mechanical thing, it is an organic phenomenon. It happens only when you are not expecting. The guest comes to your door and knocks when you were not thinking about the guest at all. It always comes like a stranger, it always surprises you. You suddenly feel something has happened – and if you start thinking about what is happening, you will immediately miss. If you say, "How wonderful! How beautiful!" it is already gone; the mind is back. Again you are in the same misery, thrown back.

One has to learn deeply that all that is beautiful is indirect. You cannot make an attack upon it, you cannot be aggressive with it; you cannot snatch from existence. If you are violent and aggressive, you will not find it.

Move towards it like a drunkard, not knowing where, not knowing why, like a drunkard – lost completely, you move towards it.

All meditations are subtle ways to make you drunk, subtle ways to make you drunkards of the unknown, drunkards of the divine. Then you are no longer there with your conscious mind functioning, then you are not there expecting, then you are not there planning for the future. You are *not*. And when you are not, suddenly flowers start showering on you, flowers of bliss. Just like Subhuti, empty...you are surprised! You were never expecting, you never knew! You never felt that you ever deserved it; that's how it is felt – like a grace, because it is not something you have brought on, it is something which has happened.

So one thing: truth cannot be taught, bliss cannot be given to you, ecstasy cannot be purchased in the market. But your mind continuously thinks in terms of getting, purchasing, collecting, finding; your mind never thinks in terms of happening because you cannot control happening – everything else you can control.

I have heard...

Once a man became suddenly rich. Of course, when it happened he col- lected all those things he had always been desiring – a very big house, a big car, swimming pool, this and that. And then he sent his daughter to college. He had always wanted to be educated but he could not be; now he wanted to fulfill all his desires, and whatsoever he couldn't do he wanted his children to do. But after a few days the dean of the college wrote a letter to him, and in the letter wrote: "To be frank, we cannot admit your girl to the college because she has no capacity to learn."

The father said, "Just capacity? Don't bother! I will purchase the best capacity available in the market for her."

How can you purchase capacity? But a man who has become suddenly rich thinks only in terms of purchasing. You think in terms of power – power to purchase, power to get something. Remember, truth cannot be got through power; it comes when you are humble. You have nothing to purchase it with, it cannot be purchased. And it is good that it cannot be purchased; otherwise no one would be able to give the cost. It is good that it *happens*; otherwise how would you purchase it? All that you have is rubbish. Because it cannot be purchased, that's why sometimes it can happen. It is a gift. It is a sharing of the divine with you – but the divine can share only when you allow. Hence I say you can learn it but it cannot be taught.

In fact in the spiritual world there are only disciples, not masters. Masters are there but they are inactive, passive forces. They cannot do anything, they are just there like a flower: if nobody comes, the flower will go on spreading its fragrance into emptiness. It cannot help itself. The whole thing is decided by the disciple: how to learn? How to learn from a flower? And a flower shows something but doesn't say it. It cannot be said. How can the flower say what beauty is? – the flower *is* beauty. You have to gain, attain, eyes to see, a nose to smell, ears to hear the subtle sound that comes to the flower when the breeze passes by. And you need a heart to feel the throbbing of the flower, because it throbs also – everything alive throbs, the whole existence throbs.

You may not have observed this because it is impossible before you go into deep meditation; you cannot observe the fact that the whole universe breathes. And just as you expand and shrink the whole existence shrinks and expands. Just as you inhale and the chest fills, and then you exhale and the air goes out and the chest shrinks, the same rhythm exists in existence. The whole existence breathes, expands, inhales, exhales – and if you can find the rhythm of existence and become one with the rhythm, you have attained.

The whole art of ecstasy, meditation, *samadhi*, is: How to become one with the rhythm of the universe. When it exhales, you exhale. When it inhales, you inhale. You live in it, are not separate, are one with it. Difficult, because the universe is vast.

A master is the whole universe in miniature. If you can learn how to inhale with the master and how to exhale with the master, if you can learn simply that, you will learn all.

At the moment when Pontius Pilate asked, "What is truth?" if he had known anything, even the *ABC* of disciplehood, the next thing would have been to just close his eyes and inhale and exhale with Jesus...just inhale and exhale with Jesus. The way he inhales, you inhale, and in the same rhythm; the way he exhales, you exhale, and in the same rhythm – and suddenly there is oneness: the disciple has disappeared, the master has disappeared. In that oneness you know what truth is because in that oneness you taste the master.

And now you have the key – and this has not been given either, remember, it has been learned by you. It has not been given to you; it cannot be given, it is so subtle. And with this key now every lock can be opened. It is a master key, no ordinary key – it doesn't open one lock, it opens all locks. Now you have the key, and once you have the key you use it with the universe.

Kabir has said, "Now I am in much difficulty. God and my guru, the whole existence and my master, are standing before me; now to whom do I bow first? To whose feet now do I go first? I am in deep trouble!" And then he says, "Forgive me, God. I will have to go to my master's feet first, because he has shown you to me. I come to you through him. So even if you are standing before me, excuse me, I have to touch my master's feet first."

Beautiful...this has to be so, because the master becomes the door to the unknown, he becomes the key to the whole existence. He is the truth.

Learn how to be in the presence of the master, how to breathe with him, how to silently allow him to move in you, how to silently merge into him, because the master is nothing but God who has knocked at your door. It is the whole universe concentrated. Don't ask questions, live with him.

Now try to penetrate this story – small, but very significant.

A monk asked Nansen: "Is there a teaching no master ever preached before?"

All that has been preached is not the teaching; the real teaching has never been preached, it cannot be told.

Buddha said to Mahakashyap, "To all others I have told that which can be told, and to you I give that which cannot be told, cannot be said." Now for two thousand years followers of Buddha have been asking again and again and again: What was given to Mahakashyap? What was given to Mahakashyap, what was the teaching that Buddha never told to anybody, that even Buddha said cannot be told because words will not be able to carry it?

Words are so narrow, the vastness of truth cannot be forced into them – and they are so superficial, how can they carry the depth? It is just like this: How can a wave on the ocean carry the depth of the ocean? It cannot. By the very nature of things it is impossible because if a wave exists it has to exist on the surface. The wave cannot go to the depth because if it goes to the depth it is a wave no more. The wave exists only in touch with the winds – it has to be on the surface, it cannot go to the depth. And the depth cannot come to the wave because the moment it comes to the surface it becomes itself the wave, it is no more the depth.

This is the problem. The truth is the center and the words exist on the surface, on the periphery – where people meet, where the wind and the ocean meet, where the question and the answer meet, where the master and disciple meet; just there on the surface words exist. Truth cannot come to the surface, it is the very depth, and the words cannot go to the truth, they are the very surface.

So what to do? All that can be said will be just so-so; it will not be true, it will not be untrue, it will be just in the middle – and very dangerous, because if the disciple has not been in tune with the master he will misunderstand. If he has been in tune with the master, only then will he understand because then there exists a rapport.

Understanding is not a question of keen intelligence; understanding is a question of deep rapport. Understanding is not a question of reason, intellect, logic. Understanding is a question of deep sympathy, or even of deep empathy; hence the central significance of trust, faith. Understanding happens through faith, because in faith you trust, in trust you become sympathetic, in trust rapport is possible – because you are not defensive, you leave the doors open.

> This monk asked Nansen: "Is there a teaching no master ever preached before?"

Yes, there is a teaching; in fact all the teaching is there, which no master has ever preached before. Then why do masters go on preaching? Why is it Buddha went on talking for forty years? Why do I go on talking, whether you listen or not? Why do they talk? If that which is to be learned cannot be said, then why do they go on talking?

Talking is just a bait. Through talking you are caught, you cannot understand anything else. Talking is just giving sweets to children. Then they start coming to you, blissfully unaware that talking is not the point; blissfully unaware they come for the sweets, they come for the toys. They are happy with the toys. But the master knows that once they start coming, by and by the toys can be taken away, and by and by they will start loving the master without the toys – and once that happens, words can be dropped.

Whenever a disciple is ready, words can be dropped. They are just a way to bring you closer because you cannot understand anything except words. If somebody speaks, you understand; if somebody is silent you cannot understand. What will you understand? Silence is just a wall for you, you cannot find your way in it. And silence carries a deep fear also, because it is deathlike. Words are lifelike, silence is deathlike. If somebody is silent you start feeling afraid and scared – if somebody goes on being silent you will try to escape from there because it is too much, the silence becomes so heavy for you.

Why? – because you cannot be silent, and if you cannot be silent you cannot understand silence. You are a chattering; inside a monkey is sitting, continuously chattering. Somebody has defined man as nothing but a monkey with metaphysics, with some philosophy, that's all. And that philosophy is nothing but a better way of chattering, more systematic, more logical, but still chattering.

A master has to talk to bring you nearer. The nearer you come, the more he will drop it. Once you are in the grip of his silence there is no need to talk. Once you know what silence is, once you have become silent, a new rapport exists. Now things can be said without any saying, messages can be given without ever giving them – without him giving them you can receive them. Now the phenomenon of discipleship has happened.

One of the most beautiful phenomena in the world is that of being a disciple, because now you know what rapport is. Now you breathe, inhale, exhale with the master; now you lose your boundaries and become one with him. Now something of his heart starts flowing towards you; now something of him comes into you.

A monk asked Nansen: "Is there a teaching no master ever preached before?"

Nansen is one of the most famous Zen masters. Many stories are told about him; one I have been telling you many times. I will repeat it again, because stories like that are to be repeated again and again, so that you can imbibe them. They are a sort of nourishment. Every day you have to take nourishment; you won't say, "Yesterday morning I took breakfast so now there is no need." Every day you have to eat; you don't say, "Yesterday I took food, now what is the need?"

These stories – they are a nourishment. There exists a special word in India, it cannot be translated. In English the word *reading* exists, in India we have two words for it: one means reading, the other means the reading of the same thing again and again. You read the same thing again and again and again – it is like a part. Every day you read the Gita in the morning; then it is not a reading, because you have read it many times. Now it is a sort of nourishment. You don't read it, you eat it every day.

It is also a great experiment, because every day you will come to new shades of meaning, every day new nuances. The same book, the same words, but every day you feel some new depth has opened unto you. Every day you feel you are reading something new, because the Gita, or books like that, have a depth. If you read them once you will move on the surface; if you read them twice, a little deeper; thrice – you go on. A thousand times, and then you will understand that you can never exhaust these books, it is impossible. The more you become alert, aware, the more your consciousness grows deeper – that is the meaning.

I will repeat this story of Nansen. A professor came to him, a professor of philosophy... Philosophy is a disease, and it is like a cancer: no medicine exists for it, yet you have to go through surgery, a great operation is needed. And philosophy has a similar type of growth, a canceric growth: once it is in you it goes on growing by itself, and it takes all your energies. It is a parasite. You go on becoming weaker and weaker and it becomes stronger and stronger and stronger. Every word creates another word – and it can go on infinitely.

A philosopher came to Nansen. Nansen lived on a small hill, and when the philosopher came uphill he was tired and perspiring. The moment he entered the hut of Nansen he said, "What is truth?"

Nansen said, "Truth can wait a little. There is no hurry. Right now you need a cup of tea, you are so tired!" Nansen went in and prepared a cup of tea.

This can happen only with a Zen master. In India you cannot think of Shankaracharya preparing tea for you. For *you* – and Shankaracharya preparing tea? Impossible! Or think of Mahavira preparing tea for you...absurd!

But with a Zen master this can happen. They have a totally different attitude, they love life. They are not anti-life; they affirm life, they are not against it – and they are ordinary people, and they say that to be ordinary is the most extraordinary thing. They live a really simple life. When I say a *really* simple life I mean not an imposed simplicity. In India you can find such impostors all over – simplicity is imposed. They may be naked, completely naked, but they are not simple; their nakedness is very complex. Their nakedness is not the nakedness of a child; they have cultivated it, and how can a cultivated thing be simple? They have disciplined themselves for it, and how can a disciplined thing be simple? It is very complex.

Your clothes are not so complex as the nakedness of a Jaina Digambara monk. He has struggled for it for many years. They have five steps – you have to fulfill each step by and by, and then you attain to nakedness. It is an achievement, and how can an achievement be simple? If you work for it for many years, if you make every effort to achieve it, how can it be simple? A simple thing can be achieved here and now, immediately, there is no need to work for it.

Nakedness when simple is a majestic phenomenon; you simply drop clothes. It happened to Mahavira – it was simple. When he left his house he had clothes on; then, passing by a rosebush, his shawl got caught in the thorns, so he thought: It is evening time and the rosebush is going to sleep, it will be disturbing to remove it. So he tore off half of the shawl that was entangled in the thorns and left it there. It was evening time and the gesture was beautiful. It was not for nakedness he did it, it was for that rosebush. And the next day in the morning, with the half-shawl left, half naked, a beggar asked him for something – and he had nothing else to give. How to say no when you still have something left to give – that half-shawl? So he gave it to the beggar. This nakedness is something superb, simple, ordinary; it happened, it was not practiced. But a Jaina monk practices it.

Zen monks are very simple people. They live an ordinary life as everybody else. They don't make differences, because all differences are basically egoistic. And this game you can play in many ways, but the game remains the same: higher than you. The game remains the same: I have more money, I am higher than you; I have more education, I am higher than you; I am more pious, I am higher than you; I am more religious, I am higher than you; I have renounced more, I am higher than you.

Nansen went in, prepared tea, came out, gave the cup into the professor's hand, poured tea from his kettle. The cup was full. Up to that moment the professor waited because up to that moment everything was rational: a tired man comes and you feel compassion for him and you prepare tea. Of course it is as it should be. Then you fill the cup – that too is okay. But then something irrational happened.

Nansen went on pouring, the cup was overflowing. Then the professor became a little surprised: What is this man doing? Is he mad? But still he waited – he was a well-disciplined man, he could tolerate little things like that. Maybe a little crazy…but then the saucer was also completely full, and Nansen went on pouring.

Now this was too much. Now something had to be done and said, and the professor shrieked, "Stop!" – because now the tea was overflowing on the floor. "What are you doing? Now this cup cannot contain any more tea. Can't you see a simple thing like this? Are you mad?"

Nansen started laughing and said, "That's what I was also thinking: Are you mad? – because you can see that the cup is full and it will not contain a single drop more, but you cannot see that your head is full and it cannot contain a single drop of truth more. Your cup is full in the head, your saucer is full and everything is flowing on the floor – look! Your philosophy is all over my hut and you can't see it? But you are a reasonable man; at least you could see the tea. Now see the other thing."

This Nansen helped many people in different ways to awake, created many sorts of situations for people to awake.

> *A monk asked Nansen: "Is there a teaching no master ever preached before?"*
> *Nansen said: "Yes there is." "What is it?" asked the monk.*
> *Nansen replied: "It is not mind, it is not Buddha, it is not things."*

Now, if no master has ever said it how can Nansen say it? The questioner is foolish, asking a stupid question. If nobody has said it, how can Nansen say it? If buddhas have kept silent about it, if buddhas have not uttered a single word, could not utter, then how can Nansen? But Nansen would like to help even this stupid man.

And there are only stupid men all around, because unless you become enlightened you remain stupid. So stupidity is not a condemnation, it is just a state, a fact. A man who is not enlightened will remain stupid – there is no other way. And if he feels himself wise, then he is more stupid. If he feels that he is stupid, then wisdom has started – then he has started awakening. If you feel you are ignorant, then you are not stupid; if you feel you know you are perfectly stupid – not only stupid but grounded in it so much that there seems no possibility for you to come out of it.

Nansen would like to help this stupid man, because there are no others; that's why he speaks, he answers. But he has to use all negatives; he says nothing positive. He uses three negatives. He says: *"It is not mind, it is not Buddha, it is not things."*

You cannot say the truth but you can say what it is not. You cannot say what it is but you can indicate it negatively. *Via negativa*: saying what it is not. This is all that masters have done. If you insist that they say something, they will say something negative. If you can understand their silence, you understand the affirmative. If you cannot understand their silence but insist on words, they will say something negative.

Understand this: words can do a negative job; silence can do a positive job. Silence is the most positive thing and language is the most negative. When you speak you are moving in the negative world; when you remain silent you are moving into the positive. What is truth? Ask the Upanishads, ask the Koran, the Bible, the Gita; they all say what it is not. What is God? They all say what he is not.

Three things he denies: one – it is not things, the world; it is not that which you see, it is not that which is all around you. It is not that which can be seen by the mind, which the mind can comprehend – it is not objects. And second: it is not the mind, it is not the subject; neither this world around you nor this mind within you. No, these two things are not the teaching, are not the truth.

But the third thing only buddhas have denied, only very perfect masters have denied, and that third thing is: ...*it is not Buddha.*

And what is Buddha?

The world of things is the first boundary around you, then the world of mind, thoughts: things the first boundary, thoughts the second boundary – of course closer, nearer you. You can draw three concentric circles: first circle, the world of things; second circle, the world of thoughts; and then remains the third – and Buddha has denied that also – the self, the witnessing, the soul, the consciousness, the buddha. Only Buddha denies that.

All others have known that: Jesus knows it, Krishna knows it, but they don't deny it because that would be too much for you to understand. So they say two things: they say this world is illusory, and the mind that looks at this world is also illusory. Mind and world are one phenomenon, two aspects of the same coin. The mind creates the dream; the dream is illusory, and the mind, the source, is also illusory. But they say that the third – witnessing, you in your deep consciousness where you are only a witness, not a thinker, where no thought exists, no thing exists, only you exist – they don't deny that. Buddha has denied that also.

He says, "No world, no mind, no soul." That is the highest teaching – because if things are not, how can thoughts be? If thoughts are not, how can you witness them? If the world is illusory then the mind that looks at the world can't be real. The mind is illusory. Then the witness that looks at the mind – how can it be real? Buddha goes to the deepest core of existence. He says, All that you are is unreal; your things, your thoughts and you – all is unreal.

But these are three negatives. Buddha's path is the negative path, his assertions are negative. That's why Hindus called him a *nastika*, they called him an atheist, an absolute nihilist. But he is not. When all these three things are denied, that which remains is truth. When things disappear, thoughts disappear, and the witnessing disappears – these three things that you know

– when all these three disappear, that which remains is truth. And that which remains liberates, that which remains is nirvana, is enlightenment.

Buddha is very, very deep; nobody has gone deeper than that in words. Many people have reached in being but Buddha has tried to be perfect in words also. He never asserts a single positive. If you ask about any positive he simply remains silent. He never says God is, he never says the soul is; in fact he never uses the word *is*. You ask and he will use the word *not*. No is his answer for everything. And if you can understand, if you can feel a rapport, you will see that he is right.

When you deny everything, that doesn't mean you have destroyed everything. That only means you have destroyed the world that you had created. The real remains because the real cannot be denied. But you cannot assert it. You can know it but you cannot state it. When you deny all these three, when you transcend all these three, you become a buddha. You are enlightened.

Buddha says you are awakened only when these three sleeps are broken. One sleep is the sleep with things: many people are asleep there, that is the grossest sleep. Millions of people, ninety-eight percent of the people are asleep there – the first and grossest sleep, the sleep with things. One goes on thinking about his bank balance, one goes on thinking about the house, about clothes, about this and that – and one lives in that. There are people who only study catalogues for things...

I have heard one story...

One religious man was staying overnight in a family. In the morning, as was his habit, he wanted the Bible to read a little and to pray a little. The small child of the house was passing through the room so he asked the kid, he said, "Bring that book" – because he thought the child may not understand what book the Bible was, so he said, "Bring that book which your mother reads every day." The child brought the *Whole Earth Catalogue*, because that was the book the mother read every day.

Ninety-eight percent of people are asleep in things. Try to find out where you are asleep, because the work has to start there. If you are asleep with things, then you have to start from there. Drop that sleep with things.

Why do people go on thinking about things? I used to stay in a house in Calcutta. The woman there must have had at least one thousand saris, and every day it was a problem... When I was there her husband and I would be sitting in the car and her husband would go on honking and she would say, "I am coming!" – and it was difficult for her to decide which sari to wear. So I asked, "Why is this a problem every day?"

So she took me and showed me, and she said, "You would also be puzzled.

I have got one thousand saris and it is difficult to decide which one to choose, which will suit the occasion."

Have you seen people?... From the very morning they start cleaning their car, as if that is their Bible and their god. "Things" is the first sleep, the grossest. If you are attached too much to things and continuously thinking of things, you are asleep there. You have to come out of that. You have to look at what type of attachments you have, where you cling, and for what. What are you going to get there?

You may increase your things, you may accumulate a vast empire, but when you die you will go without things. Death will bring you out of your sleep. Before death brings you out, it is better to bring yourself out; then there will be no pain in death. Death is so painful because this first sleep has to be broken; you are to be snatched away from things.

Then there is the second sleep, the sleep of the mind. There are people who are not concerned with things – only one percent of people – who are not concerned with things but who are concerned with the mind. They don't bother about what type of clothes they use – artists, novelists, poets, painters; they are not worried about things in general, they live in the mind. They can go hungry, they can go naked, they can live in a slum, but they go on working in the mind. The novel they are writing...and they go on thinking, I may not be immortal but my novel that I am going to write is going to be immortal; the painting that I am doing is going to be immortal. But when you cannot be immortal, how can your painting be immortal? When you are to perish, when you are to die, everything that you create will die, because how is it possible that from death something immortal can be born?

Then there are people who go on thinking of philosophy, thoughts, oblivious of things, not worried much about them. It happened once: Immanuel Kant was coming to his class. He was a perfect timekeeper, never missed a single appointment, would never be late; at exactly the right time he would enter. He never cared about his clothes, about his house, or food, or anything – never worried about it, never got married; just a servant would do, because that was not much of a problem and the servant can do the food and take care of the house. He never needed a wife or someone who was intimate, a friend – no; a servant was okay as far as the world of things was concerned. The servant was really the master, because he would purchase everything, he would take care of the money and the house and everything.

Immanuel Kant lived like a stranger in that house. It is said that he never looked at the house, he never knew how many rooms the house had, what type of furniture; even if you were to show him something which had been in his room for thirty years he would not be able to recognize it. But he was concerned much with thoughts – he lived in the world of thoughts, and many stories are told, beautiful stories, because a man who lives in the world of thoughts is always absentminded in the world of things, because you cannot live in two worlds.

He was going to his class; the road was muddy and one of his shoes got stuck, so he left it there, went to the class with one shoe. Somebody asked, "Where is your other shoe?"

He said, "It got stuck just on the way. It is raining and it was muddy."

But the man who had asked said, "Then you could have got it back."

Immanuel Kant said, "There was a series of thoughts in my mind and I didn't like to interfere with it. If I had got concerned with the shoe, the track would have been lost, and such beautiful thoughts were there that who cares whether you come to the class with one shoe or two!" The whole college laughed, but he was not concerned.

Once it happened: he came back after his evening walk...he used to have a walking-stick, and he was so absorbed in his thought that he did everything that was done every day, but forgot something. He was so absentminded that he put the walking-stick on the bed where he used to put himself, and he himself stood in the corner of the room where he used to put the walking-stick...he got a little mixed-up!

After two hours the servant became aware that the light was on – so what was the matter? He looked through the window, and Immanuel Kant was standing with closed eyes in the corner and the walking-stick was fast asleep on the pillow. A man who is asleep too much in the mind will be absentminded in the world. Philosophers, poets, men of literature, painters, musicians – they are all fast asleep there.

And then there is a third sleep: monks, those who have renounced the world, and not only the world but also the mind, who have been meditating for many years and they have stopped the thought process. Now no thoughts move in their inner sky, now no things are there; they are not concerned with things, not concerned with thoughts. But a subtle ego, the "I" – now they call it *atman*, the soul, the self, the Self with a capital "S" – is their sleep; they are asleep there.

Buddha says sleep has to be broken on these three layers, and when all these sleeps are broken, nobody is awake, only awakening is there; nobody is enlightened, only enlightenment is there – just the phenomenon of awareness, without any center...

An enlightened person cannot say "I"; even if he has to use it he never says it, even if he has to use it he cannot mean it. It is just a verbal thing, has to be followed because of the society and the language game. It is just a rule of the language; otherwise he has no "I" feeling.

The world of things disappears – then what happens? When the world of things disappears, your attachment to things falls, your obsession with things falls. Things don't disappear; on the contrary, things for the first time appear as they are. Then you are not clinging, obsessed; then you are not coloring them in your own desires, in your own hopes and frustrations – no. Then the world is not a screen for your desires to be projected on. When your desires drop, the world is there, but it is a totally new world. It is so fresh, it is so colorful, it is so beautiful! But a mind attached to things cannot see it because eyes are closed with attachment. A totally new world arises.

When the mind disappears, thoughts disappear. It is not that you become mindless; on the contrary you become mindful. Buddha uses these words "right mindfulness" millions of times. When the mind disappears and thoughts disappear you become mindful. You do things – you move, you work, you eat, you sleep, but you are always mindful. The mind is not there, but mindfulness is there. What is mindfulness? It is awareness. It is perfect awareness.

And when the self disappears, the ego, the atman, what happens? It is not that you are lost, and no more. No! On the contrary, for the first time you *are*. But now you are not separate from existence. Now you are no longer an island; you have become the whole continent, you are one with the existence.

But those are the positive things – they cannot be said. Hence, Nansen said, "Yes, there is a teaching which no master has ever preached, because it cannot be preached, and that teaching is:

"It is not mind, it is not Buddha, it is not things."

That teaching is emptiness, that teaching is absolute nothingness. And when you are not, suddenly the whole existence starts flowering on you. The whole ecstasy of existence converges on you – when you are not.

When you are not, the whole existence feels ecstatic and celebrates; flowers shower on you. They have not showered yet because you *are*, and they will not shower until you dissolve. When you are empty, no more, when you are a nothingness, *shunyata*, suddenly they start showering. They have showered on Buddha, on Subhuti, on Nansen; they can shower on you – they are waiting. They are knocking at the door. They are ready. Just the moment you become empty, they start falling on you.

Just remember it: the final liberation is not *your* liberation, the final liberation is *from you*. Enlightenment is not yours, cannot be. When you are not, it is there. Drop yourself in your totality: the world of things, the world of thoughts, the world of the self; all three layers, drop. Drop this trinity; drop this *trimurti*, drop these three faces, because if you are there then the one cannot be. If you are three, how can the one be?

Let all three disappear – God, the Holy Ghost and the Son; Brahma, Vishnu,

Mahesh – all the three, let them drop! Let them disappear. Nobody remains –
and then everything is there.

When nothing happens, the all happens.

You are nothing...the all starts showering on you.

Enough for today.

about Osho

Osho's unique contribution to the understanding of who we are defies cat-egorization. Mystic and scientist, a rebellious spirit whose sole interest is to alert humanity to the urgent need to discover a new way of living. To continue as before is to invite threats to our very survival on this unique and beautiful planet.

His essential point is that only by changing ourselves, one individual at a time, can the outcome of all our "selves" – our societies, our cultures, our beliefs, our world – also change. The doorway to that change is meditation.

Osho the scientist has experimented and scrutinized all the approaches of the past and examined their effects on the modern human being and responded to their shortcomings by creating a new starting point for the hyperactive 21st Century mind: OSHO Active Meditations.

Once the agitation of a modern lifetime has started to settle, "activity" can melt into "passivity," a key starting point of real meditation. To support this next step, Osho has transformed the ancient "art of listening" into a subtle contemporary methodology: the OSHO Talks. Here words become music, the listener discovers who is listening, and the awareness moves from what is being heard to the individual doing the listening. Magically, as silence arises, what needs to be heard is understood directly, free from the distraction of a mind that can only interrupt and interfere with this delicate process.

These thousands of talks cover everything from the individual quest for meaning to the most urgent social and political issues facing society today. Osho's books are not written but are transcribed from audio and video recordings of these extemporaneous talks to international audiences. As he puts it, "So remember: whatever I am saying is not just for you...I am talking also for the future generations."

Osho has been described by *The Sunday Times* in London as one of the "1000 Makers of the 20th Century" and by American author Tom Robbins as "the most dangerous man since Jesus Christ." *Sunday Mid-Day* (India) has selected Osho as one of ten people – along with Gandhi, Nehru and Buddha – who have changed the destiny of India.

About his own work Osho has said that he is helping to create the conditions for the birth of a new kind of human being. He often characterizes this new human being as "Zorba the Buddha" – capable both of enjoying the earthy pleasures of a Zorba the Greek and the silent serenity of a Gautama the Buddha.

Running like a thread through all aspects of Osho's talks and meditations is a vision that encompasses both the timeless wisdom of all ages past and the highest potential of today's (and tomorrow's) science and technology.

Osho is known for his revolutionary contribution to the science of inner transformation, with an approach to meditation that acknowledges the accelerated pace of contemporary life. His unique OSHO Active Meditations™ are designed to first release the accumulated stresses of body and mind, so that it is then easier to take an experience of stillness and thought-free relaxation into daily life.

Two autobiographical works by the author are available:
Autobiography of a Spiritually Incorrect Mystic,
St Martins Press, New York (book and eBook)
Glimpses of a Golden Childhood,
OSHO Media International, Pune, India (book and eBook)

OSHO international meditation resort

Each year the Meditation Resort welcomes thousands of people from more than 100 countries. The unique campus provides an opportunity for a direct personal experience of a new way of living – with more awareness, relaxation, celebration and creativity. A great variety of around-the-clock and around-the-year program options are available. Doing nothing and just relaxing is one of them!

All of the programs are based on Osho's vision of "Zorba the Buddha" – a qualitatively new kind of human being who is able *both* to participate creatively in everyday life *and* to relax into silence and meditation.

Location

Located 100 miles southeast of Mumbai in the thriving modern city of Pune, India, the OSHO International Meditation Resort is a holiday destination with a difference. The Meditation Resort is spread over 28 acres of spectacular gardens in a beautiful tree-lined residential area.

OSHO Meditations

A full daily schedule of meditations for every type of person includes both traditional and revolutionary methods, and particularly the OSHO Active Meditations™. The daily meditation program takes place in what must be the world's largest meditation hall, the OSHO Auditorium.

OSHO Multiversity

Individual sessions, courses and workshops cover everything from creative arts to holistic health, personal transformation, relationship and life transition, transforming meditation into a lifestyle for life and work, esoteric sciences, and the "Zen" approach to sports and recreation. The secret of the OSHO Multiversity's success lies in the fact that all its programs are combined with meditation, supporting the understanding that as human beings we are far more than the sum of our parts.

OSHO Basho Spa

The luxurious Basho Spa provides for leisurely open-air swimming surrounded by trees and tropical green. The uniquely styled, spacious Jacuzzi, the saunas, gym, tennis courts...all these are enhanced by their stunningly beautiful setting.

Cuisine
A variety of different eating areas serve delicious Western, Asian and Indian vegetarian food – most of it organically grown especially for the Meditation Resort. Breads and cakes are baked in the resort's own bakery.

Night life
There are many evening events to choose from – dancing being at the top of the list! Other activities include full-moon meditations beneath the stars, variety shows, music performances and meditations for daily life.

Facilities
You can buy all of your basic necessities and toiletries in the Galleria. The Multimedia Gallery sells a large range of OSHO media products. There is also a bank, a travel agency and a Cyber Café on-campus. For those who enjoy shopping, Pune provides all the options, ranging from traditional and ethnic Indian products to all of the global brand-name stores.

Accommodation
You can choose to stay in the elegant rooms of the OSHO Guesthouse, or for longer stays on campus you can select one of the OSHO Living-In programs. Additionally there is a plentiful variety of nearby hotels and serviced apartments.

www.osho.com/meditationresort
www.osho.com/guesthouse
www.osho.com/livingin

more books and eBooks by OSHO media international

The God Conspiracy:
The Path from Superstition to Super Consciousness

Discover the Buddha: 53 Meditations to Meet the Buddha Within
Gold Nuggets: Messages from Existence

<u>OSHO Classics</u>
The Book of Wisdom: The Heart of Tibetan Buddhism.
The Mustard Seed: The Revolutionary Teachings of Jesus
Ancient Music in the Pines: In Zen, Mind Suddenly Stops
The Empty Boat: Encounters with Nothingness
A Bird on the Wing: Zen Anecdotes for Everyday Life
The Path of Yoga: Discovering the Essence and Origin of Yoga
And the Flowers Showered: The Freudian Couch and Zen
Nirvana: The Last Nightmare: Learning to Trust in Life
The Goose Is Out: Zen in Action
Absolute Tao: Subtle Is the Way to Love, Happiness and Truth

The Tantra Experience: Evolution through Love
Tantric Transformation: When Love Meets Meditation

<u>Pillars of Consciousness</u> (illustrated)
BUDDHA: His Life and Teachings and Impact on Humanity
ZEN: Its History and Teachings and Impact on Humanity
TANTRA: The Way of Acceptance
TAO: The State and the Art

Authentic Living

Danger: Truth at Work: The Courage to Accept the Unknowable
The Magic of Self-Respect: Awakening to Your Own Awareness
Born With a Question Mark in Your Heart

OSHO eBooks and "OSHO-Singles"

Emotions: Freedom from Anger, Jealousy and Fear
Meditation: The First and Last Freedom
What Is Meditation?
The Book of Secrets: 112 Meditations to Discover the Mystery Within

20 Difficult Things to Accomplish in This World
Compassion, Love and Sex
Hypnosis in the Service of Meditation
Why Is Communication So Difficult, Particularly between Lovers?
Bringing Up Children
Why Should I Grieve Now?: facing a loss and letting it go
Love and Hate: just two sides of the same coin

Next Time You Feel Angry...
Next Time You Feel Lonely...
Next Time You Feel Suicidal...

OSHO Media BLOG
http://oshomedia.blog.osho.com

for more information

www.**OSHO**.com

a comprehensive multi-language website including a magazine, OSHO Books, OSHO Talks in audio and video formats, the OSHO Library text archive in English and Hindi and extensive information about OSHO Meditations. You will also find the program schedule of the OSHO Multiversity and information about the OSHO International Meditation Resort.

http://OSHO.com/AllAboutOSHO
http://OSHO.com/Resort
http://OSHO.com/Shop
http://www.youtube.com/OSHO
http://www.Twitter.com/OSHO
http://www.facebook.com/pages/OSHO.International

To contact OSHO International Foundation:
www.osho.com/oshointernational,
oshointernational@oshointernational.com